"In *The Fabric of Autism*, Bluestone gives us breathtaking insights into the workings of the mind, especially the autistic mind. Only someone with the inquisitive mind of a scientist, a heart full of compassion, and the first-hand knowledge of how autism feels could have written this book."
—Marybetts Sinclair, LMT,
Author of <u>Pediatric Massage Therapy</u>

"There is such a need to unmask the positive potential of every human being. *The Fabric of Autism* is like a beacon of light leading the way." .
—Jeannette Vos, Ed.D.
Co-author of <u>The Learning Revolution</u>

"The HANDLE concept is brilliant... Give the brain all the right ingredients and watch the magic! Using nutrition, homeopathy and movement, Judith Bluestone combines the wisdom of the body with input from the senses to produce profound changes in learning and behavior. A neuro-developmental approach to autism respects the uniqueness of each individual. Parents can now be optimistic that even the most profoundly disabled kids can function more efficiently."
—Patricia Lemer, M.Ed.
Co-founder and Executive Director of Developmental Delay Resources

"I recall Herbert Steiner said of John Perse's work: 'Nicht wir richten ueber Werke, wir werden an ihnen gemessen.' (We do not judge works, rather we are measured against them.) After contemplation of great works of art, you see the world with the eye of the artist: you do not judge the work, rather it judges you. It changes your outlook. *The Fabric of Autism* is just such a work."
—K.H
Mother and Grandmother of HANDLE clients

The fabric of AUTISM

Weaving The Threads Into A Cogent Theory

Judith Bluestone

SAPPHIRE

Enterprises, LLC

The fabric of
AUTISM
Weaving The Threads Into A Cogent Theory

Published by:

    Sapphire Enterprises, LLC
    1300 Dexter Avenue North, #110
    The Casey Family Building
    Seattle, WA 98109
    (206) 204-6000
    info@sapphire-enterprises.com
    www.sapphire-enterprises.com

Although incidents and anecdotes are based on real events, some names have been changed to protect confidentiality.

ISBN 0-9720235-2-6
Library of Congress Control Number: 2003116657
First printed in the United States in 2004 by The HANDLE Institute

Grateful acknowledgement is made for permission to reprint previously published material:
    The Uncharted Territory of Just Raising Ivy is reprinted by permission of the author from <u>The Churkendoose Anthology: True Stories of Triumph over Neurological Dysfunction.</u> Copyright © 2002 The HANDLE Institute. All rights reserved.

    This Autistic Man is reprinted by permission of the author from <u>The Light Within</u>. Copyright © 1998 Lincoln Grigsby. All rights reserved.

    Hear What I am Saying is printed by permission of the author.

Cover design by Kristin M. Adams.

Special thanks to Carolyn Nuyens and Janet Kerschner.

Printed in the United States of America.

Dedication

To my mom,
who learned to love me
as her daughter
and to like me
for the quirky human being
I am.

Contents

Contents

Acknowledgments

. . . to my three sisters: Marlene, my biological sister, and Sindy and Lane, my sisters by choice, without whose support I could not have written this book

. . . to Lane—this time as Lane Browning—for being able to switch hats from sister-by-choice to Editor and, wearing that formidable hat, helping me display the fabric in a way that others may appreciate

. . . to Lisa Brenner, who gave much thought and numerous hours to help bring this project to fruition

. . . to the staff and volunteers of The HANDLE Institute, who gave me the time and space to research and write this book, knowing that although it will never be "finished" I needed solitude to finish it

Foreword

By Tim Hutton, Ph.D., CST-D

The nervous system in general and the brain in particular are among the most complex and least understood systems in the human body. This becomes especially apparent when we try to apply our understanding of the brain to that most puzzling of situations, Autism Spectrum Disorder (ASD), which is truly becoming the disease of our times.

The application of traditional medical science and models of the nervous system to the treatment of ASD has met with only limited success, in part because our understanding of the nervous system is so rudimentary. If we do not know how the nervous system functions under normal conditions, how can we hope to apply our understanding successfully to a situation as complex as ASD?

The study of the brain presents a unique challenge since the brain itself is our principal organ of investigation, and as we investigate its function we are indeed looking directly into the mirror. The mind studying itself presents a multitude of opportunities for confusion, projection, and self-deception. To gain insight we must proceed with caution and, if we are wise, thoroughly examine all the assumptions that underlie the conclusions we hope to reach.

Among the assumptions we often implicitly make, and often take for granted, is the belief that the mind arises out of the functioning of the brain, i.e. that we think, feel, and experience, indeed that we are conscious, as a result of the cumulative electrical activity of all the synapses in our brains. We project an internal quality of our existence, the thing that we call "mind," onto the physical and biological structure of our brains. In our scientific and rational culture, we tend to identify ourselves with our brains, as if we, the brains, are simply creatures inhabiting the rest of our bodies. We look down at our arms and our legs, our stomachs and our livers, our breasts and our genitals, and don't experience them as being "us."

There is some evidence to justify this belief. We take in most of our sensory input through the face, particularly the eyes, so it is natural to associate the center of our being, our sense of "I"-ness, with a point somewhere behind the window of our vision. We know the brain is central to personality as well as to life itself. We can live without an arm or a leg, we can transplant vital internal organs and maintain life, but we can neither live without nor transplant the brain itself. Injuries to the brain can have a most profound effect upon our experience of life.

Alternatively, consciousness may be a quality fundamental to life, and perhaps even a characteristic of existence itself. Our conscious awareness may arise as the combined result of the consciousness of each individual cell, of structures within the cells, even of proteins, all working together symbiotically for the greater good of the whole. Cells and proteins make many decisions. When such decisions are made incorrectly, or there is miscommunication between the cells or between parts within a single cell, a host of health problems, including ASD, may result.

Science itself, upon which most of our modern understanding of medicine is based, has as its foundation certain assumptions, which are unfortunately usually not discussed. All science is based upon models, which we produce in the hopes that they will prove useful in predicting the future behavior of the system we are studying. The model currently prevalent in Western medicine is that the human body is basically a machine—any stimulus to the body is followed by the body's inevitable response. This is an assumption. Among its implications is that the role of the doctor, therapist, or clinician is to cure the client, rather than to facilitate and support the body's own intrinsic healing mechanisms.

The nervous system and brain are most often compared to a computer, the decision making engine with which scientists are most familiar, with the hope that in tracing nerve pathways and interconnections it will prove possible to reverse engineer the brain, as if it were a circuit board. This perspective leads to an unconscious tendency to see the brain as a centralized control unit which directs the body, despite current evidence that all cells in the body produce neurotransmitters and communicate with each other in a myriad of ways.

Science is the Zeitgeist of our age—that is, the prevailing world-view that most people in our culture unconsciously use to organize their lives. Science is the filter through which people view and understand the world around them. Like all filters, it allows only certain information to pass through, which limits our perception and thus our range of possible responses to any given situation. Scientific theories, particularly as perceived by non-scientists, are often seen as universal "truths," although many simplifying assumptions underlie such pronouncements. The simple underlying principles of all mathematics, even our belief in linear cause and effect, are in final analysis merely assumptions. That they seem eminently reasonable is actually more a statement about us and our psychological makeup than about the world itself. In reality, science is only one way to organize information about and understand the world, and not always the best way.

Carl Jung was one of the first to develop a theory of psychological types, a way of classifying how different people interact with the world around them. He observed that we take in information in two very different ways: consciously through our senses but also in ways we are not consciously aware of. That is, we are both kinesthetic and intuitive. Once we take in information, we try to classify and understand it—we are thinking creatures. In addition, we make value judgments about information and we have an emotional response to it—we have a feeling sense as well. In a healthy human psyche, all four of these methods of interacting with the world—kinesthetic sense, intuition, thinking, and feeling—are equally well developed.

Unfortunately, both individually and as a culture, we tend to value the thinking function over the other three. They come through our creative side and are the result of accessing our deeper levels of knowing. We tend to be out of touch with our bodies and thus unable to take in information reliably from our senses. When we try to observe the actions of others, their patterns of movement, how they hold themselves and inhabit their bodies, we are often unable to really see what is actually going on. In addition, we are often out of touch with our own feelings and unable to accurately detect and interpret the feelings of others, unable to empathize with them deeply. Finally we are often out of touch with our intuition, and thus unnecessarily limited in our ability to observe the world and those around us. By relying solely on our thinking function and staying stuck in our rigid "scientific" world view, we lose touch with our own humanity and that of the people around us.

Given these tendencies in our psyche and our society, what then is the state of modern medicine? And how does this relate to ASD?

Doctors for the most part are no longer taught to palpate, no longer taught to observe the client deeply, nor to rely upon their intuition. Instead, most routinely order batteries of invasive and expensive tests even before making an initial diagnosis. It is as if, in our pursuit of medicine based solely upon science, we have lost the ability to observe and to reason. Unfortunately, the human connection of the doctor to the patient is often lost as well.

When applied to ASD, this dehumanizing "scientific" approach to medicine leads to such postulates as the idea that patients with ASD do not possess a normal "theory of mind," that they are somehow less than conscious. It leads to treatments designed to suppress symptoms, without a clear idea of what is causing the symptom in the first place, perhaps making ASD patients easier to control, but often doing violence to their humanity in the process.

It does not have to be this way. Science is a wonderful and powerful tool for investigating ourselves and our environment. When used consciously with an awareness of its limitations and the underlying assumptions being made, science can contribute to a more complete and well-rounded view of the world. In particular, if science is thoughtfully combined with intuition and our emotional response in an integrated approach to investigating and interacting with our environment, spectacular insights may sometimes result.

This book is an example of just such an approach.

Judith Bluestone's history has made her ideally suited to this exploration of ASD. On the one hand, she has an extensive background in neurophysiology, neuropsychology, and neurorehabilitation. On the other hand, she herself has struggled with ASD all her life. This affords her the unique perspective of being able to perceive Autism Spectrum Disorder from both the inside and out. Her profound understanding of how the nervous system operates has led to her development of HANDLE, the Holistic Approach to NeuroDevelopment and Learning Efficiency.

Fundamental to HANDLE is that the therapist be open to communication and interaction with the client in whatever form the client wishes to or is able to use. This requires very careful observation on the part of the therapist using all of the senses, including intuition and the feeling sense—therapists must bring all of themselves to the work. By carefully observing the client and creating a profile of interactive and interdependent functions, the therapist is then able to provide the client with a customized program of deceptively simple activities for retraining the nervous system. The approach works so well in Judith's hands (or in those of other Certified Practitioners of HANDLE), I believe, in part because of the subtlety of Judith's understanding of how the nervous system operates and her ability to observe her clients deeply, but also in part because of the profound human connection between client and therapist that the approach affords.

This deep human connection has allowed Judith to develop a unique understanding of ASD, both externally as to its causes and how it manifests, but also internally as to how it feels on the inside to someone who suffers under its weight. Please join Judith for a journey into the inner world of autism, for she is truly the "compassionate translator" between our two worlds.

*I*n gratitude

. . . to the brave, generous autistic children and adults whose lives I have been trusted to join:

Bobby and Seth, who taught me the joys and trials of mainstreaming severely autistic children into school communities;

Joseph and his Grandma-Ma, who taught me patience as a guide along this difficult journey;

Jordan and Dave, who confirmed for me that speaking with my client, regardless of his assumed level of understanding, is incredibly worthwhile;

Dillon, for his amazing courage to forge a path for other autistic children in his community;

Howard, who dared to embrace communication in his thirties and whose bravery and desire for a meaningful relationship motivated him to comb his hair and to shave;

Maria, who learned not only to speak to others, but also to negotiate, all before the age of seven;

Andrew and Andrew and Andrew (yes, three of them), who learned to read and draw and write and through communication to unlock their minds and hearts;

Evan and his dad, for their willingness to keep searching, even though they sometimes looked behind the wrong curtains;

Christine, who first taught me that facilitated communication is not a hoax, and whose integrity was so strong that she chose facilitated communication over oral speech, even after she found her voice at the age of 18;

Nicholas, who has taught many people the power of first building trust before trying to assess human functioning;

Stephen, and his mom, who were willing to throw away the diagnosis of autism and address the motor planning deficits that kept him from communicating verbally and non-verbally;

Wallace, who took me at my word but tested me time and again to make sure I would not reach out to touch him, and then who plunked himself into my lap, knowing I was safe;

And Tommy, Esther, Colin, Jacob, Jacqueline, Carlos, Cooper, Chrissy, Alexa, Preston, Ben, Tara, Troy, Matt, Melinda, Sasha, Lloyd, Joel, Isaac, Sam, Jason, Bobbie, and so many other courageous children and young adults who endured my gentle probing and strange suggestions and who cooperated with their parents and their teachers to ever-so-slowly stretch their senses and their sensibilities;

Sandy, my dear Sandy, whom I somehow failed by helping her emerge from very low functioning autism into a world that was not yet ready for her metamorphosis.

And all the Certified Practitioners of HANDLE, who stretched beyond their expectations of themselves, to understand the autistic experience as part of the continuum of human function, and to guide so many families on one of the most remarkable journeys a human being can undertake.

And Leon, for being the first real boyfriend to appreciate me for who I was and to not want to take advantage of my naiveté and my need to be loved... Hoover, my first husband, for his realization of my innermost innocence and his gentle support and ease in providing me distance and space when I needed it and closeness when I was able to accept it so I could grow in a committed relationship . . . Michael, my second husband, for forcing me to become increasingly visible in my field and stretch beyond my autistic self so I might help others more . . . Jim, who, even as I was founding The HANDLE Institute, provided me a haven in which I could get respite from the rest of the world and its intrusions by returning to my earlier behaviors with total abandon, without fear of ostracism.

My incredible family of origin. My parents, who never understood, and were exasperated at what they viewed as my choices (not realizing the limitations of my autistic boundaries), but who allowed me to be and to unfold. And my sister, who also did not understand, not until we both reached middle age, that my developmental quirks fit so many labels (epilepsy, autism, PDD-NOS, OCD, ODD...). And now she is my best friend even though she understands. No, because she understands.

And unending gratitude to:

Kanner and Bettelheim and Asperger for their tardiness in proposing their labels and theories;

The psychologist who would not test me in kindergarten;

And gratitude for:

My deafness and the fact that it was reparable;

Medical advances almost keeping up with my needs;

The Pogo Stick and the community that allowed me to use it;

The Story of the Churkendoose for appearing in my life and providing me the assurance that there was a purpose for my differences;

Recent advances, and those who are researching the many threads of autism, providing me material to weave into the total fabric. For I understand the patterns, the warp and the woof.

My Ash Grove

Judith Bluestone
circa 1954

Alone in my ash grove one bleak cloudy day
I dreamed many thoughts. My mind went astray.

I dreamed of a castle in some far off land.
I dreamed of two lovers alone on the sand.

But strange it may seem to those of right mind
That in these sweet dreams myself I can't find.

A prince of a castle would not have me near.
A young boy in love would laugh in my ear.

So now I'm content to stay in my cove,
In the place where I'm wanted—my little ash grove.

The fabric of
AUTISM
Weaving The Threads Into A Cogent Theory

*I*ntroduction

Autism is a complex neurological disorder that has been observed and named and diagnosed for decades. According to the National Institute of Neurological Disorders and Stroke, autism is a developmental disorder of brain function typically manifested in three classic symptoms: impaired social interaction, difficulty with verbal and nonverbal communication and severely limited activities and interests. These symptoms generally appear in the first three years of life and may last throughout the lifetime.

Recent research into autism has led to the development of the concept of an Autism Spectrum Disorder (ASD) to include individuals with varied degrees of impairment and functioning. It is well documented that although definite similarities exist among people classified as autistic, the degree of difference from one person to another is profound. Although I will use the words "autism" and "autistic" in this book, I do so only as a form of shorthand to acknowledge that I am focused on someone whose behaviors cluster around those frequently described as being within the autism spectrum.

Initially, the term "autistic" was used by the Swiss psychiatrist Eugen Bleuler in 1911. He applied it to adult schizophrenics whose emotional behaviors and thought processes produced withdrawal from interaction in social life, but not to total removal from the social environment. In the United States in 1943, Leo Kanner's studies of early childhood development led him to use "autism" for any dysfunction of emotional contact, evident from earliest development, that leads to an autistic being—an aloneness, as implied by the Greek word "autos" meaning "self." Autistic individuals were perceived to live in a world of their own, a world that excluded all others.

In 1944, Bruno Bettelheim offered his theories on autism, based on his work with emotionally disturbed children at the Orthogenic School in Chicago. Bettelheim coined the phrase "refrigerator moms" to impart his feeling that the behaviors he saw were caused by parents' emotional neglect of their infants and young children. In 1944 in Germany, Hans Asperger reported similar autistic tendencies in early childhood development (today a somewhat distinctive syndrome of higher functioning individuals within the autism spectrum bears Asperger's name). However, it was not until 1981, when Lorna Wing published an English summary of Asperger's work, that the English-speaking world became aware of Asperger Syndrome.

In 1967 Bernard Rimland founded the Autism Research Institute (ARI) to encourage research into causes and treatments for autism and to discover ways to prevent its occurrence. His work was instrumental in dispelling Bettelheim's theories about "refrigerator moms."

As we begin the 21st century, building on Rimland's work and that of many other organizations and researchers who continue with resolve to study various aspects of ASD, the view of autism is changing, dramatically. Patricia Lemer advocates for a "total load" theory of autism in which she looks at cumulative effects of multiple assaults on the whole bodily system.[1] Her list of factors associated with ASD:

- traumatic birth
- allergies in the family
- dark circles under the eyes
- red ears or cheeks
- fibromyalgia, chronic fatigue or low thyroid in the mother
- recurrent ear, sinus or strep infections
- chronic unexplained fevers
- respiratory problems
- skin problems
- digestive problems including constipation, diarrhea, reflux
- extended reaction to immunization
- sudden decline in function between 15 and 30 months
- yeast infections
- hyperactivity
- agitated sleep
- wild mood swings
- self-injurious behaviors
- regressive behaviors after ingesting food additives
- sensitivities to chemicals including dyes, perfumes, medications
- craving for apple juice.

---

[1] Lemer, PS. "Diagnosis Autism: What Families Can Do." Mothering, Pp 44 – 47. May-June 2000.

As ASD is redefined, researchers reposition themselves to focus on one or more risk factors, particular behaviors or neurophysiological irregularities, trying to determine if we can significantly alter the symptoms or cure the "disease" by applying one approach.

Most parents are finding hope in the biomedical approaches that are developing to help them with the problems that fall into that realm: gastro-intestinal pathology, sub-optimal nutritional status, food intolerance, chronic infections and toxic accumulations. Many are combining this with behavioral programs (such as Applied Behavior Analysis) that teach social conventions, and some are combining them with programs (such as the Son-Rise program of the Option Institute, the Denver program or Stanley Greenspan's Floor Time) that teach the caregivers how to join the child in his world and help him move into the universe of social interaction.

With so many approaches and so much research currently available, why are families and professionals still searching? I contend it is because ASD is on one hand more complex than has yet been imagined, and on the other hand is more simplistic. The complexity beseeches us to apply a systems approach to understanding the problem[2], since we know that environment and behaviors (nurture) influence the structure and function of the brain (nature), although we sometimes forget that the influences continue throughout our lives and that the nervous systems, especially the brain, are in constant states of adaptation. And the simplicity will emerge once we understand how to unravel the tangled threads, gently, and reweave them into a more supple fabric. The discoveries we will make in unraveling the threads of autism will help us better understand many other disorders as well— disorders such as those John Ratey and Catherine Johnson describe in *Shadow Syndromes: The Mild Forms of Major Mental Disorders That Sabotage Us.*

As the Clinical and Educational Director of The HANDLE Institute in Seattle, Washington, I have been helping parents, teachers and other caregivers to guide individuals with ASD to more functional lives.

The approach I developed more than fifteen years ago is called HANDLE[3],

---

[2]Many researchers participating in The National Child Study, just beginning this year, will try to discover what combinations of environmental insults are affecting our children and causing so many learning disorders and other dysfunctions to occur at such alarming rates. UC-Davis MIND has just begun to study a composite effect of toxins and genetic factors to determine the cause(s) of autism in particular.

[3]HANDLE® is an acronym for Holistic Approach to NeuroDevelopment and Learning Efficiency. It provides non-drug resolution to many neurodevelopmental disorders. HANDLE is becoming recognized as a powerful tool in understanding and treating Autism Spectrum Disorders. Throughout the book, I will incorporate thumbnail case scenarios, research, and personal experience. In the Appendices of this volume you will find more details on some of the principles behind HANDLE treatment programs. I have tried to keep the information in this volume available to everyone interested in understanding autism from a systems or holistic approach.

and as I learn more from my application of neuroscientific research, HANDLE continues to evolve.

Reviewing the research and examining the developing theories about the cause of autism, I am searching not for a cure, but rather an understanding. In many ways, I return to the perspective that Bleuler adopted in working with individuals with schizophrenia—looking at the associative disturbances and interpreting what the individual is expressing through these behaviors (behaviors unique to each individual with autism, yet behaviors with many similarities). The treatment then is not aimed at the behaviors, but at the neurophysiological disorders finding expression in the deviant behaviors.

But objective studies also demonstrate that there are gifts in autistic processing and behavior patterns.

And autism is not a disease. In trying to discover The Cause of autism and The Cure for autism, many of today's researchers continue to ignore two basic neurological precepts. First, in a system as plastic and as interactive as the human body-brain-mind-spirit, it is not one specific factor that causes the wide array of symptoms that result in autistic behaviors. If there were a one-to-one relationship, ALL children would be autistic if they received certain vaccines, or ate dairy products, or had "leaky gut" syndrome, or had mothers who during pregnancy ate a lot of fish contaminated with mercury. And second, the body-brain-mind-spirit system does not receive and process information on one-way streets.

Information is processed in loops, and through these loops it's quite possible that irregular processing in the ears causes digestive problems, just as we have learned that eyestrain can cause headaches, and toothaches can disturb our ability to focus our attention on academic learning. And stress, which can affect us profoundly from shortly after conception and throughout our lives, causes shifts in all our systems. Viewing our brain-body-mind-spirit again as a roadway, not only does traffic move in different directions on the same streets, different drivers are more or less impatient at getting to their destinations, and we have detours and traffic jams with which we need to contend.

As someone who has experienced the roadway of my nervous systems as a traumatic bumper car ride, I lived basically outside the mainstream. I still do, when I can choose. And yet the cloth I donned to journey down this path was not left unaffected by society. My threads were pulled continually in attempts to understand my behaviors or to tug me in one direction or another. My fabric became snagged and frayed as I attempted to share this world with people who were not autistic.

And I learned.

I was born in Chicago in December 1944. When I was growing up, there was little understanding of autistic behaviors, as Bettelheim's erroneous conclusions clearly demonstrate. And so, for a disorder so in-your-face and so at-odds with normal social functioning, the treatment for diagnosed autism was singular—institutionalization. By escaping the label, I escaped institutionalization. But I did not escape the torment in a home and a society that did not understand.

In reviewing my life as I recall it, I realize I have been actively engaging applied neuroscience for over 55 years in order to survive and achieve in the world. At first I was doing so instinctively, from the inside out, to protect myself in the areas of my greatest vulnerabilities and to employ my strongest senses to help me learn. Decades later I began to apply my many years of advanced study in education and counseling, neurodevelopment, neuropsychology and neurorehabilitation from the outside in. During this period of more than 35 years of professional work helping others resolve issues caused by a wide array of neurodevelopmental disorders, I have helped many dozens of families in whom at least one member fit the criteria of Autism Spectrum Disorder.

So perhaps it is time for this researcher who has an applied neuroscientific approach and an interactive explanation of development to finally come face-to-face with her past and say, "I have something valuable to offer you. I am someone valuable. Do not discard me and do not discount what I have to say. I have experienced the fabric of autism from the inside out, and have studied it also from the outside in. There are obvious patterns. There are common sense solutions."

In this book, I step outside of my autism and share—in written word, the medium of expression that I have persistently preferred to speech. I share not just with those families around the world who have sought my help, but also with the world now so alarmed about the rising incidence of people like me—people who could be or have been diagnosed with an Autism Spectrum Disorder.

This book incorporates three voices. I write as a researcher sharing scientific findings, as a therapist speaking for the autistic individuals I have come to know, and as myself, an individual whose mind still feels most at home in autistic thought patterns. The book also intermingles three times: lessons from the past, current experience, and glimpses into the future. As you read the various chapters and enter the world of autistic minds, you may wonder when the pattern will become clear, when the answer will present itself. Move through this work with trust that a pattern will emerge, and you will discover many new and powerful insights into autism. These insights will form the common threads in the woof and warp of the fabric of autism enabling you to design comfortable garments to be worn proudly, for all the world to see.

I trust that this book will provide not only understanding of autism to many on the outside looking in, but also hope to those on the inside, still brave enough to look out, but fearful of the risk of interaction. I say to both, "It is okay. We can live together, respectfully. We have much to give one another."

1. The many threads of autism
Identifying some of the strands

Awoman called me in a panic. Her three year-old had just been seen by a specialist. "He says our son has Childhood Disintegrative Disorder, a form of autism. We don't know what happened. He was developing normally. Then, suddenly, he just seemed to lose everything. First his spark was gone, then his language. Now the only times he even seems relaxed and MAYBE taking us in is when he takes the freshly dried clothes from our dryer and buries himself in them. Can you help us get our son back?"

This problem was becoming all too familiar. A child who had been developing normally suddenly showed the behaviors we associate with ASD. Research was beginning to mount indicating that altogether too many children displayed similar patterns. Almost similar. But the apparent healing qualities of the recently dried clothes certainly added a different element. How could they have anything to do with the recently suspected connection to vaccinations and neuroimmune disorders? How was I going to help this family whose child certainly seemed to fit the diagnosis of autism, at least most of the time? I knew if I could study Daryl, I would be able to offer some ideas.

Daryl was like many clients I've seen, but at the same time, Daryl was unique, and this is the essential thing we need to recognize about all ASD individuals. They are individuals. There is no "magic bullet" and no "single commonality."

There are many vast and varied clusters of behavioral and physiological challenges that lead to the suspicion or diagnosis of autism. A child's label will depend on what part of the country he lives in; whether his case manager is a pediatrician, psychiatrist or the school district's occupational therapist or a speech and language therapist; and what theories the case manager embraces. The higher functioning the individual, the more difficult it is for professionals to determine if the condition meets the criteria for a diagnosis of ASD or another area of dysfunction. Recently some authorities have been clumping within ASD a grab bag of previously "separate" disorders including ADD, ADHD, dyslexia, obsessive-compulsive disorder, even Tourette's Syndrome.

There are so many threads, and viewed separately they leave one reeling. Taken as a cluster, they become tangled. But we must see each of them, and measure them, before we can begin to weave a fabric, to see the pattern, to detect the systemic nature of this puzzling disorder. The chart on page 114 provides many pieces of this puzzle. You can see these pieces do not fit together. They are a jumble. Until we find the common threads.

What most outsiders see are the problems that occupational therapists, psychiatrists, and neurologists might try to alleviate, ameliorate or cure—the self-stimulatory behaviors that those of us with autism engage in so frequently. Rocking. Head-banging. Hopping. Toe-walking. Hand-flapping. Winding strings and wires around our fingers. Twirling things. Humming or making "white noises." Smelling objects or people. Flipping pages in books. Picking bites and scabs. Various "self-injurious behaviors," repeated over and over again.

One of my favorite self-stimulatory behaviors was turning the pedals of my tricycle or bicycle while it was upside down, watching the wheels go round and round and round and round. "What are you doing?" my sister asked. "Popcorn," I replied with speech as intelligible as I could conjure.

But when I was nine, the pedals and wheels lost out to a pogo stick. I jumped on the pogo stick. Well, I didn't really jump, I actually used the pogo stick as my vehicle. In the house, on the carpeted stairs, en route to school, INSIDE school, in neighborhood shops (yes, up and down the aisles of the dime store). My sister says this was the year when she became certain I had "gone off the deep end." Looking back, I see that my behaviors embarrassed her. She says she simply found them "weird." She found ME weird also.

I had other habits that were equally annoying, and more unpleasant to observe. Chewing my clothes—cuffs if I had them, otherwise sleeves or collars would do. And picking bites and scabs and anything that itched. And searching my hair for split ends and then ripping the split portion off. And picking my nose. And rhythmically rubbing my legs together for intense sensual stimulation. And moving my toes so wildly inside my shoes that I wore holes in my socks. And wiggling my ankles so violently that I had frequent sprains.

Medical researchers are experimenting with ways to control such behaviors with medication. Behaviorists have developed approaches for controlling the undesirable activities. But I have learned that before we extinguish them, we need to understand what they are telling us.

Another major concern, particularly in more advanced societies, is the difficulty in toilet training. Autistic children either can't seem to control their urine and bowel movements, or they control them by refusing to use a toilet or eliminating only into a diaper. Some autistic individuals cannot seem to manage to clean themselves after toileting, even into their teens and adult years. And others have a com-

Stacking makes sense. It organizes things in a disorganized world. Afterwards, this little tyke needed to make sure both hands had things to hold so he could "relax" and enjoy his accomplishment, drooling all the while. Mommy and Daddy were not allowed to help to place the last four soup containers even though some extra height was called for. What would have happened had they knocked over this fragile stack? I shudder to think of the fury their two year old son would have unleashed.

pulsion for handling and smearing feces. Many suffer from constipation or leaky gut. Some professionals believe that problems of elimination indicate a deficit in the ability to feel what is going on internally and to develop the muscle control needed for toilet training.

A consistent area of concern in assessment and treatment of an autistic person is eye-contact. Professionals and families get quite upset about this, believing that if you can't sustain eye-contact with straight-on, nose-to-nose, focal vision, you're not LOOKING at them. Peripheral vision doesn't count as "eye-contact" to them. And another visual function, visual tracking (controlling the eyes in smooth pursuits to follow a line of print or track a moving object) is frequently irregular for those of us with autism.

But peripheral vision DOES count.

I once helped a physical therapist working with a six year-old autistic boy in his school. Each time the child entered the therapy room, the therapist promptly asked him to look at her so she could show him what they would be doing. And every time he turned away. She stood in front of him and asked again. Again, he turned away. Eventually the frustrated therapist tried to restrain him so he would look at her. He responded in rage, and every session ended in failure.

Finally, the therapist asked me how I had instructed others to deal with these behaviors, as they were all working successfully with the child.

"When he turns away," I asked, "is he giving you his back or his side?"

"His side."

"Then he has been doing what you requested all along. Looking at you. Using his peripheral vision. He knows that if he sits face-to-face with you, he will not be looking at you. You have been demanding that he fail. He has responded rightfully in anger."

"Oh," she said.

After that she worked successfully with the child, even though he continued to rely on peripheral vision.

Had Timmy been able, he'd have said to the therapist "I am looking at you! I just do it more easily when you are to my side."

This child, like so many others, had not developed the ability for tiny little eye muscles to bring his eyes together to converge for focal vision. We will pick up the thread of peripheral vision many times as we explore the fabric of autism. It is influenced by other threads and it in turn affects major strands. It is a thread that relates not only to looking but also to listening.

And, communication skills, spoken and nonverbal, are basic problems to those of us with autism. We may have trouble monitoring the volumes and intonation of our own voices. We are becoming much more proficient communicators now that we can rely on the Internet and e-mail. Before computer technology rescued them, some people with autism relied more on the telephone than face-to-face conversations since eye-contact was not expected and rocking or hopping or fidgeting was unobserved by the person at the other end of the line. Communicating from a distance, even if it is from across the room, is less demanding and less threatening than face-to-face, eye-to-eye conversations. One of the few times those of us with autism might seek in-person communication is to share moments of silliness and glee. We know our whole body is the communicator of these emotions.

Speech and language therapists worked with me when I was three until I was nine years old, trying to teach me how to form speech sounds and create words and sentences. If I could have given voice to my words, how much easier life would have been! My requests might have been fulfilled rather than misinterpreted. Very few people provided me pencil and paper so I could write what I wanted to say. I am sure they assumed that if I couldn't speak, then of course I couldn't write.

And almost certainly they assumed that if I didn't speak, I wasn't intelligent (a misconception still present in the minds of many people today). Today professionals might have said, "She has no Theory of Mind[4]. She cannot communicate with me because she cannot fathom what my mind captures."

But I, like so many on the spectrum, would, if able, have retorted in writing: "Theory of Mind!? What in the world does that mean? If it means not understanding how the other person's mind works, then how can anyone determine which of us it is who lacks this ability? Why is yours the one true 'mind'?"

"Because I don't look you in the eye or because I need to shield myself from some forms of sensory input doesn't mean I have no Theory of Mind. If you, who are so much older and more experienced and self-confident than I, cannot put yourself in my shoes and understand how I think, why must I put myself at risk to understand you?" And, once my indignant rage had run its course, I might have continued writing, with less energy, "Yes. I know. Other kids can do it."

Today most speech and language therapists have enough training in oral-

---

[4]Theory of Mind has become a key issue among professionals diagnosing individuals with ASD. Those who are deemed to lack a Theory of Mind supposedly cannot understand what others feel or perceive. Those, such as Simon Baron-Cohen, professor of psychology and psychiatry at Cambridge University and co-director of its Autism Research Center, who subscribe to this theory feel it is central to the communication disorder in ASD.

motor stimulation to teach a child to chew and swallow food instead of swallowing-without-chewing or just spitting it out. They would have worked with my mother to teach me how to chew and swallow and move a bolus down my esophagus, rather than having it return to my mouth, time and time again, as with a cow chewing her cud. These skills would have boosted my social acceptance at meals and sometimes hours later, when my system simply regurgitated what I had eaten.

For individuals with autism, there are many difficulties in the arena of social interactions, because we don't learn through simple imitation. It's a challenge for us to sustain attention to what someone else determines is the task at hand, but we over-focus on peculiar things that no one else is interested in. We establish rituals and routines, becoming distraught when the pattern is interrupted. We have compulsions that must be satisfied. I remember the night I absolutely HAD to count all the squashed bugs on the walls and ceiling and floor of the moonlit cabin in Minnesota where my family stopped one summer evening. Nothing interrupted me—not threats or bribes or cajoling—nothing!—until I was finished.

People with autism have many sensitivities including frequently an intolerance of haircutting or brushing. The only time my father ever struck me was when he tried to cut my bangs. Locked in a small bathroom, I squirmed and wriggled to avoid the scissors—scissors that were about to clip my sensitive hair, hair that was being pulled taut so the cutting line would be straight. I knew that sharp hair clippings were about to fall on my cheeks and neck and shoulders. And I knew my cozy visor against the glare of light—long hair covering my eyes—was about to be removed.

Frustrated to the breaking point, Dad finally smacked me with the back of the hairbrush. I didn't cry, but he did. Seeing that, I stood still—anxious but still—and the bangs got trimmed. Dad never realized why I fought him so vigorously. He didn't understand that I was protecting myself from multiple sensitivities. I couldn't tell him with words, and he couldn't interpret my rebellious fight. But he did understand my acquiescence when I saw his pain. He knew I loved him.

Today haircuts are even worse for those of us with autism. Electric clippers make whirring noises. Hair dryers sound like tornadoes and blow the tiny hairs on the back of the neck. Products emit unusual odors. And a universe of mirrors reflects light and images from every angle, distorting people and objects, and everything looking as if it is where it is not.

Nail cutting and face washing are equally upsetting. And although they may seem irrelevant to the serious problems of autism, Christine's case demonstrates otherwise. Christine was 14 and totally non-verbal when I met her. She made no eye-contact and had an extremely short attention span. Her older sister helped Christine express herself through Facilitated Communication on an alphabet board, but at times Christine had to be compelled to cooperate. We spent several months improving her functions in several areas and enabled Christine to participate in a much wider range of activities in school and in the community at large. But two years later she was very frustrated that she couldn't communicate through speech. Many people still thought she was retarded and that the message-tapping was a hoax. She also still had extreme hypersensitivity in oral-motor areas and in general in the areas served by her trigeminal nerve. She would not let us near her face. She was even more phobic about her toes. Her family tried to trim her toenails when she slept, but even that was challenging.

Christine returned, determined that I would help her free herself from this trap. She entered the room and independently tapped out "I want to learn to speak." We talked about the fact that she had resisted many of the activities that would have enhanced her ability to speak. She decided she still would not allow Face Tapping.[5] So I told her we could accomplish much the same result using the reflexology points on her feet—primarily her toes and the base of the toes—but she would have to allow me to work on them and to teach her family how to per-form the supportive form of reflexology that I have developed.

She fled to the beanbag in the corner. "You're brave," I told her, "or you wouldn't be able to get up every day and face a world that doesn't understand you. I know you're brave because you've worked through most of the activities in your programs and become increasingly independent in your interface with this world of others. And I know you are the only one now who can decide what it is that will hurt you more: the constant internal pain of not being able to communicate orally with the world or the fleeting pain of letting one of your family members touch your feet, and gently pulse certain points on your toes. So, I'll just sit here and chat with your mom for a while, and let you decide. It's your choice. It's a difficult choice. Let me know when you've decided."

The next three or four minutes were excruciating. But finally Christine re-moved a shoe and sock and extended her foot toward me, screwing up her face and

---

[5]Face Tapping is one of the more frequently recommended HANDLE activities. A description of it and some precautionary words about its implementation are in the Appendices. Throughout this book I will mention the names of various HANDLE activities. Not all of them are provided for you in the Appendices, but many are. HANDLE treatment programs integrate a number of activities specifically chosen for an individual with a particular neurodevelopmental profile. Selecting isolated activities to try at home may or may not produce beneficial results. In any case, adherence to the principles of Gentle En-hancement (also found in the Appendices) is of utmost importance in applying HANDLE treatment protocols.

first turning away so as not to see and then focusing her attention squarely on me and my hands on her foot. She allowed me to work on both feet and all 10 toes and to teach her mother how to apply the right amount of pressure to the same spots. I heard from her mother a few months later that Christine had just allowed her to cut her toenails with no complaints and the family was celebrating with a cake, a "Toenail Cake," which grossed out the younger brother and left more cake for brave Christine to enjoy. And then another letter from the mom a few weeks later: Christine was speaking. She had indeed chosen which pain was more intolerable, and she had chosen to allow herself to open to her sensory vulnerabilities in order to be opened to express her sensibilities.

Despite hypersensitivity around the mouth, perhaps not as extreme as Christine's, most of us with autism appear not to notice food on our faces. We can build a behavioral program of eating followed immediately by face-wiping, whether or not there is food on our faces. We can even be programmed or maneuvered into keeping our clothes on even if we would rather rip them off. And sometimes we can be bribed into taking off an extra jacket or long pants, although we feel much too exposed and vulnerable. Contradictions? No. Idiosyncrasies of neurodevelopment.

Have I just been sharing a series of disparate thoughts, this listing of complaints that people with ASD experience? It may appear that way to the uninitiated. But these are some of the threads of the autistic experience that we must explore in order to understand how this fabric is woven and how we can intervene successfully to create a full tapestry without unraveling or knotting the delicate threads.

Every event provides sensory input. For those of us in the autism spectrum, the input frequently also causes discomfort and stress. Just the thought of these events can elicit anxiety. Anxiety about most of the elements inherent in dynamic social interaction certainly explains why "difficulty in social interaction" is always cited in descriptions of individuals with ASD. Yes, we are anxious. We have difficulty communicating verbally and nonverbally. We engage in weird behaviors. Others do not understand how our minds work. We don't interact comfortably with typically developing children. We can manage better in the company of adults. Adults are generally more predictable and more patient, and the things they do—sit around and watch movies or read books and talk—require less multitasking.

Ultimately, we prefer the companionship of people like us or people who do the things we do well. In that way we're just like everyone else.

Most of the characteristics mentioned above have been cited for decades.

More recently we have added other threads to the fabric of autism. There is growing concern about poor basic nutritional levels in autistic children, levels so low they fail to support basic body-brain functions on a cellular basis. Most children with autism do have digestive problems. Again, bowel function issues unify most of us in the autism spectrum. Bowel problems are frequently related to allergies and other gastrointestinal problems. Some theories relate these problems to yeast infections that result from antibiotics taken for frequent ear infections and other illnesses. Others relate them to allergies to dairy products (casein) and wheat and other grain products (gluten). Yet others feel that the body may not be producing enzymes and hormones (such as secretin) in quantities sufficient to complete the processing of food.

Allergies are not unrelated to irregular functioning of the immune system. It appears that a large percentage of autistic children do have weak immune systems. They seem to be subject to many infections, particularly ear infections. More recently parents are convinced that autistic behaviors are linked to elements in vaccinations. But most children who receive these vaccinations, of course, do not become autistic. So why is it that for so many children, the MMR vaccine developed with thimerosal (with mercury as a preservative), seems to trigger the plunge into autistic behaviors?

Often mentioned, too, are environmental toxins such as mercury, arsenic, cadmium, lead, organochlorine, dioxin, which pollute the systems of our children. Most likely relevant to the MMR debate, toxins are being found to cause many of the serious health problems people face today. These substances alter the way the nervous system and body interact and are particularly detrimental when exposure occurs in fetal development or early infancy. Yet it should be obvious that not everyone who has been exposed to certain toxins becomes autistic, not even if that singular exposure occurred at a specific age in early development. However, the ways in which toxins interact with our unique neurophysiological makeup can predispose us to certain disorders. And if we have been exposed to a multiplicity of toxins, interactions among them can cause more damage, since the whole is greater than the sum of its parts. Then all we need is the catalyst to pull the trigger.[6] Different catalysts for different people. And once the trigger is pulled, there is no going back.

But that doesn't mean there is no resolution.

I believe my story began with toxicity. Not from one source, and not at one

---

[6]Studies recently reported by Lathe and LePage, at www.newscientist.com, indicate that hair samples of children with autism are providing researchers evidence leading to a hypothesis that autistic children do not excrete mercury adequately; therefore the mercury in the vaccines places the system on overload.

specific time, but from multiple sources, in high concentrations, throughout my mother's pregnancy with me, and continuing through my critical developmental stages. Both my parents probably influenced my toxic development. Mom began to dye her hair just about the time of her pregnancy with me. She also drank huge amounts of coffee and ate fish that had spawned and grown in the Great Lakes— probably the most highly polluted body of water outside of India and Asia at that time. And she smoked cigarettes—not a lot of cigarettes every day, but this was just one more element in combination with the other toxins in my prenatal and neonatal environment.

My father was a research chemist. In the mid-1940s—when my sister was just turning two and had already moved through her most critical developmental stages—Dad began to develop pesticides and insecticides that were to become widely used in agriculture. He was involved with developing five of the "dirty dozen" insecticides and pesticides recently recognized as neurotoxic and banned in a treaty among 127 countries. I was conceived when his sperm would have been contaminated with these toxic elements. Mom's pregnancy with me was fraught with tension. Her life had been endangered during her pregnancy with my sister, and the doctors had warned her not to risk a second pregnancy. But she did, and into that pregnancy, Dad unknowingly must have brought toxins home on his clothing. His shoes transferred them to the carpets on which I crawled. I know he later sprayed experimental pesticides and insecticides on the lawns and trees and shrubs surrounding houses in which we lived when I was a young child. I know, too, that I have had more allergies, food intolerances, and severe illnesses than any-one else in my family.

And, I, too, had an untoward reaction to the measles vaccination I received at age three. My sister was in first grade and had been exposed to the measles. My pediatrician, aware of my fragile immune system, worried I would be seriously threatened by a bout of the measles. The measles vaccine was new, and Dr. Schick actually paid a house call to vaccinate me. My mother watched for any reaction. Within the three day period Dr. Schick had thought I might react to the vaccina-tion, my left foot developed a red raised rash—measles! The rash remained local-ized on my left foot for about two days. And then my entire body was overtaken by the most severe case of measles my doctor had ever seen or heard of. Did my autis-tic behavior become more pronounced at this time? I don't know, since my delayed speech was already evident. Perhaps I became more hypersensitive to light and touch after this. I don't know. I do know it was not the vaccination that caused my problems, since I already had signs of neurodevelopmental differences.

Despite my peppering this book with examples of my own autistic tendencies and experiences, the book is not about me. It is about autism. And, yes, my toxic start and compromised immune system most likely predisposed me to many problems that I would encounter throughout my life, just as it does for many people in the spectrum. (The chart on page 121 illustrates the core role of toxicity in most of the issues that define the autistic experience and other medical and behavioral challenges.)

The last thread that needs to be picked up before we can begin to weave this new fabric is the concern that autism is a genetic disorder. My sense of this issue is that siblings and families share so many factors—physical environment, basically similar nutrition, modeled behaviors that become reinforced as brain patterns, and, yes, genes—we can't single out heredity as the cause of autism. Even children separated at birth have shared the same fetal environment, with whatever toxins and nutritional deficiencies and stresses were part of that experience. Researchers will be hard-pressed to prove a genetic link since despite the current deluge of autism in today's children there are negligible reports of autistic behaviors in most of those children's families of origin. Genetic predispositions? Perhaps. But epidemics, such as we are currently seeing in autism, are not caused by genetics alone.

As I begin to weave these many threads into a coherent theory on autism and help reduce its negative impact, I leave the thread of genetics behind. I do not know how to alter genes. I choose to focus on the other strands, those I have helped families resolve through a **H**olistic **A**pproach to **N**euro**D**evelopment and **L**earning **E**fficiency.

2. Nutrition
It's not just about food

C hildren with autism have eating problems. Indisputably. Concerns about nutrition have galvanized parents, allergists, naturopaths, homeopaths, physicians, pharmaceutical companies, and manufacturers of nutritional supplements. The concern is very real: a malnourished body-brain will have difficulty functioning, but not all children who are malnourished present with autism. So what is going on?

Chewing. It's largely about chewing.

The seemingly mundane process of chewing is integrally related to the serious issue of nutrient absorption. Digestion begins in the mouth. If food reaches the intestinal tract and cannot be absorbed, it is very unlikely that the problem is, as some specialists have theorized, due to a lack of any particular enzyme such as secretin.

The digestive SYSTEM is just that, a system. It relies on food's being processed all along the path. The work of this system begins in the mouth with chewing and salivation. Of course these two processes need to go hand-in-hand. Most people with autism do not chew their food. Instead they tend to swallow it almost whole. So when the food reaches the stomach, it is not ready for the mechanical churning process or the enzymes secreted for digestion in the stomach. And because inadequate chewing also means that the food has spent less time in the mouth, the taste buds have not had adequate time to signal the brain what types of enzymes to send to the stomach for the food it is about to receive. Food then reaches the intestinal tract not prepared for the mechanical and chemical processes that occur there. The results? Stomachaches, bowel problems, and inadequate nutrition.

But why would people not chew their food? Most people with autism have irregular tactile sensations in their mouths so they do not like the feel of the food. In addition, they have weak muscle tone in general and especially in the muscles of the mouth—those used for sucking and chewing and articulation. Muscle tone is not the amount of strength that you can call into the muscle group, but rather the degree of tension in the resting muscle. That explains why some people with autism can chomp down very tightly when biting the hand of another child whose behaviors or proximity seem threatening, or when chewing a piece of surgical tubing, but are not ready for the coordinated series of movements involved in chewing and swallowing. The movements required for chewing and swallowing and breathing (an extension of the earlier suck-swallow-breathe instinct) depend on a sequence of timed interactions among cranial nerves, nerves that develop during the embryonic stage of development.

People who are hypersensitive to sensations in the mouth and on the face are particularly bothered by one of the twelve cranial nerves—the trigeminal nerve. (See Figure 1 below.) This nerve not only services each of our teeth, but also the

Figure 1

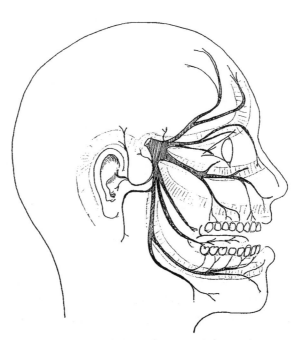

Scheme of distribution of the Trigeminal Nerve
Cranial Nerve V

gums, the tongue, the nose, the cheeks, the eyebrows, the forehead, even the corneas. When your trigeminal nerve hurts, you can't concentrate on anything else (if you've ever had root canal work or orthodontia, you'll know this).

The sensory-motor cortex of the brain, where tactile stimulation from our whole body as well as our motor responses is processed, devotes approximately half of its area to the information provided by the trigeminal and facial nerves. We are made not to be able to think of much else if these nerves are being stressed. Yet, we are also made to become aware of twinges of pain, to react to sudden intense pain with definite displays of distress or fright or affront, and to ignore constant nagging pain, so we can get on with life. When there is a change in location of the annoying stimulation, such as in chewing, face washing, tooth brushing, shaving, and even speaking, this may be interpreted as pain—felt pain that continues to irritate as it stimulates a different part of the trigeminal nerve with each movement. Many avoidance behaviors in individuals with autism are therefore a sign that the trigeminal nerve is distressed. But when the distress occurs in one place and does not travel (such as when we have food on our faces), we simply do not allow the sensation to continue to register. To feel it would open our senses to overwhelming pain.

This child is unaware of the food on her face. This phenomenon, common in those diagnosed with autism, is frequently related to hypersensitivity to touch. Because the sensation is painful, we block it. Blocking sensations restricts movement of the face and interferes with the development of the muscles needed for speech development and other important functions.

I understand this pain. Until I was 56, my trigeminal nerve was battered by a strangely constructed jaw, surgical procedures, and other assaults. In order to feel what my mouth was doing, I needed to allow myself simultaneously to feel unbearable pain. Movements of my mouth and jaw and tongue needed to be performed on a relatively conscious level. It certainly dampened the enjoyment of eating anything other than ice cream! I also had a hard time understanding why people enjoy kissing. And to this day, when I see someone vigorously chewing gum, I either hold my face and jaws to diminish the vicarious pain I feel or suffer silently, with a good deal of my attention drawn to the pain and away from the social interaction.

The mother of a three year-old nonverbal autistic youngster was more devastated by her son's not kissing her than she was by his not speaking. "I just wish he would kiss me," she kept saying plaintively. "Oh, sure, he sort of puckers a little but he just won't plant a real kiss. I would give almost anything for one kiss from his sweet little lips." She needed that kiss as evidence of his "love."

After several weeks of Face Tapping, following the pathway of the trigeminal nerve, her precious little boy began to give her kisses and not just when asked. He definitely loved his mother, not as a result of his HANDLE program but because he felt a strong bond to the woman who bore him and who loved him so. But before his program helped alleviate the pain and organize the sensation in his trigeminal nerve, he just couldn't bear the pain to demonstrate that love with a kiss.

While tactile concerns are important in relation to nutrition, anticipation of the awful texture of something would more likely prevent the food from ever entering the mouth, or would cause gagging before the food proceeded down the gullet. In truth, the sensory limitation that most often prevents autistic people from chewing their food and moving it from side to side in their mouths until it is chewed is *hypersensitivity to sound*. Listen to yourself sucking a hard candy, making little slurping noises, banging the candy into the walls of your teeth, swallowing. It is *loud!* If you can't see the activity, and the noise is not only blaring but unexpected, wouldn't it sound like an avalanche? Can you imagine being frightened by the sound of yourself chewing?

Two clients of mine finally began to chew their food after I told them my perception of what it sounds like and invited them to sit ear to cheek and listen to me chew. One of them had just begun to speak but her speech was labored and slurred. After a moment of listening, she pulled away with wide-open eyes to express her amazement, and then said "Again" as she again placed her ear on my cheek to hear the shockingly loud sounds as I chewed a carrot stick. We repeated this several times, each time with her command "Again" when she was ready. Finally, after many repetitions, she pulled away from my cheek with a relaxed face, having overcome her fear of the mysterious loud sounds in the cavern of my mouth.

We moved on to crunch contests, where we picked up foods like corn chips and carrots and celery, said "Ready, Set, Go!" and on "Go" bit into the food to see who could make the loudest initial crunch. We argued over this, since to each of us the crunch in her own mouth sounded louder than the crunch across the table. I played similar games with both clients to help them accept and even enjoy some of the auditory input that occurs in chewing and swallowing food. These clients, ages 19 and 20, were finally able to chew their food whenever and wherever they ate.

Why might someone be so hypersensitive to noise that the sound of his own chewing (or sucking as an infant) is aversive? And what other effects might this have on autistic behaviors? If protecting our ears affects our digestion, is there a corresponding effect that causes digestive problems to change how our ears function? Let me explain.

For years occupational therapists trained in Sensory Integration Therapy have been addressing the vestibular system in the inner ear to enhance the functions of individuals with ASD and many other children with irregular neuromuscular control and responses. The vestibular system is not a closed system; it shares structures and fluids and stimulation with the mechanisms of hearing and is open to other influences through the outer and middle ear and also from the nose (and indirectly, the mouth) via the Eustachian tubes. (See Figure 2 below.)

This figure shows you the relative positions of the middle ear and inner ear, including the vestibular system. As you look at the hand that is drawn to hold back the outer ear so you can see the approximate location of this system, you will

Figure 2 Vestibular System: Inner Ear

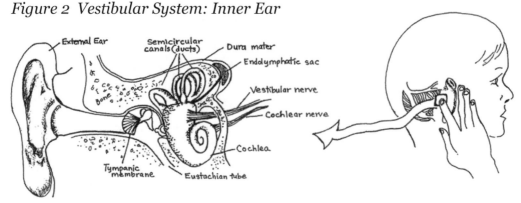

probably recall this rather typical autistic behavior of placing hands to ears.

Not only does this behavior help protect the ears from bombardment by noise, it also points the way to an area of major concern in treating the root causes of autistic behaviors. So the ears, like the trigeminal nerve, are important enough to draw our attention.

Although I knew for years that sound sensitivity is pivotal in the behaviors associated with autism, I had a moment of profound revelation one summer day in 1998. At various points in the day, I was working with three autistic clients—one four years old, one eight, and one in his thirties. It was a hot and humid day. The air conditioner was on. And each client covered both ears, humming and rocking as he moved away from the cooling window unit, even though these self-stimming behaviors had been nearly absent in our previous sessions. When we turned the air conditioner off, the clients calmed down. Then it became too warm, so we opened the window and the door slightly to get some cross-ventilation. As the street noises entered the room from both sides—street noises from streets that were at least a hundred feet away from us on either side—back came the ear holding, humming, and rocking; but this time the sound was coming from two directions, so they couldn't move away and instead began to walk in circles in the room.

We decided to swelter for the duration of the session.

By the end of that day, I realized how I began to journey through my autism. During my early years, unbeknownst to my parents, my doctors or myself, the bony structures in my middle ear continued to grow, eventually closing the opening completely by the time I was eight and a half. I had gradually been losing my hearing as speech therapists inadvertently taught me to lip read while trying to teach me to speak intelligibly. A few months before my ninth birthday we learned that I couldn't hear a thing.

And that was my salvation: I was saved from classic autism by deafness! A surgical procedure called fenestration restored my hearing, and for a period of time my autistic behaviors intensified until I learned that I could shut down the stimulation in my inner ear by jumping on a pogo stick.

The inner ear and vestibular system shut down when they experience rapid movement and sudden stops. Spinning, jumping, head-banging. All ways to shut down an overwhelmed middle and inner ear system. Some therapies incorporate these movements. HANDLE treatment programs usually do not, because most clients who need these tools find them on their own. And professionals who try to extinguish these forms of "negative self-stimulation" fail to recognize how essential they are to individuals with ASD. The ability to shut down an overwhelmed vestibular-auditory system on demand can even save some people from seizures. I do not want to ponder who I would be today if my parents and teachers had tried to stop me from jumping on my pogo stick until I had worked through my need.

So although we don't need help to find a means to stop the movement of fluids in our inner ears, what we do need is help to incorporate the slow controlled movements that enable the ear to process the information that will help us be in touch with the world. We want to be in touch with the world.

Failure to chew properly requires further exploration (beyond its role in causing indigestion and stomachaches) in order to be appreciated as an important part of the fabric of autism. What do you do when you have a stomachache? You bend forward, hunch your shoulders, and get into a semi-fetal position. If there is any intestinal discomfort, you might start to rock, forward from the hunch and back to the hunch. You won't extend your body to rock back and forth; rather you'll rock forth and forth, because to extend backwards would stretch your stomach and exacerbate the pain.

Thus the postures so frequently associated with ASD, and some of the mannerisms, too, are similar to those people assume when they have digestive problems, problems that can stem from not chewing the food, from sensitivity to sound, and usually also from trigeminal nerve irritation.

However, by adopting these self-protective, soothing postures and movements, we further restrict the range of movement that provides stimulation to the inner ear and therefore to the vestibular system. This becomes a vicious cycle that requires intervention, not forcefully, but with respect. Gentle Enhancement[7] of weak systems allows them to open and develop. Abrupt stimulation and over-stimulation causes them to shut down.[8]

Of particular significance in the postures and movements adopted by most of us with autism is most probably that the endolymphatic sac in the vestibular system—a soft tissue organ like a long-necked balloon—does not fill. Recent studies have shown that when this sac fills with the fluid in the inner ear, the sac actually touches the outer lining of the brain—the dura mater. When this occurs, the rhythms of the body as translated through the vestibular system share their input in

---

[7]Gentle Enhancement is pivotal to successful neurodevelopmental therapy. Its significance will be discussed in later chapters. Gentle Enhancement[SM] is the trademark of HANDLE treatment programs.

[8]Dr. Daniel Amen's research on ADD using SPECT scans demonstrates that the brain shuts down when it is overwhelmed by stimulation. This phenomenon is true for other disorders as well.

yet one more way, immediately and directly, with the rhythmic flow of the fluid whose flow establishes a form of communication to the entire brain and spinal cord (this fluid is the cerebrospinal fluid that flows between the dura mater and the pia mater—the meningeal lining that is next to the brain). This process is aided by therapeutic modalities that influence craniosacral adjustments.

***

Caregivers of individuals with autism cannot understand why they will not agree to eat nutritious food, even food other people just love, but will happily munch on and even devour a Styrofoam cup. Can this behavior, too, have a logical explanation?

A voracious appetite for Styrofoam and other non-food items (a disorder in its own right—pica) might indicate deficits in certain minerals or microbes. The cup eater might be trying to balance his pH or reinstate friendly bacteria into the intestinal tract. He might like the tactile aspect of the cup. Perhaps he is seeking some form of constancy. Food items look and feel different outside of the mouth from how they do inside the mouth (raw tomatoes are one of the most deceiving and confusing foods from the standpoint of anticipation of the tactile experience). From years of chewing and sucking my clothes, I can attest that there is a certain predictable nature to materials that do not readily decompose when chewed. And certainly those of us in the ASD seek perceptual constancy.

Other typical autistic behaviors are also linked to the digestion issue. Toe walking, for example. In the Chinese practice of reflexology, points on the soles of the feet have been mapped, and the heel of the foot bears reflex points for the intestines (these are not reflex points that are connected directly to the nervous system). Despite the fact that acupuncture, acupressure and reflexology employ theories not yet explained to the satisfaction of Western medicine, the approaches have become acknowledged as valuable diagnostic and treatment tools for physiological problems.

Viewing toe walking from this perspective, we see that when the intestines are unhealthy and tender, we change our gait to avoid putting weight on our heels, shifting forward onto our toes. Gently stimulating the appropriate reflex points on the feet, and gently enhancing the other interactive systems that make up part of this fabric, can bring an end to toe walking without any direct attention or therapy to the gait, and without resorting to surgery or injections of Botox to release the Achilles tendon.

So from head to toe, autistic behaviors signal ways to deal with the digestive issues. But if we view the behaviors merely as self-stimulation or annoying quirks, and we use medications and behavior modification to mask the symptoms, the problems will not resolve. The underlying issues will return, and usually with a vengeance, and will explode in violent releases of the energy that has been trapped inside our bodies.

3. Integrating the senses
Sound and light

W̶e are energetic beings in an energetic world. What we perceive as sound and sight and touch and movement are all waves of energy that are received through our different sense organs. When functioning smoothly, we integrate these scattered forms of energy into congruent wholes and perceive the world "as it is." Reality is in the eyes of the beholder—and the ears and the skin and the muscles and tendons and stomachs.

But those of us in the autism spectrum differ markedly in our perception of the world from individuals deemed "neurotypical." Dr. Temple Grandin, one of the world's best known persons with autism, detailed quirks about her visual perceptions and visual memory in her book *Thinking in Pictures*. The movie *Rain Man* also depicted the savant ability to take "mental snapshots" and process them from inside one's head rather than in the here and now (roughly 10 percent of those of us with ASD seem to have this savant ability, but accurate figures are difficult to obtain because most people with autism cannot communicate their perceptions well enough).

My visual memory is very reliable. I can navigate in strange cities after only a brief look at a map. I also immediately translate verbal directions into maps so I can find my way. Situations where I don't know what to expect visually and need to trust someone else to tell me where and when to turn stress my sensibilities. I'm like the child who needs to know where her toys are, and cannot tolerate their being rearranged even slightly. Reality and the "mental snapshots" must coincide to make sense. And if they do not make sense, I can't be calm.

Five year-old Danny had a passion for dinosaurs. Many boys his age share that passion. Danny knew the names of more dinosaurs than I had heard of. He also knew what each one looked like. His mother, a talented artist, was able to draw dinosaurs with accuracy. We were working together—Danny, his mom and I. Danny already had accepted that I could not fulfill his demands to draw dinosaurs. He wanted a T-Rex drawn while his mother and I were conversing. His screeching, beseeching "Draw a T-Rex a T-Rex a T-Rex" got him only this: "Here's some paper. You can draw it yourself. We're busy."

Danny tried. Sheet after sheet of paper with the beginnings of a T-Rex. Not a perfect one. Not one that fit the mental snapshot. No matter how many times I said in all honesty, "That's better than I could draw, Danny," he was inconsolable. He needed a T-Rex that looked exactly like the T-Rex in his favorite dinosaur book. Flinging sheets to the floor in anger, Danny threw tantrums until finally his exasperated mother drew him one perfectly fine T-Rex complete with every requested detail—"Teeth, Mommy," Danny ordered with great expectation. "Toes, Mommy," he said, flapping his hands as the image began to conform to the one in his memory. Imagination and approximation were not choices. Things need to have constancy, in this case visual constancy, or the world is not a safe place to be.

But there are wonderful advantages to the savant qualities of an autistic profile. Imagine how much easier studying for a history test would be if you carried in your head a photo album of the pages of the book, and if you could take those snapshots one after another in rapid succession, and trust they would not fade for many days! And can you imagine the clutter if you couldn't delete photos you no longer wanted, and the delayed response time if you needed to sort through all of them to locate the one you were searching for? Zoning-out is frequently zoning-in, attempting to find the right snapshot that answers the question, but it is mixed up with innumerable others and won't surface. Some of us develop the ability to categorize and create a filing system for those images so they are more generalized. This wonderful skill combined with another—to archive the photos I rarely need—has helped me process information more rapidly than most people, no matter what modality they use.

My eighth grade social studies teacher, Mr. Paller, had never encountered someone like me, nor even heard about people like me. Special education as we know it now did not exist when I was in school, and after I began to sit relatively still in class and speak fairly intelligibly, I tested as gifted, even a "genius." Mr. Paller knew little of my history. He did know that I was a straight-A student, with a gift for expressing myself in writing, but that I rarely spoke in class. Sometimes I contributed to discussions, if I had time to rehearse my answer first inside my head.

Mr. Paller was an inspired and inspiring educator. He developed interesting projects for us and rarely assigned humdrum homework. He also constructed tests that required analysis of the material and creative thought to discern comparisons and contrasts, to ascertain reasons for sequences of events, to challenge our thinking about the facts. I usually read the assignments quickly, sometimes barely glancing at the page. Except once.

On this occasion I reviewed the chapter the night before the test on it, and glanced at it again in homeroom. Mr. Paller's test that day was a hasty assemblage of the bold headings introducing the sections in the text. Headings such as "Why did the Rhode Island colonists place freedom of religion in their charter?" I didn't know that this is what Mr. Paller had done. And he didn't know that I had photographs of all the pages in that chapter inside my head—headings and all. The next day, he asked me to see him after class.

In an accusing voice he asked me "Why did you cheat? And how could you have thought you would get away with it? Having your textbook open and copying paragraphs verbatim!"

I was dumbstruck. My favorite teacher, accusing me of something so horrific.

While I hesitated, Mr. Paller warned me, "It won't help your situation any if you lie. Just tell me the truth. Why did you do it?"

Suddenly I realized what must have happened. "Open the book to any page and ask me any of the bold-faced questions," I said.

He did. I quoted the book verbatim. And we both learned. He learned there were people with visual scanners in their heads. I learned to take the time to check what I was writing against my scanned image, to make sure I wouldn't find myself in trouble again.

My abilities to speed-read and to photograph the pages helped an 11 year-old I saw a few years ago. His parents knew that Mark was very intelligent, even though he had not yet spoken intelligible words. He was, however, a good one-finger typist on his Light Writer, and the remarkable machine gave voice—albeit robotic—to his ideas. His muscle tone was so weak that he needed to have his elbow supported by a facilitator much of the time. His cynical teachers thought the facilitator was inputting ideas and that Mark was simply the equivalent of a ventriloquist's dummy. But I knew his facilitator personally, and she was a terrible speller. The spelling on the Light Writer was flawless. Mark was clearly the author.

Mark had many self-stimulatory behaviors. One of his most frequent was flipping the pages of books and magazines, over and over and over again, then discarding the book or magazine to flip through another. One of the goals in his school-mandated individualized education program was to reduce and eventually eliminate this self-stimming. I was appalled.

"Yes," I said, "he's self-stimming. But not in the way you think. He's providing himself with mental stimulation. He's reading those books and magazines!" His parents told me they knew he could read, but no way was he reading in that fashion.

Moments later Mark typed out a message conveying "At last. Someone understands."

After that, we convinced his teacher. She gave him a book he had never seen before. He flipped and flipped until he tossed the book away from boredom. Then the teacher handed him questions on the book. Assisted at the elbow by his facilitator, he typed out the correct answers and earned a B+ on the book report!

So why might such a youngster become outraged when someone takes away his magazine and then insists that he focus his vision on the face of the interloper in order to see or hear a direction to perform some other task? Not only is he interrupted in the process that is satisfying a need for stimulation, but he is also being expected to change the mental picture and, worse, to sustain focal vision on something directly in front of him. To sustain eye-contact.

When I was younger I didn't sustain eye-contact. People thought I was shy. I was, but in addition to shunning the social interaction, I took snapshots. I worked from the indelible image in my head. Among the images I'm sure I held some faces. But face recognition is a significant problem for many individuals with ASD. In fact, researchers are studying a specific area of the brain—the fusiform face area—for clues into the experience of autism.

When I take a snapshot of a table and then view the table again, it doesn't change. When I take a snapshot of a face that's leaning toward me and smiling, and then I look back at that same face, now leaning slightly to one side with a slight furrow in its brow, it's not the same face. Sometimes it's flushed and sometimes it has a pallor. Sometimes it's moving rapidly and almost never is it truly still. Human faces have so many details and more possibilities of altered expression than animals' faces. Inanimate objects provide constancy and therefore security, that is, until they become marred or rearranged in relation to the other objects around them.

I was working with a family whose seven year-old had been diagnosed with Tourette's Syndrome—a movement disorder characterized by tics usually of the face, and sometimes of the throat, the neck, the shoulders and chest, rarely of the legs, accompanied frequently by "mental tics" or obsessive-compulsive thought patterns. In my first meeting with Evan, I noticed his inability to sustain eye-contact and his reliance on peripheral vision. His muscle tone was weak, facial muscles as well as his body in general. He had difficulty controlling his vocal tone, speaking in a monotone punctuated by loud and squeaky notes, all without prosody (the natural rhythmic flow of spoken language).

Evan had no idea how to play with other children. He couldn't focus his attention on tasks in class; he tended to daydream. I suggested he didn't have Tourette's at all, despite the throat clearing and blinking and other tic-like behaviors. I felt that a psychiatrist would diagnose him with Asperger's Syndrome—that the tics were a combination of an allergic reaction to foods and a stress response to the strain he was placing on his various systems in order to focus more intensely and longer than they were able to withstand.

But the diagnosis was irrelevant. We began to work on Evan's muscle tone and his ability to engage in focal vision. We reduced sensitivity to peripheral sounds and increased focused listening and response time to questions and instructions. It was not easy, but his family was diligent in performing the specially selected activities and in returning for monthly re-evaluations so we could alter the program in keeping with Evan's progress.[9] As with all HANDLE programs, no skills were taught, no behaviors were practiced, and Gentle Enhancement was the key.

Actually, the diagnosis WAS relevant because the misdiagnosis led the parents to pursue many "cures" for a "disease" their son didn't have. When they finally focused on the allergies and the detoxification process necessary to reduce the allergic reactions, Evan began to apply the gains we had made in his sensory systems and their interactions, to have a consistency of internal response to stimuli organ-

---

[9]HANDLE activities are not just exercises. They are discretely designed subtle movements—some passive and some active—specifically prescribed to enhance each individual's weak systems without stressing other systems. These activities are shared freely with families and professionals in relation to specific cases. HANDLE courses also provide venues for people to learn activities from the HANDLE repertoire and to learn the principles behind the construction and application of each activity. Just as it can be dangerous to give a diabetic the same midday snack as others in his group, asking a person with one neurodevelopmental profile to perform the activities developed for another is irresponsible. I would rather err on the side of caution. Several activities are included in the appendices.

ized within a healthy body. But the work needed to occur in concert, so that the stress of being unable to meet the demands of the school day and social engagements did not create more neurotoxins that would then, again, need to be cleared from his systems.

Evan is just one of hundreds of children whose behavioral symptoms were red flags calling our attention to the systems that needed strengthening. Instead, he received medication in attempts to mask these behaviors, and suggestions of behavior modification therapies designed to replace those rituals that served his needs with routinized behaviors and scripts that served the needs of his social group. But his symptoms persisted. Why? Because they must, until they are recognized and treated developmentally as integral parts of the system, not as separate annoying traits.

And so, what may cause difficulty in sustaining focal vision? And how does it interact with the nervous systems and thereby with our general development?

Cameron's mother, Vicki, was exasperated by years of futile attempts to have her now 11 year-old ASD son develop eye-contact and also to tie shoelaces. "In his case," I explained, "these two phenomena are related to his inability to focus his two eyes on one target, making it difficult for him to look at anything straight on, and also difficult to distinguish foreground from background."

In addition to activities to develop his binocular functions I suggested teaching the behavior of lace tying in a special way—totally outside of the HANDLE paradigm of not teaching specific skills, but wanting to show Cameron and his mom how his visual challenges were an obstacle to lace tying. I suggested they practice tying with a lace that was half white and half red.

Vicki wrote me "I finally got it together to dye a shoelace half red and he was able to tie it!!! What a wonderful accomplishment. What I notice is that where he used to seem to look away when he was trying to do it, he now seems to be able to look where he is working. I had this realization that if I took my eyes and defocused them so that I had a double image, then turned my head far enough so that I had a single image, that I looked like he did when you asked him to focus on something you were trying to show him. Is that what has been going on for him? I am so excited!"

I was excited, too. For both of them.

Many things can prevent an individual from using his eyes to team in creating focus. Most people who have suffered traumatic brain injury have difficulty with this, too. But because autism is a developmental disorder, we need to look at what affects this ability developmentally. And the reasons we discover may also apply to those whose neurodevelopmental differences express themselves through different obstacles to learning and social interaction, such as attentional disorders and learning disabilities.

Developmentally, babies are programmed to have a strong sucking reflex, so they will be able to get nourishment and survive. In order to suck we need to engage our lips and tongues and allow tactile sensations in these areas as well as on our nose and cheeks. When a sucking infant feels safe, she closes her eyes and relaxes into the experience, after first latching on and gazing at her mother's face. With eyes closed, beneath the eyelids, her eyes actually converge with each suck.

If an infant keeps his eyes open to suck, because he feels insecure, his eyes do not converge as he sucks. Instead, they are scanning the environment in vigilant self-protection. If he is, in addition, hypersensitive to the sound of the sucking and swallowing, his experience is fitful and can be frightening. And if he is distressed tactually, he keeps his eyes open and his Autonomic Nervous System (ANS) stays in fright mode, altering his breathing and many other internal responses.

Two-finger sucking can create irregularities in binocular vision that translate into challenges in sustaining eye contact. Compromised focal vision can cause difficulty in listening to conversations, distractibility or irritation in environments with background noise, and other problems of auditory attention.

This difficulty compounds itself, because when infants do not practice sucking, small roots of the trigeminal and facial nerves do not stimulate little muscles in the middle ear that control mechanisms that dampen sound. And the eyes do not send messages of focus to a part of the brain designed to direct a contingent part of the brain where the auditory nerve would receive the message of "Focus forward. Don't let the peripheral environmental sounds draw your attention." When this does not happen, language sounds and non-language sounds intermingle. The rhythms of language get lost in the hubbub of extraneous sounds. (For those of you who wish to explore this connection further, the parts of the brain in question are the superior and inferior colliculus.)

Another influence on our sense of hearing comes through the very important trigeminal nerve. When it is overly sensitive and perhaps our sinuses are impacted from allergic reactions, we may cut off sensation that would send messages to our ears about our own voices via bone conduction hearing. But if sensing this is too painful, we will speak louder, to project our voices out into the periphery and hope we can distinguish it from the din of all the noises we are indiscriminately hearing through unfocused air conduction hearing.

Mark, the boy who self-stimmed by flipping through books and had not yet spoken, discovered the sound of his own voice the first afternoon I worked with him. After first demonstrating the use of a Tok-Back voice reflector, and having his parents also demonstrate it, I offered the gizmo to the child.

He grasped it lightly and looked to his parents for help in putting it on. Then he stood absolutely still, breathing and making other quiet noises into the reflector, looking into the reflector and into his own head, trying to comprehend the mystical event he was experiencing. He made a few language sounds, and again his being said "I am trying to fathom the immensity of the moment." He took the voice reflector off. He put it down for a moment. Then he picked it up, put it on again, and experimented a while longer.

When he finally removed the device and sat down, slowly, almost in reverie, I waited until he seemed settled in his body and his seat, and asked him, if he could, to tell me what he experienced. On his Light Writer, he typed "It helps me understand just plain my voice."

How perfectly he captured the profundity of the moment. For the first time in his life he had heard his own voice, outside of the din of the environment. He knew he existed not only because he could feel pain and movement and pressure, but because he could hear and feel his voice. I sent him home with the voice reflector and a number of other activities that his family engaged in with him a few minutes each day. Several weeks later his older brother returned home from school and asked his mom, "What's Dad doing home so early?"

But it wasn't his dad. It was Mark, talking in another part of the house. Trying to "find" his voice, he first found the one he had heard the most and the clearest—his dad's. He moved through the repertoire of family members' voices in a short period of time, and eventually truly found his own. Within a few months the nonverbal autistic eleven year-old was sustaining eye-contact, engaging in an ever decreasing amount of self-stim, and reading six to ten sentence speeches to his classmates.

Was a part of his brain damaged or dormant? Had he found a way to awaken the dormant parts or reroute the messages to intact areas? I imagine we will never know. But I do know that by using an approach that takes into account the interactions of systems, and which gently and respectfully enhances systems in developmentally sound ways, we created function where there had been dysfunction.

So as we continue on this journey of interwoven senses and intertwining nervous systems, know that if it were possible to explain autism in a totally linear-sequential way, others would have already done it. It is my task to try to guide you through some known and some unknown territories that loop back upon one another, and to hope I don't lose you in the process.

In a way, you will be experiencing the apprehension and fear of an autistic person, entering an unfamiliar building, wondering if you are safe and if you will be able to find your way out if you need a quick escape. What is behind the doors we are about to walk through is obvious only to those of us who have been here before. I will guide you and at times throw you a familiar concept as a rope, or a new neurological discovery as a beacon. So, now, with our eyes and ears focused, we move on.

4. The forgotten sense
The smell of danger

T hese doors we're entering are both expansive and confining. Imagine yourself with weak focal vision and poor perception of three-dimensionality. Your hearing doesn't filter out extraneous sounds. Your tactile system feels tickled when air moves across your skin. You're about to enter a space where someone may touch you, where lights and sounds may assault you, where you may be asked to sit up straight or walk slowly when your muscle tone and balance cannot support those activities. You may be yelled at or demeaned because you can't process the information and respond appropriately in two seconds. If you respond inappropriately, you may be ridiculed or simply ignored. You do not know what to expect, and EVERYthing makes you afraid. You are not safe, either physically or emotionally. Yet you need to feel safe before you can accept your new surroundings.

Safety. It's essential for all of us.

How do autistic people develop that sense of safety? How do they internalize the concept of boundaries so they don't invade others' space or feel violated when others move closer? Our primal senses of touch and smell try to take over, but we can't control them; so we trust the one that has proven most reliable.

Smell.

While the sense of touch develops in the first month of gestation, it is practiced in a wet environment and almost all of the tactile stimulation we receive until the moment of birth is self-stimulatory. When we emerge from the womb, the sense of touch goes through a tremendous and abrupt transition, because we are being touched by others in a dry world. For some reason, most children on the autistic spectrum have difficulty with that transition and with so many others. Perhaps it is from too sudden of a birth (vaginal or Cesarean delivery) that did not allow a gradual introduction of "roughing up" of the trigeminal nerve. Or perhaps it was too long of a labor, during which the ganglia of the trigeminal nerve took a beating as the plates of the skull continued to be pushed against it. Or perhaps forceps squeezed the trigeminal nerve severely, or a suction mechanism traumatized both the trigeminal nerve and the optic nerves and the optic chiasm. Or perhaps any number of other factors (including heavy metal toxicity) caused the newborn to be challenged by this transition into a world of tactile discomfort.

Olfaction (the sense of smell), however, which develops in the second month in utero and is also well practiced before birth, is honed in a dark, wet environment and is stimulated by chemical elements outside of our control. Because this does not change at birth, smell becomes our most reliable sense. And we need something to rely upon.

Another reason most people with autism are extremely sensitive to smells is simple—survival. We must protect ourselves from unseen toxins, molecules that our bodies know will push us over the edge. And we must be able to identify the position of these enemies and the position of our friends. When I introduce a new object to a person with autism, his first response is often to smell it, sometimes to bite it. I don't try to interfere with that behavior, because it helps me see how the individual's systems function naturally so I can learn the strengths and weaknesses as a prelude to creating trust.

Again, imagine that you're entering a new space, perhaps an elevator to take you to a new doctor. The doors open. You need to move aside so you will not be touched by the people who are rushing out of that box with oh-so-many lights in it. You lean into your mom, who is embarrassed by the fact that her 14 year-old daughter is frightened by the elevator and the people in it and around it. She tenses. You approach the door and step across the threshold. And then you notice it. A pungent cologne. The woman in the navy blue sweater is wearing Replique. Your throat and nostrils close. You can't breathe. You are in a box, surrounded by people, lights reflecting and sounds ricocheting and smells assaulting. And the box is moving, stopping periodically, jolting, and taking off again at uneven speeds. The door opens. You bolt, bumping into people and greatly upsetting your mother, who races after you before the doors close and separate you. You don't apologize, because you have achieved your goal: survival.

I have been that child. I have climbed 17 flights of stairs to avoid elevators full of scents that would overpower my respiratory system. I am the 18 year-old who returned to consciousness surrounded by an emergency medical team crowded into a dentist's office in Cleveland, Ohio. I had passed out in the chair, before any procedure had been performed. I didn't faint from fear; I passed out because of the smell of ripe bananas. As the scent neared my nose, my lungs began to shut down. It turned out, the dentist had planned to prepare my gums with a drop of banana oil prior to injecting me with Novocain. I couldn't escape the scent. I passed out.

I am allergic to bananas.

And with the scent still in the room, I needed medical intervention—an oxygen mask—in order to regain consciousness. I vividly remember that when I came to and saw all the confusion and concern, I responded to quizzical looks and questions I could vaguely hear. In a breathless voice I said one word.

"Bananas."

Banana oil is an extremely potent and volatile chemical compound—iso amyl acetate. Placing a thin film on the outside of tubing is actually the oldest method of testing respirators, since iso amyl acetate has a strong, readily identifiable odor that will be recognized immediately if the respirators' seals don't fit. Can you imagine the challenges I have had in supermarkets, in restaurants, on airplanes where breakfast bananas were being served, and even in friends' homes and at gatherings with baked goods that have as a "hidden" ingredient the very nutritious and moist and flavorful banana?

So of course I allow my clients to smell things. Perhaps, they, like I, need to protect themselves from overwhelming toxins their noses will ferret out. Although in our clinic we insist that our cleaning crew use only unscented products, and we advise everyone entering our premises not to wear colognes, hair spray and other highly scented items (clothes that have been dried with fabric softener sheets are highly scented), we cannot totally eliminate scents. And that's good, because they sometimes provide valuable information. But we try to keep the atmosphere as clear as possible of irrelevant odors, and we stock lime spray because lime is the universal odor neutralizer. There is enough to process with the scents that are in fabric, emitted from bodies, naturally found in foods, in virtually everything to those who are hypersensitive.

Scents trigger memories and can facilitate a beneficial form of sensory integration deemed rare in people with autism. In her book, *Nobody Nowhere,* Donna

Williams said she can be in only one sense at a time. Usually when people say this, they are unaware of how dependent they are on their sense of smell, operating in the background.

Smell integrates by its very nature, through its connections to the limbic system—an intricate part of the brain that is the seat of emotional response and motivation and memory. Some recent studies show that those of us with autism have strangely ordered limbic systems, as well. So I let my clients sniff, and we both learn: I learn about "triggering" smells, and the clients learn I can be trusted.

Sometimes, as a child, I could override my hyper-vigilant nose. When no one new entered my environment and I could sit in a corner or move surely in a familiar space, then I could almost relax. If someone new entered the space (preceded of course by his scent), the level of my arousal—my fright—would heighten. If I were not too tired, I could cognitively piece together elements of this person's energy. I could tell myself, "Poise yourself for flight or even fight. But wait. This person is not moving in a threatening way. He is not using a threatening voice. He is not shape shifting as he moves from one field of light to another. Whew! He is not emitting any other form of threatening energy. Perhaps I can tolerate his presence. Perhaps I do not need to continue into a fight or flight response. But I must remain vigilant. And that means I cannot continue with what I was doing. He has interfered with my enjoyment of my safe and familiar pastime. Maybe if I'm lucky, he'll leave soon."

However, when I was tired and expecting certain olfactory experiences but had others forced upon me, I couldn't control my responses. I usually sought a rapid escape, not worrying about what was in my path. Or I squirmed more vigorously and covered my nose and mouth and let loose a muffled scream. Or I clenched my fists so hard that my fingernails dug holes in my palms. I didn't become abusive to others, unlike my nine year-old client, Isaac, whose high-level of functioning most of the time did not prepare his teachers or classmates for his explosive behaviors when overwhelmed by smell.

Isaac's special education teacher, Mrs. Walker, had referred him for assessment. She pleaded, "I need to know what I can do to help Isaac. I know he doesn't mean to destroy others' property or to harm the other children, but he just loses control. Usually just before lunch he begins to get very edgy, and during lunch he rampages the room, terrorizing the other children. And at recess, after lunch, he goes for one or two of the children and simply attacks them. We've tried everything. We thought that perhaps he was suffering from severe blood-sugar swings, so we gave him high protein snacks mid-morning. We thought he might need to sit at a separate table, or at a table with the children he seemed to like the most. Nothing helped. I don't want to give up on him. Most of the time he is so sweet and he is so smart. But I can't endanger the other children."

Next, I interviewed Isaac's mom. She, too, was at a loss. Actually, she said, "I've been at a loss since Isaac was first placed in my arms moments after his birth. He seemed to reject me. My firstborn child," she continued, almost choking on her tears, "and he just couldn't seem to relax in my arms. We never bonded, and he still seems to reject me. Whenever I move closer to him, he squiggles his nose and moves away, sometimes even pushing the air between us as if to increase the distance. And we can't take him to malls or parties or anywhere there are people he doesn't know well, or where people come and go. It's as if there's something unseen that he senses that deters him from others. His dad and I are as much at a loss as his teacher. This special class was our last hope for Isaac. Just tell me what I can do to help. . ."

Isaac's mother and teacher had all the information I needed. His nose squiggling. His edginess around lunchtime at school. His earliest rejection of his mom in the delivery room with all of its unfamiliar odors. His mom's use of cologne (which my sensitive nose discerned as mildly offensive, too). His pushing away the air between himself and others who were approaching him.

Isaac needed to know what to expect in his olfactory environment in order to feel safe.

I assessed Isaac to see if any of his other senses were weak, which could explain his inability to let his sense of smell rest. Isaac was not the most willing partner in the assessment procedure. He kept shrugging his shoulders and saying, "Just leave me alone."

He did cooperate enough to let me know that he had some irregularities in his visual functions. And also in his sense of body in space. But he was coping. At least from his perspective he was. He had explanations for his attacks on others. "They just won't stop annoying me." And when I asked him what it was that annoyed him the most, he replied, "Their food stinks. Mustard and pickles and orange juice and hard boiled eggs. And especially salami and peanut butter. They get close to me after lunch and breathe out their salami breath on me on purpose."

Why hadn't he told this to others? Probably because they hadn't created trust. They may have entered the situation with preconceptions about his behaviors. They had not opened the Pandora's Box of senses to explore. Perhaps they wore clothes that had been recently dry-cleaned, or used highly scented hand-lotion. Anyone who smelled like that couldn't be trusted, wouldn't understand.

While we were working to strengthen Isaac's weaker senses, so he could rely less on smell in relating to his world, we needed to help him so he could remain in school. We arranged that the parents of every child in his class would send a complete menu each day and that the teacher would read these menus one at a time, before each child opened his lunch box. Mrs. Walker obligingly read the menus, willing to sound like a waitress placing orders in a family restaurant if this might help Isaac and restore peace to her class: "Jason has an Oscar Meyer bologna sandwich on whole wheat bread with French's mustard. He also has a bag of Frito's corn chips, some carrot sticks, and a red Delicious apple. His drink today is Tropicana orange juice. Jason, you may open your lunch now. And Lynne has a tuna salad sandwich made with light Bumble Bee tuna, hard boiled eggs, chopped onion and celery, and Miracle Whip . . ."

Once Isaac knew what to expect, and could prepare himself for the odors of each lunch, one at a time, he could contain himself. He was still not relaxed, but he could predict his olfactory environment and allow his classmates to enjoy their lunches in safety. And after lunch, before going out on the playground, Isaac was reminded which children to keep a distance from on the playground so their odiferous breath would not trigger his lion to rage once more.

Within less than 2 years, Isaac returned to his neighborhood school, mainstreamed and doing well. His social interaction problems were behind him. And his formerly weak senses were stronger, so he would not need to fall back on smell for protection again.

Luckily for Isaac, I knew his olfactory challenges well, and knew that anticipation of odor was an important factor in preparation for any transition, especially when we are tired. Traveling in the back seat of our car with my sister beside me, I would need to go to sleep. If she didn't want me to use her rump as a pillow, she or my mom would toss me a pillow. Any pillow. But if they tossed me my sister's pillow, I would squirm and fuss or kick and scream, not able to sleep, beating the pillow and tossing it around wildly. And they had no idea why. I couldn't explain that the pillow had my sister's scent and not mine.

If they'd known, they might have asked, "How could you sleep using her rump as a pillow or with her beside you? Doesn't her skin have her scent, even more so?" Of course. But her scent is part of her, and I expected that. But my pillow should not smell like my sister! It should have only my scent on it. Why could others not understand this?

Perhaps this is one reason that when those of us in the spectrum have stuffed noses our behaviors change dramatically. We may be less volatile but much more irritable. We can no longer rely on our sense of smell to guard us. So how can we determine with whom we are safe and where we can find comfort? We need to get close, perhaps in someone else's most personal space—in her face—and sniff her hair and her skin to determine if she is friend or foe, mom or stranger.

Some of the children I've worked with go through cyclical periods during which their customary attachment to their mothers dissolves. For four or five days they seem not even to recognize their mothers. It turns out that these intervals of confused withdrawal coincide with the women's menstrual periods. Mom smells different, so mom is frightening and unfamiliar.

More than 30 years ago, as a teacher in self-contained classrooms of children with a variety of special needs, I would warn my class. "In the next few days you may notice that although I look like the same person, I will smell a little different. It's okay. I'm not sick and this is just part of what happens to most women every month or so for a few days. Remember? I've told you that before. So if you notice that I smell different, you'll be right! But it will still be the same Me you know and trust, and we'll be able to do our work together and have fun together just the same."

Remember, preparation helps us to set our systems' upcoming experiences. Those of us whose systems become readily overwhelmed need warnings about the sensory experience, so we can anticipate it and set our filters. Once warned, we are not so frightened. This warning is not related to behaviors. It is not a "you need to calm down if you want to watch your video" type of statement. It is preparing the senses for transition. It is not enough to say, "You need to stay beside me and be quiet in the library."

First you need to describe the situation in minute sensory detail. "When we walk into the library there will be a lot of posters hanging on the walls telling people of upcoming events, and then when we go through the next set of big doors, we'll be in a big room with rows and rows of bookshelves and tables, some of them with computers on them and some empty. The library has fluorescent lights, and you may hear them hum and see them flicker. It's okay. They do that. One thing you'll probably notice as unusual is that almost no one will be talking, and if they are talking they'll be whispering. People need to be quiet in libraries. Another thing you'll probably notice is the smell. There are lots of books, and new books have that strong smell of print that you know. Old books have a special scent of their own. You'll sense them, I'm sure. I don't know exactly what the ventilation system sounds like today, but since it is very hot out, the air conditioning will probably be on and you may feel cool air blowing on you." That's the kind of information many people in the spectrum need in order to make sense of their autistic world before you can expect calmer behaviors.

Seventeen year-old Nedhi was like a terrified deer. Eyes darting from one person or space to another, neck strained, body ready to spring off in any direction at the slightest movement toward her. Frightened by her mother's arms extended toward her to perform Face Tapping or Skull Tapping, and yet wanting to endure them because she truly wanted help out of the trap of her autism. During the first two days of her program, both mother and daughter cried a lot. I told Kiran, the mother, "Perform the activities on yourself for a while. Let Nedhi see you doing them. She will learn to anticipate what it feels like." My advice brought relief, and a few weeks later, disbelief, as Kiran reported, "She is calmer now. She wakes up cheerfully, humming. She is happy!"

But Nedhi was still resistant to each new activity, until her mother performed them, not always with great ease herself. Eventually fear subsided in this beautiful and graceful ASD teen. And, almost as if from fear that exuberance would blow away the fragile gains, reports from home and school came in with quiet excitement. "She is listening more, taking in what is going on around her at home and school, processing the information and learning," they said.

But she still had tantrums out of frustration when she could not meet the demands she felt were put upon her.

I understood so well.

"Why can't you just be normal?" my mother would ask me almost every day during my teen years. She could not listen to the plain truth: I was differently made. It was harder for her now to keep my differences in mind. Perhaps because she was tired of focusing on them, but more likely because by my teens, I was quite deceiving. I could do almost anything, so outwardly in many ways I appeared "normal." But I did "normal" things not with ease and not with grace, and I paid a price afterwards, and those around me paid too.

Even today I frequently become overwhelmed by needing to be the patient, comfortable receiver of others' disorganized nervous energy, and the compassionate translator between two worlds or two "theories of mind." But I have learned to contain this chaos until I am in a safe space. And as a professional who is frequently in public, I don't find such places easily.

Late in my life, I "found" two people in front of whom I have felt safe to be Just Me: my sister and my partner. They let me wiggle and squirm; they help me remove my socks when my toes can no longer tolerate them. And as they help with my socks, the lights begin to bother me. And while they are adjusting the light, the fold in the fabric on the upholstery cover pinches and itches me. And then someone begins to chew gum on a movie on the television, or there's a commercial for food with melted cheddar cheese dripping from it. I am continually overwhelmed, until I make a conscious decision to ignore the environmental stimuli. And then my toes again become unhappy, and the only thing that will quiet the energy running amuck inside me is to have someone place a pencil between each toe and its neighbor.

And then with resolve, to ignore the external stimulation, I pull myself inward to the machinations of my mind, and become silly, unrelentingly silly.

"How come?" I ask. "How come?"

"How come what?" my partner asks, trying to make sense out of my question.

"No!" I holler. "Don't ask me 'what'! Jus' tell me 'how come'!"

"Okay. You've just got a case of the 'how comes' I guess."

I continue to ask "how come" to every sentence I hear or imagine.

I try to calm down by drinking some cold water. I fill my mouth with water and pop my cheeks to spray water across the room.

Giggling wildly, I burst into a full chorus of "Djever see a djever go this way and that way, and djever see a djever go this way and that," almost to the tune of "Did you ever see a lassie?" Soon my giggles turn into peals of laughter as I picture wild images that defy words—donkeys with helicopter heads flying overhead. I begin to cry as sense and nonsense collide inside my mind.

I cannot make sense now. Sense requires being in touch with my surroundings, and they are overwhelming. Especially the tactile components of them. I know of only one way to get away from the tactile interferences of the world, and that is to return to the womb.

I fill a large bathtub to the brim with hot water and bath salts, and I turn down the lights and shut out as much sound as I can, listening to my own heartbeat or to the white noise I create to block out environmental sounds that are still impinging on my senses. I strip, immerse myself in water, nothing touching me but myself, or things I can anticipate and that help me define my boundaries—the definite walls of the tub or the rough washcloth or loofah in my own hand. And I roll over and do little buoyant exercises, almost recreating the sense of floating in the womb, relaxing my spine and my entire being.

And then to bed. Before I fall asleep, I can simply tell myself I will not allow the tactile sensations to bother me. But I cannot set those conscious filters to ignore tactile input when I'm asleep. So if I'm alone, I can manage by tucking the sheets in military style or discarding the top sheet altogether. Top sheets move, and their corners attack your cheeks and necks and shoulders, especially if you're sleeping with someone else who dares move in the bed, pulling the sheet with him. Some autistic people need to have heavy blankets rather than sheets and lighter weight blankets. While this can help reduce the movement of the blanket and therefore the tactile annoyance, there is another reason for seeking the weighted blanket. We'll explore that later, but for now let's look at tactile sensitivities.

If one person can be *hyper*sensitive, another can be *hypo*sensitive. But hyposensitivity, when the nerves and other mechanisms are intact, is merely a way for the brain to protect an individual, autistic or not, from extreme hypersensitivities.

Deborah assured me her teenage daughter with autism didn't feel things. "She doesn't feel food on her face. When she was four, she closed her hand in the door of the car and didn't cry. She never seemed to notice if her sock was twisted inside her shoe." Yet Deborah also said, "She complains about hair brushing and face washing and tooth brushing and nail cutting, and she prefers soft clothes and no turtlenecks."

I explained to Deborah that her daughter, Bobbie, was not hyposensitive to touch, rather her apparent hyposensitivity is just a way to turn off one more thing that would make living in the world intolerable. Even still, signs of hypersensitivity emerge in situations easily anticipated, when the autistic person feels doubly abused. Bobbie saw the hairbrush approaching and knew what it would mean.

"Oh, stop squirming. You know this doesn't hurt," she heard. She wanted to respond: "Doesn't hurt? Have you explained to me how things feel to you? How it feels to you to wear synthetic clothes that trap your energy inside and keep you on edge? Oh, it doesn't feel that way to you? I can't tell you how it feels to me, because everything is so intense and I don't have the words to describe it."

Sometimes we can get beyond our tactile hypersensitivities and do what needs doing. I spent several years wearing pantyhose while I was working in schools in New York. I wore pantyhose and shoes with leather soles and sat in wooden chairs. It was okay. I had some natural materials beneath me and around me that allowed for a transfer of pent-up energy.

But 15 years later, when I once again needed to conform in "corporate America," things had changed. Shoes now had "man-made soles"—synthetic. When I wore pantyhose with those shoes, my energy went wild and recycled in me, becoming more and more aberrant (synthetics don't allow for transfer of energy from one medium to another). And then someone seated me in a fiberglass chair and momentarily I put my hands on the Formica-topped table in front of me.

My body shrieked at the insult of compressed resin and mineral layers laminated with who-knows-what glues onto a pressboard tabletop, and I could barely maintain my composure as I stood to begin a presentation. And then a friend, knowing I like to fidget with something to help release trapped energy, handed me a glob of some goopy synthetic substance. Momentarily it touched the palm of my hand, and I couldn't drop it fast enough. I lost all color, could no longer stand, and was unable to speak.

My speech ability returned about 10 minutes later after the shock wore off. I buried my hand in linen for a few minutes, wiping it furiously until the hideous sensation was gone, and then, standing, away from the fiberglass chair and Formica topped table, I resumed the posture of the consultant invited to present a talk on a subject I knew well—neurodevelopmental perspectives on disorders of behavior and learning.

Aha! The three year-old you met in Chapter One. He had "suddenly" become autistic. However, he seemed comfortable and almost back to himself when he burrowed into the all cotton clothing piled on top of the synthetic carpets in his home. That's because a synthetic environment can interfere with energy transmission, and in so doing cause further bedlam—chaos, disorganization of the bodily systems. Natural fibers allow the release of chaotic energy and help us become calm, organized, responsive.

I know this subject from the inside out and the outside in. But the 7 year-old nonverbal boy, who bites and kicks and smears his feces on others, whose various diagnostic sessions have ended abysmally, but always with the diagnosis of low-functioning autism, does not know this, as he enters a small room in London, where I have been invited to work with him. He comes in with his mother and father and younger brother. He glances at me with his very best peripheral vision.

He hides behind his mother in the farthest corner. The room is adjacent to another clinic space, where someone is providing massage therapy with scented massage oils. He is overwhelmed by two new people (my intern and me) and by the claustrophobic new surroundings. There is only one door and two windows. He entered through the door and is sitting, behind his mother, on the floor by one of the windows.

I calmly introduce myself from the far side of the room, keeping my hands at my sides, not moving toward him or anyone else. I talk calmly about not much for a minute or two, getting him comfortable with my voice. "You don't need to worry," I'm saying. "I won't ask you to do anything, nor will I touch you if you don't want me to. I merely want to learn some things that might help me help you. I will learn these by observing whatever you do and when and how and what you choose not to do."

"It looks like you are curious, Wallace," I say, "bothered by the sounds and smells coming from the room next door?"

His breathing shifts. I caught him off guard. I understood.

"The sounds and aromas bother me too, but I've had more time to get used to them. And although I'm sensitive to those things, too, they haven't harmed me, so I am trusting that today they won't harm me or you or anyone else in our room. And I know it might seem strange, but the people in the other room are probably enjoying them."

I keep talking, in a slow, warm voice. His parents interject now and then, telling me, "It's fine if you want to try to push him into things. He's used to it; he's had so many assessments."

But I wait. Wallace is taking all of this in. His massive dark eyes beneath thick black curls suggest he's beginning to believe he can trust me. But he has not yet tested me in the area of his greatest vulnerability: tactile hypersensitivity. What would happen if he were close enough for me to reach out and touch him? He moves from behind his mother, and sits on the floor in front of her. I don't budge.

"The light from the window is a little bright, isn't it?" I say, continuing to share the sensory aspects of the environment with him. "The room itself is a little small for 6 people. If it gets stuffy, we can open the window. But then we'll hear the noises from the street—the cars going by and the children playing on the play-ground across the street."

"This is Cris, my intern. He helps me help children who have a hard time with some things. Cris knows that it's important for him to stand quietly in his cor-ner of the room by the other window until you want to play with him. You can trust him." Cris nods to acknowledge the introduction.

Wallace is baffled. Why aren't we touching him, pulling him across the room, pushing him into a chair, making any demands of him? He moves closer to me, then quickly scoots back to sit by his mother. He repeats this behavior several times, each time getting closer to me but returning to his mother. "You're using your hands to pull yourself toward me," I say. "The carpet is kind of rough, isn't it?"

Then he stands up, walks over to me, stands directly in front of me, waves his arms around in front of my face, and reaches out to touch me. I am still a talking object. I have been constant. I am safe. Soon Wallace and I are on the floor. He is in my lap and we are gleefully engaging one another in touch and play.

It's a first. It's a beginning. A beginning on which we built, slowly and surely, with trust, training a young woman to help his parents integrate his HANDLE program with an Son-Rise program so that Wallace could rely on each of his senses and integrate them into meaningful perceptions, opening a world of communication to him.

What would have happened if I had shaken his father's hand? Wallace would have feared invasion of HIS space as well. This was a boy who stiffened to touch, who interacted with force rather than gentleness, who appeared not to understand language. Why should he do as directed, when the directions require that he pick up things with his sensitive fingertips, or that he hold someone's hand to walk down the hall. A hand? One of those things that someone else moves around on your hand, in unexpected ways while you are walking? That twitchy, slippery, cold or warm thing with many moving parts? That part that connects me to someone whose will is different from mine?

He knows only too well that the world of human interaction is fraught with tactile experiences. All the sensory tables—box-like tables designed to provide tactile stimulation to hypersensitive hands—filled with rice and beans have not changed that. And these unpredictable experiences of human interaction involving tactility are truly overwhelming. People with ASD need help to sort out the various elements of the total experience, gently—this is what you hear, this is what you see, this is what you smell—and to allow the tactile experimentation to come from within rather than being forced from without. Then we have a chance.

Lincoln Grigsby, an autistic man who expresses himself via facilitated communication, self-published a volume of his poetry, *The Light Within*. He gave me permission to share the poem on the following page—one of several expressing the effects of sensory overload.

THIS AUTISTIC MAN

THIS AUTISTIC MAN
KNOWS FROM A DIFFERENT PLACE
SEES ODD THINGS
THINGS SEEM STRANGE
SOMETIMES SENSELESS
TO SENSES UNLENSED.

SENSES OPENED
SEEING TOO MUCH
UNDERSTANDING SOME
BUT NOT ALWAYS UNDERSTOOD.
OVERLOAD, OVERLOADED
I GO DEEP DOWN
TO BLOCK OUT ALL
THINGS THAT ARE SENSELESS
SO THAT I CAN SEE
THINGS THAT ARE SENSED
DEEP INSIDE
THIS AUTISTIC MAN.

Because it is all about safety.

5. Safety
Secure with our place in space

There is another form of safety that most people with autism understand. It relates to proprioception, which I define simply as the brain's unconscious awareness of the sense of body in space. Proprioception and tactility are the two ways we develop our boundaries. And the two senses are interwoven, because proprioceptive receptors are part of the tactile system, and provide us information about the relative position of our body parts, one to another. But the proprioceptive sense goes beyond this tactile component, and it integrates with our other senses to tell us where we are in space and how to move easily and safely in space, how to move through crowds without losing our sense of self and our sense of security.

Most of us with autism don't inherently know where we end and the world begins. It's one of the reasons we need to investigate unfamiliar surroundings[10]—to know where we are, and to see the possibilities of where we might be or where others might be. It's not enough to be told about these other rooms and people. We need to take our snapshots. When we're uncertain of where we are and what awaits us just around the bend, we're like Temple Grandin's cattle[11] in a poorly con-

---

[10]The difficulty in establishing boundaries may be one of the reasons some individuals with autism urinate in corners of rooms, or spread their feces on walls. They may need to mark out spaces with their scent—again relying on the most organized sense to help gain constancy in their environment.

[11]Temple Grandin understands proprioceptive insecurity and has designed special chutes that provide a sense of security to calm cattle as they move on an unknown path to their death in slaughterhouses. In her chutes the cattle are less anxious in their last moments. This is not only more humane but also helps the beef industry since calmer cattle yield better meat as they do not engage the fright/flight/fight response that causes physical injury and also pumps hormones into muscles, changing the composition of the meat.

structed chute. We panic, causing injury to ourselves and to those around us. We scream. We destroy property. *"Will someone please help me know where I am and where I am not!"*

Sometimes wearing cowboy boots and carrying backpacks helps teens with proprioceptive insecurities contain themselves in their surroundings. Being squeezed in a machine, in a bear hug, between two gym mats can also provide a sense of Here I Am. But this is a compensatory measure with limited applicability. We cannot go through life between two heavy gym mats. And even if we could it would not really help, since the brain attends to novel stimuli and then ignores the stimuli once it becomes humdrum. That is why weighted vests and weighted lap pads may calm some people with ASD, but only if used intermittently. Otherwise we are not just calm, but almost numb.

Those of us in the spectrum need to know our own bodies' beginnings and ends: how they feel when we're still, when we're being moved, when we're actively moving. And after learning this, we must learn it again, almost moment by moment when we enter puberty and have growth spurts and shifts in balance points, and seemingly new and unfamiliar body parts to become acquainted with and accustomed to. Puberty can be a time of great confusion, of tremendous anxiety, as the old sense of self no longer fits. We don't know that everyone else our age is going through a similar struggle. They do it so much more easily. They have a firmer base from which to experiment since they had an organized perception of themselves in the first place. And they have friends and communication skills to share these experiences and, through sharing, to increase their significance and reduce their fearfulness.

How do people develop proprioception? A great deal of information comes from our eyes, assuming they are providing accurate data on three-dimensionality. Our noses provide information as to proximity to objects with specific scents. Tactually, energetic stimulation of our skin also creates a sense of how close people and objects are in the environment. Then this information is integrated with messages received from receptors deep in muscles and tendons and joints—proprioceptors, part of the tactile system. Interpretation of the messages from these receptors relates back to the ears.

Again, the ears and more specifically, the inner ear with its vestibular system. Through a very sophisticated system, the movement of fluids and little microscopic he clumps called otoliths communicates to other parts of the brain how tense the muscles are in every part of the body, whether or not equilib-rium is sustained, how the pull of gravity is affecting the body and each of its parts and the speed and direction of any movement made. The ear also sends information on relative position in space based on hearing and the ability to echolocate—to judge distance from objects by the speed at which sound arrives at each ear.

In a way that researchers are only recently uncovering through sophisticated forms of magnetic resonance imaging, the information from each ear is sent to another part of the brain called the superior olive. It is here that the cues are processed enabling echolocation—the process through which the sounds we hear help us, like bats, know where we are in space. The olivary complex, it appears, has an extremely significant effect on the cerebellum—the part of the brain that has been associated for many years with balance and coordination, but which plays many other roles as well.

The cerebellum comprises only 10 percent of the brain's volume but contains more than half of the neurons within the brain. It is constructed to receive input from internal and external environments, to compare them and also to check if the real action matched the intended one. It gets a great deal of information via a closed circuit projection from the vestibular system. It also receives sensory information from various parts of the body, largely via the spinal cord, and it coordinates this information into a number of fractured brain maps that have more to do with the bodily parts involved in performing a particular function than to the actual body schema. In addition, it interrelates with the motor planning areas of the cerebral hemispheres and is crucial in the ability to respond in a specific time or to a particular rhythm.

Brain imaging is now showing that the human's cerebellum is active in many varied functions that may not be directly related to movement at all. One such finding indicates that the cerebellum helps process quick and accurate perception of various forms of sensory information, as well as playing a significant role in attention, higher cognitive processes, short-term memory, emotional response, impulse control, executive functions (the ability to plan tasks), and appears to be important in both schizophrenia and autism.

The cerebellum receives information from many parts of the nervous systems and organizes this information, synchronizing the input. Via a network of very large and specially shaped cells called Purkinje cells, the cerebellum sends messages to the cerebral cortices—those "right-brain/left-brain" areas we think of as governing our sensibilities. The Purkinje cells get a considerable amount of their information from other nerves with welcome familiar names such as parallel fibers, climbing fibers, and others. It is via the climbing fibers that the olivary complex affects the cerebellum. Each of these fibers, rooted in the inferior olive, climbs and wraps around a Purkinje cell, hugging it and in the hug, sends hundreds of synaptic messages.

Whew! From feeling lost in unfamiliar space and needing to know where we are in strange surroundings and seeking deep input—hugs, squeezes and the like— to getting lost in unfamiliar parts of the brain. There is a metaphor. Picture the climbing fiber wrapping itself around the Purkinje cell to give it the messages it needs to be able to respond adaptively as it guides us in dynamic interactions of our body in space. Just like other behaviors showing the way to affected systems, once again the behaviors that may annoy others but are vital for our sense of comfort with our bodies in this world—those weird little quirks are apparently there to guide the way. Recently researchers at a number of universities and medical research centers have reported abnormalities in the inferior olive of the brains of individuals in the autism spectrum[12]—the part of the brain where those tenacious climbing fibers are rooted.

Consider the 37 year-old woman who had been in psychotherapy for more than 20 years trying to resolve her feelings of insecurity in social gatherings, her inability to develop an intimate relationship, and her need to dress like Heidi, ready for a trek across the Alps with all of her belongings on her back. Laura knew something was wrong. She was never diagnosed in the autism spectrum because her verbal communication skills were quite good, but she had some ASD traits (in fact, when we look at unusual behaviors, an understanding of autism provides insight into so many other dysfunctions, because the autistic experience is so complex in its disorganization). Neither psychotherapy nor medication was helping. Laura was suffering.

At a talk during which I described some proprioceptive irregularities, she heard me speak of feeling like an astronaut, drifting unmoored in space and needing to be held down by anything available, about difficulty sleeping without weighted blankets or being held, about fear of closing your eyes and accepting the embrace of another without a panic of not knowing where you were or if you were. I mentioned how these problems frequently manifest themselves in difficulty with mathematical concepts, because permanence and balance and other proprioceptive experiences provide our brain with the basis of mathematical thought.

Hearing all this, Laura burst into tears. She recognized her life, and before

---

[12]General information on these studies and their outcomes is available at www.imfar.org and www.naar.org, the organizations providing funding for this research.

long she became my client. We worked on the root of her problems, by strengthening her inner ear's tolerance for slow controlled movements, her proprioceptors' ability to pick up on information from her joints in particular. We integrated the information her eyes and ears and body were giving her. The energy from the various organs and systems through which we process disparate forms of energy needs to be organized so the brain can interpret a reality that makes order from chaos. Then we can create a reality aligned with what others who share our environment experience. When we can do this, our experience is no longer one of scattered, confusing stimuli. We feel more secure. We can relax. And within a few months, Laura was able to ease herself into a meaningful relationship, her panic and confusion overcome.

Her change was so dramatic after she realized that proprioception was the root of her problems. And for so many years she had looked so normal, but was so dysfunctional. Her life in some ways paralleled that of someone with ASD.

One client incident haunts me still, nearly four years after it occurred. I was working with Cameron, the 11 year-old mentioned earlier who couldn't tie his shoelaces. He had significant language delays and fleeting eye-contact, his social skills were extremely immature: the students in his class tolerated his companionship on a rotating basis, because he became burdensome to any one person. (Working with Cameron reminded me of the three mature girls in my elementary school who were assigned the rotating duty of staying with me at recess so I wouldn't hurt myself on the playground equipment.)

Cam had no concept of mathematics, but no one was particularly concerned about that issue. They focused on his more basic deficits in communication and socialization.

I was concerned about his extreme anxiety and his inability to identify or move parts of his body if he couldn't see them. Vicki, his mom, had an understandable hope: "I hope that someday he will be able to sleep for even a few hours without my being beside him in the bed. Ever since he was born, I have had to be touching him, enshrouding his body with mine, or he would awaken. Awaken with extreme anxiety, screaming and sweating and with a racing heart."

I told her, "From what I see in his waking behaviors, he simply does not know where his body is or IF it is unless he can see it or unless it is defined by your body."

As I was teaching his mother to perform a particular massage[13] to balance

---

[13]This massage, the Peacemaker Massage, which I developed nearly twenty years ago, is in many ways similar to Tellington Touch, a massage technique developed and used to calm animals.

issues of muscle tone and tactility, to enhance proprioception and to induce a state of calmness, I narrated the path through which I was moving a special ball with firm concentric circles on Cam's right shoulder and on the back of his right arm. As I returned to his neck, I told Vicki to match on his left side the movements and verbal narration I had done on the right. She concentrated so fully on the movement of the ball and the path through which she was to move it that she forgot to mention what part of his body was in contact with the ball and where the ball was moving to next.

Within a second, Cameron began to cry out frantically "Where are ya now, Mama?! Where are ya now?!"

It was a dramatic demonstration of Cam's challenges.

While his mother continued to focus her attention to the massage technique, I gave him the verbal information he needed to direct his brain to where the sensation was focused. Cameron relaxed. And his brain learned.

Within a few months' time, Cam allowed his mom to transition from sleeping with him through the night, to staying beside him until he fell asleep, to sitting in a chair beside the bed until he fell asleep, to just saying "Goodnight" and leaving the room. And in the daytime, with his eyes open, his movements were more adaptive, he had greatly reduced self-stimming, he could listen to directions and conversations while he moved. All this because his brain and body had found connectivity and peace.

Less than eight months later, Vicki proudly reported, "It's almost magical, but he can now express his own feelings, speak in a natural tone of voice. He is successful in his schoolwork, although he is still not working at grade level. Even his memory has improved and his sense of sequence. In math, he has begun to grasp the concept and computation of fractions. I can tell that this is just the beginning of a long journey."

Everyone needs to be secure with his or her own body in space before freeing the energy to interact with others. When we are proprioceptively or tactually insecure, we cannot open up to the world and its multitude of stimuli. Some people with ASD (notably Tito Mukhopadhyay[14] and Donna Williams) feel they can focus only on one form of sensory input at a time; however, Cameron demonstrated so poignantly that the brain and nervous systems need to receive input from many senses and integrate that information for synchronous processing if we are to re-

[14]Tito is the severely autistic Indian teenager currently under intensive and extensive neuroscientific study funded by Cure Autism Now (CAN). Tito's ability to express himself through facilitated communication is providing researchers many insights into autism.

Finally, years after wishing to be able to ride a bicycle, this twelve year-old mastered the two-wheeler. First his balance and ability to judge distance (3-dimensional perspective) needed to be stronger, and he needed to be able to sort out the actions of one side of his body from the other, with upper body and lower body each moving in different dimensions. Those are real challenges to overcome when proprioceptive and tactile systems provide irregular input and when binocular vision is not well developed. This youngster learned to ride his bicycle, with great pride, shortly after he stopped bumping into things in his path when he walked and also shortly after he began to speak in intelligible sentences. Most children don't master bike riding until a few years after attaining these other mileposts, but those of us with autism frequently play "catch up" once our systems are strengthened and integrated, once the fear dissipates.

spond dynamically to our continually shifting environment. And because the cerebellum processes much of this information, it is not surprising that some theories suggest that the proprioceptive deficits in people with autism stem from abnormalities in the cerebellum.

Several studies indicate that in people with autism the cerebellum and its

Purkinje cells are not organizing and transmitting information properly, resulting in overwhelming the system with sensory input that cannot be handled. These observations add credence to the cerebellar influence on autism. Individuals with autism may take two to three times as long to shift their attention from one element to another, and then they lose information on the content or context because they have lost the continuity of the total experience. This problem may relate to a finding that individuals with autism have significantly fewer Purkinje cells and therefore have increased difficulty organizing sensory input and inhibiting sensory overload.

The events of life will not stand still for us, will not give us a chance to have the words coincide later with the snapshots we archived. Or if they do coincide later, and we respond to them when this occurs, we are out of sync. People will wonder "where did that come from?" If we don't feel secure in our bodies, we can't feel secure in the world. When our conscious attention goes to protecting our bodies or simply staying in touch with our bodies, so we know *that* we are, then we have difficulty knowing *who* we are. Operating in this ethereal state, it is much easier and safer to relate to static objects than to people. People move. Children move more than adults.

How unfair that just as someone is working to establish that she is and who she is, she is also being expected to interact with pesky peers who demand that she attend to everything about them and herself at once. No wonder I flunked kindergarten but reveled in escaping into a corner with a book.

Tito Mukhopadhyay provides the most current high-profile example of just this challenge in the autistic experience. His mother, wisely, removed him from the environment of children to teach him at home, and she did not let him fixate on any one sensory modality. Today, Tito's extreme intelligence and ability to communicate through writing provide special insights into autism. But after focusing for a period of time, Tito, for all his brilliance, loses it. Loses what, exactly? His sense of self. His proprioceptive input.

And when Tito loses it, what does he do? The very same thing most people with autism do—he flaps and spins and moves rapidly. He says this puts him in touch with his body. It certainly provides visual and proprioceptive input to his vestibular system. And when the movement is very rapid, it may even provide him a few minutes of respite by briefly shutting down an overwhelmed system. In Tito's case it may not be possible to learn what his brain is actually doing, because his hyperactivity precludes functional magnetic resonance imaging.

As we continue to weave this fabric, it seems that the inner ear and the areas to which it links most directly remain prominent. If a person can't use this linked system to help calibrate equilibrium and a generalized sense of body in space, then he deprives the system of the practice it needs to regulate muscle tone. And muscle tone is so important that at birth every newborn is tested on it five different ways. The test is called an APGAR. Ratings of zero, one, or two are given in 5 different areas: respiration, heart rate, skin color, reflex response—all of course dependent on muscle tone—and lastly, on muscle tone itself. It's obvious, then, that to gain a more complete understanding of human functionality and how it might go awry, specifically in relation to the autism spectrum disorders, muscle tone demands consideration.

6. Muscle tone
Readiness to respond

Muscle tone, if present at birth, supports most vital functions as well as movements. It is not synonymous with muscle mass or muscle strength but is the degree of tension in the resting muscle. It provides a readiness to respond to stimuli, both according to plans that have been processed and also reflexively, as the body reacts to stimuli that trigger automatic responses. Some of the muscles that need to respond are governed primarily by the Central Nervous System (CNS) and peripheral nerves, and some are governed more by the Autonomic Nervous System (ANS) and certain cranial nerves that are a part of the CNS. Muscle tone is pivotal to so many functions, but in connection with the central theme of autistic behaviors it is frequently overlooked. It needs attention.

When we are relaxed and something touches us, depending on our stage of development in a process called reflex integration, we should respond by moving only certain body parts. For example, when the doctor scrapes the bottom of a newborn's foot, her whole body should display a flexed startle reaction. That's a good sign. It means the nerves and muscles throughout the body are connected, that signals are received in the brain and messages to respond are received in the muscles.

But as the infant matures, the response becomes integrated until only the toes of the scraped foot react.

When human beings respond reflexively—something we are all programmed to do for survival—they engage their Autonomic Nervous Systems, which have received a sense of threat to survival. Then according to the programs built into all of us, we send most of the available nutrients including oxygen to the muscles that need to respond—not just the muscles that move our bodies but also those that move within our bodies, such as our heart and our lungs. When we relax, the muscles have a chance to return to a state where they are again ready to respond to new messages they receive from the brain.

So what happens when anyone feels continuously threatened by the environment? Muscles tense and the brain receives a different set of messages and nutrients to use in processing information. Remember, the brain learns to turn off things like chronic pain and prolonged tension (such as the pressure of a weighted vest). Ten or fifteen minutes of intense pain is extreme. Most people innately rub areas that have been injured, to diffuse the pain and reduce its intensity. Through different strategies, the brain may ignore the area, and the tension in the resting muscle may become lax and it may not be able to respond in time to new information. During early development, when a state of tension caused by reflexive response and chronic pain is status quo, coordination, concentration, socialization, learning all suffer.

People with autism rarely know how to relax, and this is not something that can be taught. Remember that cartoon of a person all tied together with high-tension wires, with the caption of "It's only stress that's holding me together?" That's me.

In a group I belonged to several years ago, a renowned Gestalt psychotherapist from Cleveland asked for a volunteer to demonstrate the techniques we had just discussed. He wanted someone to choose a state of being he or she had never experienced, and to then work with him through the process of attaining that state. No one volunteered. After an interminable minute, I raised my hand and said I would be willing to try.

What state had I heard about and wondered how to achieve? *Relaxation.* Well, we worked and worked, moving through years and tears of my existence and my perceptions and my conceptions, and as the tension surged through me during the process, the facilitator realized he had met his match. Gestalt therapy could not help me relax. In fact, he advised me not to try to relax, because—you guessed it— he felt it was only my tension that was holding me together.

So transfer that to the infant, overwhelmed by sounds and smells and touch and light, and trying to organize through the one more constant sense—smell.

Coming naked into the elements, being rubbed down by towels, having wisps of hair fondled by his proud parents, experiencing the harsh chemical smells and bright lights of the hospital birthing room, and the sounds, the overwhelming sounds. If this infant has autistic tendencies, he has just been introduced to a kind of hell.

If I am that infant, you don't need to scrape my foot to see me startle. The world startles me every day, every hour, every minute. I have not completed the processes of habituation and classical conditioning through which I recognize familiar sensory stimulation and moderate my response as appropriate. So I tense. But I can't hold the tense posture forever. I exhaust my resources. I try to sleep, but again I tense. Finally the tension is unbearable, especially in my face. I can't suck if I'm tense. I can't swallow. I can't breathe. I relax, but then I relax too completely. I can't find that balance between tension and relaxation that is normal muscle tone. I can't find it because of my hypersensitivities. And as I grow, I can't develop tone, despite many therapeutic attempts, because I have chosen to close down the input in my inner ear. I can't deal with the sounds. I can't feel the proprioceptive shifts.

The little hair-like nerve endings in my inner ear—the cilia—are overwhelmed by movement. Or I limit their responsiveness by jumping on a pogo stick, or simply clenching my jaw and tightening my neck. Or any other means I can find that does not violate another area of my hypersensitivity.

And so I don't develop the tone I need for so many forms of response. My smile doesn't have the energy in it that other people's smiles have. My facial expressions are limited. Others cannot read my mind well and I don't have any knowledge of what a face feels like when it is relaxed or happy or impatient. So I cannot accurately read the expressions that are on the faces around me, or in the bodily postures around me.

But my eyes—perhaps they can reflect my thoughts, even if I may not be able to control their movements well. Yet who will look at my eyes, especially if I cannot sustain contact with theirs? How will they know what I feel and why? It's not that I don't have emotions. I can't express them through speech and my muscles won't cooperate to express them nonverbally. IF I allow myself to feel, I feel pain and tension. If I don't allow myself to feel, I can't get the energy to move. Maybe someone will notice my eyes, and maybe someone will notice what it is that makes me tense and stop the tension from overtaking me. Maybe.

I was fortunate. My eyes worked fairly well together. But sometimes my vision played tricks on me. Light would not stay fused. I saw fractured segments of the various frequencies of light. As a youngster, I recall seeing colors of light danc-ing inside my head as I listened to music. The sound waves transferred into light waves, and I couldn't control these. The lights that bothered my vision were easier to control.[15] And I needed to control them in order to be able to read and do jig-saw puzzles, to excel in something and boost my self-confidence when possible. Yet I couldn't always keep the light waves from breaking into blobs of color that jumped onto the objects in my visual field, or couldn't keep the white spaces inside letters from mushrooming out and gobbling up the black outlines until I couldn't see the letters any more at all.

I turned lights off, just as quickly as others turned them on from their con-cern that I not ruin my eyes. I learned it was easier to use my hair and my hand as visors to block the light, and whenever possible to read and play under the huge dining room table. And there in the near dark I increased my visual prowess.

If I could coordinate the muscles of my eyes, head, and hands fast enough to capture the words inside my head before these tricks happened, then I would be okay. So I channeled almost all of my control to my eyes. And I lost touch with so much of the proprioceptive input that my body might have given me.

I stood with my knees locked, getting deep proprioceptive input regarding my stance and my balance. Some people sit in a "W sit," with their legs splayed out on either side, forming a W and giving them a broader proprioceptive base. This posture can help them concentrate better, speak longer, be more a part of the world. If they sit or stand like most people do, some of their energy is going to sus-taining muscle tone, (because bones and locked joints are no longer supporting them) and to feeling insecure about their position in space.

I don't remember what postures I adopted when I first started to speak. If I was like many of my autistic clients, I probably leaned into the corner of a couch or lay on my bed in order to have enough support for the muscles of my body, to know that I was gravitationally secure and protected from tactile and proprioceptive surprises. Then I could concentrate on learning to move the many muscles involved in speech so I might begin to articulate words that others could understand. Most

---

[15]However, as I was working on this book, going back and forth from the computer screen to printouts to books and re-search articles, hour after hour, I had a momentary recurrence of this fragmenting of light. For minutes after feeling totally disoriented and frightened because blobs of color were overtaking the objects in my space, I could not read or even see the silverware on the kitchen table; and the face of my lunch companion became first blotched and then gobbled up by the most amazing array of colors, like fireworks. I closed my eyes, and the pyrotechnic displays continued inside my head. I allowed myself to enjoy them, and as I calmed down, they dissipated and I was able to return to life as usual. Usual since I have inte-grated this sense. But what a flashback to what life was like before I had control of this pervasive visual processing disorder—a disorder that educational psychologist Helen Irlen has named Scotopic Sensitivity Syndrome or Irlen Syndrome.

people never need to think about finding control of the tongue and the muscles that control the jaw and the pharynx—that three-tiered muscle that starts behind the ears and goes through the neck, helping to control the flow of air through the larynx. Those of us in the spectrum do.

So frequently there is a monotone or strained tone in the speaking voices of people with autism. The word "tone" is not unrelated to muscle tone: just as on a violin or guitar, the tighter the tendon the higher the tone when it vibrates. Trying to adjust different strands for different tones is truly challenging. I marvel at how people can tune a stringed instrument. I marvel more at how natural and easy it is for most people to tune their vocal cords, and to coordinate the movements of tongue and jaw and vocal cords and lungs to speak. And to do this without apparent thought and without needing to lean on something for security. How can they still be upright?

Before I turned 10, I learned to control the sequence of tension and relaxation in these muscles, most of which I cannot see even if I look in a mirror. I produced speech sounds. At least most sounds. I continued getting speech therapy sporadically, until by the time I was 14 my speech was fluent and relatively clear. I practiced incessantly, making up tongue twisters and singing along with the commercials on the radio: "You'll wonder where the yellow went when you brush your teeth with Pepsodent" was a particularly challenging jingle to master.

It takes so much energy to process thoughts into words and words into intricate sequential movement patterns that demand muscle tone in places most people don't even know they have muscles. But I know. I feel them. I feel my tongue. Literally. I need to know my tongue so I can get it to cooperate with my jaws and other articulators in order to move and remember the series of movements, the amounts of tension in various places, so I can develop muscle memory (kinesthetic memory) of how to say these sounds and words. But it is not automatic. And if I need to think of an answer to your question and phrase that in my own words, spontaneously, I know my muscles will not cooperate. I will lose the thought. I will appear ignorant. I will lose my self-esteem as I trip over the sounds and the words.

So I repeat the words you said. If it was not silly or ignorant for you to say those words, I will be accepted if I repeat them. And I watch how you moved to make them—perhaps surreptitiously, using peripheral vision. I focus on your mouth, not your eyes. What help could your eyes give me in learning how to form the words?

But now that I have worked so hard to figure out how to make the same sounds you do, to form them into words and even sequences of words—now you ridicule me. Because I am a parrot. But the practice I get from repetition— echolalia—will help me develop more fluent speech. Then, maybe if I learn enough scripts, I can have answers to your questions and comments to insert into your discussions.

Let's see. "Hi!" followed by another voice saying "How are you?" answered by the first voice saying "Fine, thanks." I can practice that from both sides of the conversation. I can learn a few hundred of these conversations. I can practice them over and over again until they trip off my tongue just as easily as they do for other people.

Greg was 8 years old when he strode confidently into my clinic. My schedule book noted he had been given these diagnoses: autism, pervasive developmental disorder, hyperlexia, Asperger's Syndrome—definitely on the autistic spectrum. Yet here he was, all stagger and pluck, announcing himself with "Hi! My name is Greg."

"Hi. Where's your mom?" I responded.

Greg nearly fell onto the couch, knocked backward by my words, which violated the script. His gaze turned inward, as he waited for a prompter to provide the next line in this new script.

Scripts are something I know a lot about. Virtually every Broadway musical, folk song, romantic medley, Shakespearean work I heard more than once or twice is still recorded somewhere in my head. If an unsuspecting guest says ". . . and while we're on the subject. . ." off I will go: "Your servant?! Your servant?! Indeed I'm not your servant . . .." Not until I have finished Anna's lyric tirade from "The King and I," not until I have moved past the children, the sheep and the toads to the point where I beseech the King to kick me as one of his loyal subjects, not until I exclaim "Oh! That was good, your majesty!" would I stop.

Oh, yes, I can read the nonverbal communication that tells me the other person is moving from surprise, to amusement, to amazement, then to someone-better-stop-this-crazy-woman. Sometimes I can stop the recording in my head from bubbling out of my mouth. But until I have completed the sound-track, it will keep emerging and interrupting other conversations. This is how I learned to speak. Someone else's voice and words and practiced scripts. I could match my voice to another's. I could play with the speed. I could laugh at my tongue getting twisted. It was okay. It was safe. I wouldn't forget what I was going to say, because it was a script. And now, I must admit, I sometimes wish these hundreds or thousands of scripts would leave me in peace. The effort it takes to hold back the flood of words is sometimes so great that I have difficulty listening to my own ideas or to the thoughts of others.

But not when I am working with someone with autism or another unusual disorder. At those times I can abandon myself and become a receiver. I know that I need do this for a few hours at a time and then I will be able to go home and release the trapped energies that would have interfered with my ability to help someone else get far enough through this journey that they will be somewhere close to as functional as I am. Most of the time.

An interesting phenomenon of the relationship between muscle tone and language was reported in 1974 by William Condon and Louis Sanders agreeing with the observations made by Dr. Alfred Tomatis in France in the 1960s. They noted that infants who showed no muscular response to phonemes (the smallest element of human speech) were later found to be autistic. Not responding to speech sounds, these infants do not practice the experience of becoming alert and ready to use language and communication. It's plausible that this lack of response is due to the brain's tuning out a painful experience—listening to language through sound-sensitive ears is painful.

This phenomenon has more far-reaching effects when considered in light of the neurological concept of habituation, the progressive decline in responding to stimuli, which is found to occur in a healthy fetus between 23 and 29 weeks. You can demonstrate this by providing repeated auditory stimuli or vibration through the mother's abdominal wall. Initially the baby should respond with whole body movements, but with repeated stimulation, the response should become inhibited or integrated. This is very important because it is the beginning of the ability to filter out background stimuli and allows the developing fetus to relax, to screen repeated sounds such as the mother's heartbeat and save energy for healthy total development.

In her book *What's Going on in There?: How the Brain and Mind Develop in the First Five Years of Life,* Lise Eliot clearly states the importance of this phenomenon. "Nor is habituation trivial on a neural level. It is not simply a consequence of sensory adaptation or muscular fatigue but involves long-lasting changes in the electrical properties of cells and synapses in the CNS. Babies whose brains are compromised in utero because of oxygen deprivation, genetic abnormality, maternal smoking, or other prenatal problems do not habituate normally. Fetal habituation can thus be used clinically to predict a baby's neurological health and mental development."[16]

And apparently habituation is necessary before the fetus can begin to develop the process called classical conditioning, in which he responds with a learned association to specific stimuli. Music and the human voice are two of the more influential such stimuli that the fetus responds to in utero, assuming that habituation has occurred. If these did occur the baby is born with memories of filtering out irrelevant background noises and listening for mother's voice, for particular musical melodies, and even for favorite poems and songs. Although these earliest memories are not available to the baby through conscious recall much beyond the first few days or weeks of life, the influence this experience has on the neural level is certainly bound to be significant to his ability of reciprocity in relating to his environment and the people in it. And therefore this phenomenon looms significant in understanding autism and the relationship between muscle tone—readiness of the muscles to respond—and communication.[17]

Another frustrating detail about muscle tone and its relation to language is that it supports all forms of communication, not just speech. Unfortunately, writing and typing and nonverbal communication also place demands on muscle tone, which is developed when the inner ear responds to proprioceptive insecurities and claims victory over equilibrium and gravitational pull.

We all need to move through the several ranges of movement that activate the flow of fluids and otoliths through the saccule, utricle, and endolymphatic sac, as well as the three bony semicircular canals (each canal orchestrates response to a different axis in the three-dimensional world). If not, then the cerebellum, the midbrain, and the areas influenced by the rhythmic flow of the cerebrospinal fluids—all of these will be weak. What chance does the autistic youngster have of developing communication, if, in order to survive in a world of irritating and confusing stimuli, he shuts down vestibular input and cannot even communicate with himself?

Enter Sandy, an 18 and a half year-old client—not yet a young woman, but difficult to describe as an adolescent. Sandy was not autonomous in any way but for her ability to refuse, usually in a loud screaming voice, and to become physically abusive if people wouldn't listen. For 15 years she had been labeled autistic and profoundly mentally retarded. She dragged her feet, although she could walk with more energy if she locked her knees and splayed her feet to provide her a large balance point. She spent most of her time sitting, hunched over, sometimes rocking,

---

[16]Eliot, L. P. 137

[17]Eliot discusses the damaging effects of excessive noise on the developing ear in the fetus. Juxtaposing the importance of the ear to the development of language and communication in general with Eliot's findings points to another possible reason for the dramatic increase in autism in the past decade—the use of ultrasound tests and particularly the Fetal Acoustic Stimulation Test which is becoming more common to determine fetal well-being late in pregnancy.

sometimes slapping the table or her thighs, sometimes biting her own hand, usually jiggling a small block or stone in her fingers. Frequently she performed what looked like a little belly dance, moving her diaphragm up and down in something almost resembling a tic. Once in a while she would struggle to raise her eyes in the sockets to see what the person across from her was doing.

If asked a question, Sandy realized she was expected to answer, so she would mutter "yah" in a monotone, maybe repeating it a few times. Every now and then she would change her form of response, and repeat the last word she had heard. Her older sister had teased her about this often when the two girls were alone, asking her things like "Do you want a hamburger or a hot dog?" and when hearing "ot dog," would then ask, "Do you want a hot dog or a hamburger?" and upon hearing "ambuhgu" would howl with laughter at her "retarded" sister. Humiliated, my client would become aggressive, and she was reprimanded for lashing out, because she could not explain her behaviors.

At our first meeting, Sandy's mother Barbara had a few very focused concerns about her daughter. She did not expect much. She hoped that before Sandy turned 21 she would be able to carry on a scripted conversation like "Hi. How are you? Fine, thanks." She also wanted her to either notice when food was on her face or not become belligerent when someone tried to wipe it off.

And she had two more goals—for Sandy to climb a flight of stairs, without needing to hold onto a person or rails for support; and for Sandy to wipe herself after toileting.

Reweaving the loops already covered here, I knew I needed to attend to awakening, not too rapidly, the senses that had been turned off due to pain and confusion. I knew we needed to increase muscle tone in all of her muscles, but that could not happen until she would allow herself to receive proprioceptive and vestibular input. I knew I must respect her intellect, because Sandy was bright enough to know when she had made a fool of herself. She was also intuitive enough to sense I was her ally, that I respected her and understood some of the choices she needed to make that dictated how she would and would not respond to the environment.

We worked, gently tapping on the roots of the trigeminal nerve, and placing cool packs on her forehead and temple afterwards. I gave her a crazy straw—one with many loops that requires strong sucking—and asked her to drink a glass or two of water through the straw each day, with her eyes closed when she took sips if that was not too threatening. We tapped and bounced information into her joints when she was in different positions in a chair or on the floor, so she could learn where her body was and how it felt, while still having some constancy of feedback from a stable object. I taught her how to rock gently, not just forth and forth from her hunched position, but back and forth in a special legless rocking chair, because her muscle tone was too weak to support the movement unaided. We couldn't do this without bringing her feet along, with her being hunched in a near fetal position, or we would have caused distress to her poor distended stomach.

Sandy's stomach had probably "digested" several pounds of cellophane in her life, as behaviorists rewarded her with candy. Candy was a good incentive, but unwrapping the candy was much too noisy for her hypersensitive ears, so down the hatch, in one gulp, cellophane and all, unless of course, someone unwrapped it first in another room.

I taught Sandy to sit with a broad supportive base, and to rock slowly from one side to another, trying to look at something in her line of vision so that her muscles and ears would learn to calibrate the sense of body in space. In each rock and roll, the moment there was a state change sign—that is a change in breathing, flushing, muscle tone shifts either to tension or flaccidity, eyes losing focus, feeling of disorientation or dizziness—I taught her to stop the activity, even if she had performed only one eighth of a roll or one tenth of a tip. She learned to feel her state changes and to stop activities before they created stress and shut down the very systems we were trying to open. This profoundly retarded autistic youngster was so motivated by what she could feel happening in her body and her mind, that she practiced her activities a few minutes each day at home in her bedroom.

A little bit at a time. We had two and a half years to achieve those goals, remember.

Yet 60 days later, Sandy and her mother returned, and the mother was overwhelmed. Sandy was talking nonstop. That very week the young woman who had been trapped inside that overwhelmed and non-responsive body for so many years had exploded with "What are they doing?" and "Why?" and "Why not?" and "How come?" What happy frustration! But now, as the mother's goals shifted to a laughing "Can you get her to shut up?" I turned to Sandy to ask her about her goals. After all, we needed new goals. She was completing toileting on her own. She was taking stairs up and down without hanging on to anything and even carrying small bags or baskets. She noticed food on her face and washed it off on her own. She combed her hair. She started using lotion on her face and experimented with lipstick on her mouth and nose and wherever else it landed.

Sandy laughed and expressed herself with non-verbal as well as verbal communication. Her muscles and inner ear, and all those various parts of her brain were connecting. And as they connected, it was clear that Sandy was not retarded. Retardation is a concept reflecting a rate of learning, not the amount of learning someone is able to demonstrate. This young woman learned more in two months than "normal" children learn in two years. And, yes, there was more left to learn. And, no, she was not normal. But she was on her way.

On her way to achieving her new goals. Sandy wanted to learn how to read enough to be able to read a TV guide and directions for heating prepared foods. She wanted to be able to multi-task—to carry on a conversation while she was engaged in another task, so she could socialize at work. And she wanted to work in competitive employment, or at least in a sheltered workshop with high functioning young adults. A far cry from the first set of goals. But attainable, as Sandy proved over the next eighteen months, not without some backsliding when she became stressed. And when taxed, her communication skills—developed so late in life—suffered.

7. Communication
Interpreting the meaning

C ommunication is such an amazing process, and so vital to our being able to interact socially, to demonstrate our intelligence, to live in this world with others. Controversy exists among theorists as to whether sensory-motor development or emotional development is the foundation for intelligence and communication. Personally, I know that my sensory-motor development made it nearly impossible for me to communicate effectively with others and for others to bond with me. It is difficult to feel loved when the person declaring love for you transmits verbal and nonverbal messages that she doesn't understand you and wishes in her heart-of-hearts that you were someone else.

My mother, a nurse, was extremely caring. She held me and fed me and read to me. She took care of me—of the me she thought I was or she wanted me to be. But I couldn't relate to this caring, which at times felt so abusive. "Put on a sweater because I am cold, dear" became a family joke as we remembered how my mother imposed her feelings on an overheated child. But that regular occurrence, compounded many times every day with other miscommunications because Mom and I were operating from different sensory-motor baselines, took its toll.

I still remember my anger when Donald Black mailed invitations to everyone in the class (the rule in our sixth grade class was that every class member be invited to parties), instead of distributing them in school. Mom took in the mail and saw the invitation before I could destroy it. "Oh, how wonderful! You're invited to a party!" she said. "You'll see, we'll get you a new dress and you'll have a wonderful time!"

Me? Have a good time at a party with the same classmates who ignored my presence when choosing teammates in gym. Me? Snickered at when I couldn't keep the beat to music let alone learn a dance step. Me? Not knowing how to start a conversation if it was not based on a topic in which I had a profound knowledge base. And then frequently not knowing how to stop when others were no longer interested. How could my mother think this invitation was a "good" thing?

This very same Me was the Me who was a fussy baby. Hard to feed. Hyperactive. Uncontainable in a playpen. Disturbing my mother's sense of orderliness and her need to be on a regular schedule, to have her own quiet times for reading. Looking back, I can see that my mother only wanted me to be happy, and the only frame she had for happiness was what made her happy. Just as the only measures she had for body temperature were either a thermometer (which she frequently plunked under my tongue) or her own sense of heat, which was very different from mine. But she didn't understand that my senses and sensibilities found contentment and happiness in different ways.

Did she not empathize with me? I think she did not because she could not. Between the ages of 9 and 12 I wrote poetry, volumes, daily. I expressed my innermost thoughts and feelings and dreams. My poetry was dark, brooding. Yet whenever Mom requested, "Come, show me what you've been doing up there in your room," and I brought down a heart-wrenching poem, she would read it word for word and look at me with a smile on her face, saying, "Oh, how lovely!"

I wanted to scream that "lovely" was not the response I was hoping to elicit. Sometimes I did. "How dare you call that 'lovely'? What's wrong with you? Can't you tell that I'm expressing deep sorrow? What's 'lovely' about that? I don't know why you pretend you want to read what I write. You obviously don't want to try to understand it!" And then, grabbing my poems from her hands, I would run upstairs to my room and sob inconsolably, kicking the bed until I fell asleep from exhaustion.

Later in life, I learned that my mother did not understand metaphor so I better understood her inappropriate responses to the poetic sharings of my inner world. But at the time, there was little empathy between us. We had roles. She was my caregiver even though she began to realize that she didn't understand me very well and that she didn't like much of what she did understand. And my job was to survive my early years with minimal scarring of others, and trusting with a blind faith that I would someday find a place where I would be accepted, where I could be comfortable.

The empathy I did feel was from my dad, who amazingly has no recollection of how significant a role he played in my emotional survival. He left early in the morning to go to work. He came home tired and had lots of fix-it jobs to do around the house. I'm sure many of his jobs revolved around fixing the things I had destroyed in my attempts to defy the constraints of a playpen, to find things that interested me, to keep myself busy. Later I channeled some of this need to be busy into working with Dad on tiling the floor and paneling the walls of our family room, or mowing the lawn, or working on science projects for school—all things involved with toxins, as I see now, but so nurturing to my soul.

It was my dad who would calm the storms Mom inadvertently created. Dad didn't calm me with words, but with silly faces and postures and music. He was able to remove himself from the minute-to-minute frustrations of caring for a sick, fussy, strange child and by so doing, was able to provide me emotional support.

Yet, my affective development certainly was altered by my sensory-motor problems. And in large part the activities I sought didn't provide me positive feedback from the outside world, but rather security and an intuitive sense of nurturing to my being. This unusual developmental pattern didn't interfere with my intelligence. In fact, my need to understand how to interface with a chaotic world may have helped me develop skills that later translated into high intelligence. Perhaps because there were no methods to control my behaviors—no medication and no behavioral modification programs to constrict me arbitrarily—I was able to explore and make sense of the world using the tools I was given. And my tools worked. Differently. I knew what I wanted because it was what I needed. I also knew how to satisfy these needs. Not unlike so many of the children I see.

The first youngster with whom I identified was Charles, a not-quite six year-old with a brother a few years older. Charles entered my suite hanging onto his mother's skirt and then sat in the corner of the couch—but only for a moment. As soon as he sensed I was safe, he got up and ran across the room, with awkward gait and arms flapping. He had seen the PUZZLES. He did them, over and over again. I joined him, and he jumped back from the table anytime my hand got near his.

Then, mumbling something incoherent, but with intonation that made it sound like spoken language, Charles ran into the bedroom and began to strip. His mother tried to restrain him, insisting that he keep his clothes on. He pulled away, struggling to remove his pants over his shoes, mumbling in a huffy voice something that sounded like "dunoaiaineedabindis."

"Charles," I said, "You don't need to be in all of your clothes, and I'm sure you're more comfortable without them, but we're making a video of our time together today. And you're the star! So I need you to keep your underpants on. You can take all the rest off if it makes you more comfortable."

Charles froze and looked at me. I understood so completely. He didn't know why he needed to be in those clothes that poked and tickled him. He didn't understand the reason behind the seemingly arbitrary demand that he remain clothed, but when I made the leap to let him know I knew his intent and he did not need to defend himself, he relaxed and joined me. He DID try a few more times to strip completely, but each time he accepted the rule: "No clothes means no video."

While we continued to work, his mother said, "You can imagine how embarrassing it is for the whole family, but especially for his older brother, to have Charles behaving like this. Why, he can't even have friends over because Charles is running around naked, plopping himself in the middle of whatever anyone else is doing, muttering things we don't understand, and then throwing a tantrum when we ask him to get dressed and behave himself. If you can just get him to accept his clothes, and help his speech become clearer, we could become a family again—go places and do things together."

As she was talking, Charles showed me some of his tricks, some of those very antics that irritated others. He mumbled something gleefully. It sounded somewhat like "animuhkeydu." Then he started moving around on the floor in strange patterns making even stranger noises. Actually, the noises and movements weren't so strange at all. I helped his mom understand that he was sharing his deep love for and knowledge of many animals. He was trying to show what he learned watching "Animal Kingdom" on TV. Once his mom relaxed, she laughed at his imitation of a bear, and a walrus, and his attempt to be a pelican. And she realized that he understood how they got food and slept and cared for their young.

"I feel awful," she said, beginning to cry. "All this time, we didn't really pay any attention to what he was trying to share." Because Charles couldn't communicate with words and no one had taken the time to see his repertoire of movements and sounds and put them into context, his stories had gone untold. Everyone around him made him STOP his eager communication, thinking he was just acting wild. How sad, and how puzzling for the bright energetic youngster.

But Charles' mom was still concerned. Charles was almost six. Teachers and other children would not take the time to interact with him from his level of need. How could there be any hope for her beautiful dark-haired little boy?

As I was about to tell her my own story, to give her hope, my sister, whom we had been expecting, called to tell me she was in the lobby. Charles' mom was happy to have her join us for the last few minutes. I opened the door for Marlene and as she entered she took in the scene. And she, too, was sent back in time. Had Charles been female and considerably thinner, he would have been my double. Marlene, who had functioned as my interpreter when I was little, immediately understood his speech, too.

Charles' mother was stunned.

"Does Charles remind you of anyone?" I asked my sister. And Marlene said, "That's exactly how you spoke! He is so much like you, I can't believe it!"

Charles' mom knew then that there was hope. And she worked hard with Charles to perform all of the activities in his HANDLE program, almost daily. And later that summer, when her parents came to visit, Charles kept his clothes on the entire time, and interacted with a better sense of boundaries, knowing he was understood and appreciated. And, of course, his speech became clear and, of course, he is still a child who is different from his peers. And each of his peers is different, too.

So, having looked at my later childhood experiences and Charles' earlier childhood experiences, and realizing that we each developed cognitive functions and communication skills, because we were understood, I need to approach the concept of Theory of Mind.

I shared my bias with you earlier: I believe that those of us whose sensory-motor experiences are unusual, who cannot sustain our attention as others might on continuous shifts in the nuances of facial and bodily expression of someone in our immediate environment, who cannot allow ourselves the sensations of discomfort or pain to move in ways similar to those of the people around us, and who therefore cannot fathom what other people are feeling because we cannot allow ourselves to feel what we are feeling—we may not understand what drives another person's behaviors, and therefore we may be deemed to have no Theory of Mind.

However, the other person, in turn, does not understand what drives our behaviors. Is it only because the other is in the majority that we are deemed to be lacking this quality? And might it not be that we have already felt energetically what the other was transmitting, and so we did not need to stay attentive to gather their intent? And might we not then assume that the other person could possess the same ability?

I remember countless times being driven to distraction because others—usually my mother or my teachers—would want me to listen to their monologues to the end. I would wring my hands and twist my ankles, look down, move around, and writhe internally as I stood listening. And I needed to stand listening longer, because they assumed I wasn't listening. After all, I did not sustain eye-contact.

Why wasn't I listening? Because I had already understood the subject from their first few words, and their mood from a quick glance at their stance, and their intent from a rapid sense of their energy. I already knew what they were saying, what they wanted me to do. Occasionally someone would ask me "What is so difficult about standing still and listening to the end of what I have to say?" My answer "Because I already know" was not well received. If she put me to the test of "Okay, so what was I going to say?" I would be right every time.

I realize I must have annoyed many people when I didn't sustain reciprocal visual contact with objects as I pointed to them and asked for them. I probably STILL annoy people with this behavior. I assumed that a fleeting glance and the energy in my intent could be read by others just as I could read theirs. I didn't know about the concept of Theory of Mind. I didn't show my Theory of Mind because I didn't move through a certain dance with the other, so he would know my intent. The pragmatic me says "what a waste of time" and the sensorily overwhelmed me says "I have other things to spend my energy on. I don't need to play this silly game." And in a way, that ties into Baron-Cohen's theory about us autistics. He feels that we have a well-developed sense of "folk physics"—that is that we understand how things work—but that we have poorly developed "folk psychology" and do not understand social causality. This may be true.

But looking at the Theory of Mind, and joining to it Baron-Cohen's theory that most autistic people function from a strong sense of the "male brain"—relating to mechanistic and systematic functions—with little engagement of the "female brain"—relating to the intuitive and empathic—several questions arise. Why can't we simply conclude that people have different ways of relating, based on their neurophysiological and experiential make-up? Marriage and family counselors recognize the angst in their "neurotypical" clients who bemoan "He doesn't understand how I feel about things," or "I just can't seem to communicate with her. Whenever I share what is important to me, she just sort of tunes me out." This is normal behavior.

This situation is compounded in individuals in the spectrum. But the reason for it cannot logically be that those of us with ASD have no Theory of Mind. We have other problems that make it difficult for us to sustain focal vision, read non-verbal communication, get in touch with basic feelings.

Stanley Greenspan, child psychiatrist and professor of psychiatry at George Washington University Medical School, captured the connection to the inner affect that provides the fuel for intentional movements and communication when he posited "As the ability to form symbols emerges, the child needs to connect her inner affects (intent) to symbols to create meaningful ideas, such as those involved in functional language, imagination, and creative and logical thought. The meaningful use of symbols usually emerges from earlier and continuing meaningful (affect-mediated) problem-solving interactions that enable a toddler to understand the patterns in her world and eventually use symbols to convey these patterns in thought and dialogue. Without affective connections, symbols like action plans are used in a repetitive (perseverative) manner (e.g., scripting, echolalia)." [18]

Viewing the connection to inner affect as a part of transformation of affect could soften the blow that a family feels when told their child has no "Theory of Mind."

In his Affect Diathesis Hypothesis, Greenspan goes on to state that what appears at a later date as primarily a biological deficit might actually be the result of insufficient reciprocal affective interactions that are rooted in earlier biologically-based processing disorders influenced by such things as hypersensitivities to the elements of the outside world—light and sound and touch. This is congruent with my personal and clinical experiences. Such a life-situation impedes learning social skills, but I question if it necessarily is an obstacle to the development of intellectual skills. My own experience and that of my clients—young and adult, in various ranges within the spectrum—says No. Our intelligence and ability to function intellectually may be unimpaired. We may, however, need to engage in some behaviors deemed inappropriate in order to access these abilities.

And, again, especially in light of Greenspan's acknowledgment, I return to question the Theory of Mind. Why cannot the other—the adult or child who does not have these abnormal neural messages interfering with his ability to communicate—why can he not understand my intent? Why would Phil's aggressive jabbing at caregivers as he gazed peripherally at someone moving in his environment not be interpreted by them as his fear that his space was about to be encroached upon? Why did they assume that this large 30 year-old intended to harm them, rather than concluding he was beseeching them to assure him he was safe?

[18]Greenspan, S. (2001) p. 3

And why did 21 year-old Kyla's respite caregivers not realize she was merely trying to warn them that her blood sugar levels were low and she needed to eat? She didn't have the wherewithal to engage her relatively newly developed language abilities. So why couldn't they understand that a hypoglycemic state ruled her behaviors and when she saw another resident eating ice cream, her incessant asking for ice cream was not a more generalized cry for FOOD? Period. Instead of offering her other food, they simply refused her the ice cream, inciting a fight that put her in a straight-jacket, after which she was whisked away to spend over a week shackled to a bed in a locked mental ward. Her respite caregivers were missing important pieces of information: Kyla was hypoglycemic and only recently had learned to speak.

I frequently am missing some very pertinent information when working with adult autistic clients. Did he or she have a good strong suck in his or her first few months? How does this relate to the communication problems of a Phil or a Kyla?

In part, the inability to maintain the simultaneous visual and auditory filtering and focusing that is necessary to observe the other's gestures and facial expressions while listening to their words—that alone, not yet deriving meaning from these—goes back to the connection in the colliculus mentioned earlier. The eyes tell the ears where to focus, unless the ears are picking up on messages that say "Danger!" And as research has shown, autistic children have not moved through the stages of habituation and classical conditioning to sound. So not only has irregular sucking as an infant made it more difficult for the two or three year-old to sustain visual and auditory focus, normal speech sounds do not elicit muscular readiness to respond, and filtering out figure from background is not well developed. So what exactly is it I am to focus on, if not the global sense of the event?

If I am to develop speech and begin to speak for the purpose of communicating, I need to focus on many things. Studies have shown that ASD adults with normal intelligence focus their vision more on objects than on people, and when focused on people, they tend to focus more on the speakers' mouths than their eyes. That little quirk may very well be one of the things that helped me develop lip reading as I was trying to learn to speak. I probably did the ASD thing of focusing intently on mouths of speakers, not their eyes. But while mouths give us some information as to urgency and mood, eyes do so much more.

So what am I to focus on? Lips? To learn to speak and to feel safe, because they are not looking back at me? Or eyes, to read into the soul of the speaker, but perhaps then to miss the words, because my ears cannot filter out the background noise and focus on the speech sounds? Of course, I need both, but to deal with both simultaneously demands abilities I do not yet have—not until I have been able to work first on one, then on the other. And in school I keep hearing "Use your words!" So that must be my first point of focus, even if I miss out on much of the intent, at least for now.

With so much focus on the language and social deficits of people with autism, no one talks about the communication tools we DO have. Avoidance of a situation is communication. Tension surrounding certain events or stimuli is communication. Performing "inappropriate behaviors" is communication.

My client Jordan, 11, was trying as hard as he could to participate in his session with me. He dragged his listless, low-tone body from the corner of the room where he had been flapping his hands, and came over to stand next to me at the table, trying to accommodate my request: "Write your name on this paper." He knew how to spell his name and how to hold a pencil. What he couldn't do was bring enough tone into the muscles of his arm to support and energize the writing.

He needed me to balance his elbow so he didn't have to feel the weight of his unsupported forearm pulling down on his shoulder.[19] With my assistance he wrote his name, so faintly it was almost invisible, but he wrote it. And he was proud. But if I'd next asked him to draw a square, or a person, or a tree; or to button a button or pick up a fork, he would have balked. An angry outburst would have been his natural way to say: "I need to recoup before trying to focus my energy on a specific muscle group again, especially on the same group."

While he was writing, Jordan looked at his hand and the paper on which he was writing. As soon as he stopped writing, he looked away, and at almost no other point in that day did he make the effort to bring energy into the tiny muscles that make the eyes converge on a single target. Peripheral vision is so much less demanding, and the stress of focal vision needs to be reserved for when it is essential.

Later that day Jordan taught his parents and me another lesson. He had cooperated with me for more than two hours. Granted, much of the time he was standing apart from us, rocking, and flapping his hands and humming—awakening his body, keeping his vestibular system energized through its connection to the visual system watching those hands flap and flap while they released trapped energy, and blocking out invasive sounds with the comfort of his own humming—but he had cooperated.

---

[19]This is why a number of individuals with autism can express themselves in writing with the assistance of a properly trained facilitator.

Finally, we were finished. His parents were helping Jordan with his coat and heading toward the door. Jordan was eager to go home to familiar and comforting surroundings. And then, as we were standing in the doorway, his parents asked just one more question. They'd done this before, obviously, in other settings; but this time Jordan would not have it. He looked into my face and spat, drenching my cheek from a distance of about three feet.

His parents were mortified, and Jordan knew it. He knew his behavior was reprehensible. "Jordan! You know better . . .!" they began, but "No," I said, "Wait."

"No," they said. "He knows better. He's been taught that he can't do that ."

"Of course he knows how rude that is," I said, "and he WILL learn to stop. But please don't punish him now. You know his verbal communication skills are nonexistent and his nonverbal communication is challenged by his diminished muscle tone. And he has severe tactile hypersensitivities, too. He 'talked' to us the only way he could, from a distance. He was protecting himself, and he was angry about the broken promise. He thought you were leaving, and when there was an additional question, he panicked. Knowing I was in charge, he correctly directed his anger at me. He needed me to stop talking to you. He communicated that clearly."

Jordan sent his nonverbal message across the room, engaging focal vision and energetic mouth movements, knowing he would "get in trouble" but needing desperately to be "heard."

His parents stopped short, momentarily speechless. Then his father said, "We never looked at it that way before. But it does make sense. And chastising him hasn't really helped, as you just witnessed," he said, embarrassed.

Until that moment, his parents hadn't understood the intent behind such behaviors, nor the courage and strength that went into these outbursts. Their son eased into a calm, and I sensed that he wanted to thank me, somehow, but didn't have the means.

But I did have his attention, and used it. After all, his parents were right, and we did not want to reinforce this totally unacceptable behavior. He needed not to do such things.

"No," I said to Jordan, "I don't like being spat at. In fact it really does bother me a lot. But I know you had no other way of communicating your thoughts to me and to your parents. So I don't want you to be punished for what you did, and I don't want you to punish yourself. You communicated clearly. I hope the next time you meet with me or with someone else whose conversation or other demands irritate you, you will find another way. Perhaps you will find words."

And he did. Not magically, but once again, through working on those intertwined systems that support human function and give energy to the human spirit.

8. The language of emotions
Cracking the code

Words and language. Language and communication. How do we develop one without the other? Must we understand language in order to utter words? If we utter words, does that mean we understand language? Not necessarily. But the relationship between language and communication is undeniable. Then how do we learn which words in language communicate what events or feelings?

The first words most people learn are nouns. Nouns label objects that maintain constancy, even for visual learners. A table is constant as a category of all pieces of furniture with flat tops and spaces below them for legs. Of course, then we need to alter that group, to understand that there are also geological tables and mathematical tables and tables of contents. And sometimes we visual learners still picture four legged tables in our minds and chuckle at our own private joke when someone talks about a table of contents. Or we cannot accept a second meaning for a word and must create a different word or tag a modifier onto the word, so it can fit a different set of pictures. As such, we may laugh at things that no one else finds humorous or not laugh at things that others see as double entendre.

Adam's mom, Rita, could not complete a single 20-second Face Tapping procedure. "He just starts laughing so hard that it's impossible to tap on him," she said.

"Show me what's going on," I replied.

As Rita positioned herself to tap on the face of her son who was sprawled out in a beanbag, he immediately began to laugh. Rita started tapping, and with the tapping, to sing in order to distract Adam from the experience. She began singing "The ants go marching one by one, hurrah, hurrah . . .," Adam howled with laughter, making it impossible for his mom to complete the tapping pattern.

"See," she said, "that's what happens every time. And when I tell him to stop laughing, he does. But as soon as I start tapping again, he bellows."

"I see," I said to Rita and then said to Adam, "I want to know what's so funny" (thinking all the time that what's funny to me is that most of the time people don't ask for explanations of perceptions, particularly when someone has severe language delays).

Adam laughed some more and mumbled "anniesoo," which made little sense to me. But his mother now began to laugh, too. "His Aunt Sue, my sister, is a really dignified woman. He must be picturing her marching, and sucking her thumb, and all of the other things he hears in the song. He always used to laugh when he heard the song on his video, too, but I just thought he was enjoying it. I'll have to tell Sue next time I talk with her. We'll all laugh! My little literal thinker unknowingly made a pun!"

And then Rita went on, "I wonder how many others times when I think Adam's laughing at nothing, he's seeing these, well, puns, and just not able to explain himself."

Other words more so than nouns can be much more challenging for people with autism to learn. Words that relate to tactile sensation, for instance, may make no sense (and in any event, we hate some of those feelings). What is "smooth" or "rough" or "silky"? And how can we determine the meaning of words that relate to relative position in space (words such as "under" or "between") when we don't know where we are in space?

We need to be taught painstakingly, over and over again, to put a ball under a chair and pick up a piece of paper and put it under a book. Our response time to such requests will be halting. Sometimes it is so slow that others think we didn't hear or comprehend or that we are simply defiant or lazy. So they repeat the demand, louder and with impatience, "Pick up the paper," they say, tapping impatiently on the edge of the paper, "and put it under the book," now tapping on the book under which they want us to put the paper.

Verbs are a little easier to deal with, because even if we have never jumped, we see other people jumping after the direction has been given. I can create a picture of that movement. The verb "to be," however defies this internalization, especially if we do not feel present in our own bodies. "Where are you? How are you? Are you hurt? Are you ready yet?" These seemingly simple questions are so abstract. What are they asking? And of whom?

Pronouns are the most challenging for nearly everyone in the spectrum. As part of what defines our place in the spectrum, most of us have not yet established a true sense of ourselves proprioceptively and emotionally. People around us talk to us in the third person when they talk to us. "Esther looks so pretty in her new dress," they say to Esther's face. And they say "we" and include themselves with us in experiences that are ours alone.[20] "We're having a hard time remembering to keep our shoes on in school," the teacher says to mom at the end of a school day. How are we supposed to figure out where we end and they begin, if in speech others confuse us and in our bodies we don't have the ability to discern this?

And we are supposed to be clear on what each of us intends and to whom we are directing our thoughts in order to have a Theory of Mind? So let's look at one of my Andrews. I first met Andrew when he was eleven and a half. He had a few almost distinguishable words and phrases to communicate the important things, like "bafroom." He had already been exposed to many theories and many treatment protocols, and he still spent most of his days not engaging with others, apparently disinterested in conversations and social activities, although he really wanted to learn to ride his bike.

Assessment revealed that Andrew's tactile and proprioceptive senses of his body were almost nil. His muscle tone was very weak. He was so hypersensitive to sound that he shut down his auditory-vestibular functions most of the time. He could not go beyond his body because in a sense he was not yet in his body. I guided his parents in special forms of tapping and massaging to establish this primary ability, and we also encouraged sucking and blowing activities more so to strengthen his visual focus than to enhance the function of his articulators (tongue, jaw, cheeks) coordinated with breathing.

At his third monthly follow-up session, Andrew's mom entered the room noticeably excited. "What happened?" I asked with concern.

Her stunned reply: "On our way to your office from the freeway, I was

---

[20]I have been having a very difficult time writing this book, trying to keep my personas unified. I began using "we" to mean myself and others in the spectrum. But I am beginning to move across that boundary, as I near 60 years of experience relating to myself and others in this world. I find that I more readily see myself these days as part of the "we" of the general population. And, of course, there is the "we" of the human race. But I am sensitive to the use of pronouns, and I hope that in this book so far I have used them in a manner that is not confusing. As I use "we" to include myself with each population some of the time, I trust you will understand through the context which "we" I am referring to.

muttering to myself, as I frequently do when I drive, saying 'Is this the right street? Now which way am I supposed to turn here..?' And Andrew's voice, projecting clearly from the backseat, asked, 'Are you talking to me?' as he made eye-contact with me through the rear-view mirror. I can't believe it! Attention and speech and pronouns, and can I assume, a Theory of Mind . . .?!'"

What next, once someone has learned all of these words and parts of speech, not in a grammar lesson, but dynamically and pragmatically? We need to put them together into meaningful communication, words expressing our inner-most feelings.

But how do autistic people know their feelings? Bobbie, the young woman who was 18 years old when I first met her, shed some light on this. She was considered non-verbal, had only occasionally mumbled some words or blurted out a short sentence. She was alternately hyperactive and lethargic. She was silly or sullen, remote or overly demonstrative, slumped in her chair or chasing someone around the room. Extremely sensitive to sound. Her mother, you may recall, thought she was hyposensitive to touch.

"I know it appears as if Bobbie doesn't feel most of the tactile input that you would, but I think she is simply blocking feeling, because it is so painful." Yes, I have mentioned this before, but it warrants repetition.

Approximately one year after she began her HANDLE program, which had been modified according to her progress, Bobbie wrote this for attendees at a state-wide autism conference:

"I love HANDLE because it has changed my life. I can now know what everyone else does. I feel like you feel, I hear like you hear, I see like you see, and I can move like you move. I think all of you take these fine abilities for granted, but I don't. These abilities for me have been a long time in coming. Before, I had gotten trapped in a body that had hobbled along. Just to move was a mental and not very easy problem I had to solve. Now I can move without thinking. I feel free to do things I got stuck on before. Now I just have to work longer on my jumping, to work harder on my speaking, and I have to get to the point where I can go to college and be on my own. I believe I can do this in a few years time. I not only believe this, but so does my mom. If I can, so can others like me. Kind of hopeful isn't it? Mothers are great, so is Mom. I will hope for the best."

She could give voice to her feelings only after she could allow herself to feel, and after she could move without thinking about movement—a full range of movement. Her movements had been so restricted her whole life, and her balance so challenged, that you can imagine the surprise of her family when she came down for dinner one evening, about three months into her HANDLE program, and said to her folks, "Watch me!" as she held both hands in the air, lifted her leg over the chair and sat down.

Yet, even at this stage in her growth, Bobbie was more comfortable capturing her ideas in writing, rather than by speaking. I am like Bobbie in this way. Writing is my preferred mode of communication. It requires less energy to write, and there are fewer stimuli to filter out so I can keep track of my ideas. I get much less input into my still sensitive trigeminal nerve when I write or type than when I speak. And I am not exposing my thoughts to others until I have composed and edited them. I am more in charge.

It is less interactive of a process, granted. But when we need to choose between no communication and written communication, the choice should be obvious.

That is the reason a growing number of families with autistic children—children of many different ages, some of them older than I—are turning to forms of augmented communication. Picture exchange techniques have been available for years. Typewriters required much too much muscle tone for most autistic people to rely upon. Electric typewriters and computers began to open a whole new realm of communication. And the newer facilitated devices will even read aloud the messages typed.

Some autistic people (including some you have already met in these pages) are aided by a technique called Facilitated Communication (FC). A reliance on FC seems alarming to some. I have seen it abused and I have seen it used to great advantage. Without FC, the poem included on page 49 of this book would not exist, since Lincoln Grigsby was released to express his thoughts verbally through FC. He is one of many. He is only recently developing adequate muscle tone to hold his body upright and find the sustained strength to support his arm above the keyboard. He is working on it. He has not yet had the tone to keep himself balanced and coordinate all of those little muscles needed for speech. He is working on it.[21]

With an intricate interplay between balance and muscle tone, bodies are supported as they move through space and perform tasks, including that extremely important task of speech. Muscle tone again enters the scene as a prerequisite for virtually every movement and every way in which feelings are communicated. Listen

---

[21]Between my original writing of this book and its final preparation for publication, Lincoln began to speak. At the age of 42, six and one–half months into his HANDLE program, he began to name the letters he was typing, and then words. And one of the first words he uttered was "HANDLE."

to the idioms commonly used: "What is it that moves you?" means tell me your reasons for doing something or seeking particular stimulation. "Can't you move on to something else?" is asked in exasperation when someone is stuck in their response to a demand.

Even not doing something, the restraint of a motion, requires muscle tone. It requires more muscle tone to go downstairs than to go upstairs, because going down there is a need to resist the pull of gravity. Muscle tone comes into play when I need to stop before I bump into someone, especially if I am running instead of walking. These are manifestations of muscle tone that most people can see. But the same factors also come into play in our verbal and nonverbal communication: control of vocal tone and volume; development of prosody, so our speech conveys the spontaneous rhythms of our feelings rather than the monotones of a string of words put together into an utterance.

Usually when we run instead of walk, it is because if we were to slow down, we would need to worry about resisting gravitational pull—another way in which balance and muscle tone and the inner ear interact. When I start a memorized song and can't stop once the momentum has overtaken me, is it that dissimilar? Moving and not moving, doing and being all require action from those parts of us that move us—our muscles. And our movement patterns create mental patterns, brain patterns that then shape our behaviors. Intertwined again, the body and the brain, the physical and mental and emotional beings.

Intertwined. To include synergistic reactions among toileting and muscle tone and expressive language functions. Muscle tone, for everything: the peristaltic movement of food from the mouth, through the digestive tract and out the other end for elimination—bowel and bladder control. All relying on round, ring, sphincter muscles, the same type of muscle that regulates constriction and dilation of the pupils of our eyes. The sphincter muscles most of us learn to control consciously before any other are those of the lips. And the more we practice and strengthen the sphincter muscles in any part of our body, the more we strengthen them in every part of our body. Weak sucking may lead to difficulty in developing bowel and bladder control.

Corey was stuck in a number of ways. He was stuck in a compulsive fascination with numbers and measures, he was stuck in his inability to use language as a medium for communication rather than a tool for rattling off calculations that flashed onto the screen inside his brain, and he was very stuck in the bowel movement department. He simply would not allow himself to move his bowels, clenching his entire body into a C-shape and gritting his teeth and holding the feces inside until they became brick-sized blocks that would cause him to bleed. He was terrified to release them.

His general movement patterns were also stuck, that is not fluid. His speech was without prosody. His parents said he never cried. He was obsessed with blinking lights and long chains.

Corey bravely attempted almost any activity I suggested, but he staunchly refused to close his eyes and rely on his proprioceptive sense.

I was certain that a great deal of his proprioceptive insecurity stemmed from a condition he had in infancy. A large hemangioma—a sac filled with blood vessels—bulged around one of his eyes and on the eyelid. Because the pupil was covered, his vision was threatened, so he wore an eye patch on the "good" eye for four hours a day to force the threatened eye to "see." His parents worked hard to keep him "using" that bad eye, dangling things in his face and not letting him doze off.

When I met him, he was just shy of 4 years old, and he would not close his eyes. Whether his need to keep his eyes open was due to deep-seated memory of his medical history or some other unknown quirk in his make-up, he needed to stay vigilant. Yet he also needed to retreat behind those eyes into the snapshots in his own head, which were his only source of visual perceptual constancy. He had a conflict, and the schism between the world and his mind's eye's view of it was apparent in his behaviors and his speech.

As we worked through this eye-closing resistance and he learned that he and the world were still here when he opened his eyes again, not only did he gain more confidence and more emotional responsiveness, he gradually became more willing to release bowel movements. He grew to trust his environment and was able to try such frightening things as standing on an uneven surface and riding an escalator. That eyelid may have been a much more important factor in his development than anyone would have anticipated. From a systems perspective, it probably kept him in some ways from a natural flow of opening and closing and taking in and releasing himself and the world.

If I can't feel and control my body parts adequately, how am I supposed to feel and control my emotions? Many high-functioning people with autism say they didn't start to feel emotions until they could allow themselves to really feel their bodies.

Sean's parents were worried that he lacked empathy. He slapped and pushed people and felt no remorse. He laughed when others fell and hurt themselves. He offered defiant glances and continued his bothersome behaviors when his mother entreated, "Stop running and shouting, Sean. I have a really bad headache." His mother voiced her concerns, "I truly fear that my son is asocial, and as he gets older he will seriously injure others and run amuck of the law. I can't even honestly say that I love him. I can't trust him. I don't understand his total lack of empathy."

As Sean's tactile system became integrated and he learned to modulate the movements of his big muscles, he became increasingly aware of his feelings. He cried from the pain of a physical injury for the first time when he was almost fourteen. He cried for the first time from the pain of an emotional injury a few weeks later. As he became integrated with his own sensory-motor systems, he began to feel and to be moved—first sensitive to his own experiences, and then to others. His mother shared the day that Sean noticed she was not feeling well and asked, sweetly, "Mom, is there anything I can get you? You look like you're not feeling well."

Developmentally, people are not moved by things and events outside their bodies until they can deal with their own movement first (unless they have severely limiting physical disabilities in which case other principles come into play). This concept, then, sheds another light on the issue of the vestibular system and cerebellum and their interconnections. They provide more than just support for movement of the body, but also are intertwined with our motivation to be. Movement and life are, after all, synonymous. And movement is necessary for learning. People move to accomplish things they are motivated to do. Everyone needs to be moved to move. And everyone needs to move to be moved.

9. Unity of the senses
The formation of patterns

Our senses are unified. I have problems sucking and swallowing. This caused me to have digestive disorders. And my sucking-swallowing also are in large part responsible for light sensitivity that bothered me until my trigeminal nerve was organized enough to allow me to exercise the sphincters of my lips in a natural, unstressed manner. Typically developing people don't need to understand these connections, just as they don't need to be taught to stand up and walk. But those of us with autistic tendencies need to create patterns. We might find them in our bodies or in the arrangement of our toys or in street maps and jigsaw puzzles, and we may find solace in the patterns formed by numbers. We are seeking order in a disorganized world. We are fulfilling with a vengeance our human mission, to create entropy from chaos.

Seven year-old Nick explored my office space and came across the microwave. His parents winced, knowing about his fetish. Pushing buttons, watching numbers appear, hearing tones, and repeating the sequence was his bliss.

Bouncing on his tiptoes, and flapping his hands between stabbing motions at the touch pad on the microwave, he squealed, emitting gleeful little sounds.

Of course, his parents prevailed in their request, "Nick, stop playing with the microwave. We need you to come sit down with us in the other room now," they said, as they grabbed the belt loops of his jeans and walked beside him into the evaluation room.

But every few minutes, after attending to my directions to the best of his ability, Nick needed to retreat[22] into something that he could control and enjoy. He returned to the microwave. Never pushing the Start button, fortunately. Just looking for patterns and listening to sounds more distinctive than the whirring of the motor of the oven. He might have been seeking a particular sequence of numbers or series of tones, or maybe he liked the lights. He never told me. It was most likely the congruence of the various sensory elements, consistently forming integrated patterns.

Looking for patterns in mundane events is something I understand. In one sense, that is how I have created HANDLE. Looking for patterns in behaviors in order to understand what is at the root of those seemingly unrelated behaviors.

That driving need to look for patterns underlies another of my quirks: Digital clocks drive me nuts. I can't work with one in sight, nor sleep with one by the bed. Number patterns are too intriguing, so if the clock says 12:13 I might watch it a bit and mutter "Stupid clock!" Because even though it marched nicely along with 12:13 it didn't then move to 14:15, 16:17.

One of my favorite times is 12:34, and I usually get excited when I see the numbers marching in such neat progression. I actually recorded a remarkable event that occurred on the afternoon of January 17, 2003. I was checking into a hotel in Portland, Oregon. I was going to hear a lecture by Dr. Oliver Sacks, whose insights into neurological functions have excited me for years. The clerk in the hotel handed me a form to sign and my key card in a little paper holder. Numbers popped out at me. My room number was 1516. My sign-in date was January 17 and my sign-out date January 18. 15-16-17-18. I knew the world was in order. I still wonder what the clerk thought as I began to muse and chuckle about this.

Digital clocks can also cost sleep. If I wake up at night and see "1:37" on the LED, I must think whether or not that's a prime number. And I don't remember all the prime numbers, so I need to sit up in bed and divide 137 by as many of the lower prime numbers as I can until I satisfy myself that it is in fact a prime number. I've been known to try to engage others in the activity, so I can return to sleep sooner. I try to stay away from digital clocks. The small one on my computer screen right now says 7:11, so I'm distracted by wondering why the convenience store chain uses the name 7-11 when its hours are much longer than that.

Most people in the autism spectrum seek patterns. And they find patterns, frequently different from the patterns others see.

---

[22]Give the word "retreat" another look. "Re" meaning again. "Treat" meaning pleasure. If we discard the "military" context and see this word as "repetitively seeking something pleasurable in the midst of an arduous task," it is a wonderful word.

A brilliant second-grader with excellent verbal skills and a whirling imagination just couldn't make friends. At recess, try as he might to enter games with the other children, they shunned him. Sometimes they ridiculed his tone of voice or his delayed and awkward motor responses, as they ran around the play area, chasing one another and interacting with no apparent rules, no clear patterns to their behaviors.

Chaos. Ken knew chaos. He battled an out-of-control right brain constantly, trying to ground himself in logic, in sequence. But that blasted disorganized right brain kept interfering. During one diagnostic activity of drawing circles and triangles with both hands simultaneously, with his eyes shut, Ken thought his sides were working synchronously. His results surprised him and worried his parents.

Ken's drawing was virtually identical to the circles and triangles drawn by the youngster who was able to isolate his voice from the rest of the world's noises only after using the voice reflector. The near total lack of organization in the production of the left hand reflects disorganization of the right brain, which controls the left side of the body. It is not by chance that this pattern appears in the drawing of many individuals in the spectrum. The right brain is out of control.

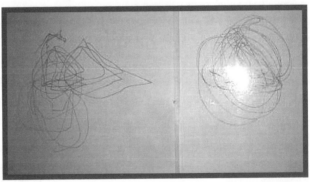

As much as Ken needed patterns so his left brain's logical, sequential sensibilities could help him organize his behaviors, he could not stay in this organized mode without stifling his creativity—a right brain function. When I first asked Ken to write his phone number for me, he looked to his dad to tell him the number. His dad began telling Ken the numbers. "Seven," he said, and after a momentary pause he continued, "four, seven . . ." As his dad was about to continue with the rest of the numbers, Ken stopped writing, waved his arms around with great excitement, and exclaimed, "Our phone number is an airplane!" And he was off flying! He did settle back down and completed the task, but later, when he thought of his phone number again, the airplane returned.

So patterns can be "good"—giving order to our world—or they can be "bad," distracting us if we need to find order and they give us none, or directing us to associative images that no one else sees and understands.[23]

Again, witness the fury of the child whose ritual has been disturbed, who needs to perform things outside of the routine pattern of events. Or the adult who throws an adult-sized tantrum because one of the cars in his collection of models has been moved to another position. The pattern is broken, the energy is shifted, the world is not right.

One way we develop meaningful patterns is through rhythm. Rhythm and music are wonderful organizers and integrators of numerous brain functions. Most people learn to sing the alphabet long before they can retain the visual or auditory (but non-musical) sequence of those 26 letters. Many people cannot alphabetize words without humming the alphabet to keep their place.

Patterns and our need to organize a chaotic world can lead to social challenges beyond those of not allowing others to move one's precisely ordered belongings. Children's play is not organized. Rules to games change every few moments, depending on the whims of a leader or the joint decision-in-action of the children involved. But five and a-half year-old Maria couldn't join in. She had incorporated scripts, including movement patterns associated with some games. So she got upset when the rules changed and her rehearsed behaviors no longer fit. Her teachers and her mother have had to remove her so many times from altercations, with her kicking and screaming, "I want to play! I want to play!" But Maria wanted to play the "right" way—the way she had rehearsed.

Maria's behaviors perplexed everyone around her. After nearly three years of providing her services, the school district referred Maria for a HANDLE assessment. One of the questions I was asked: Is Maria Autistic or Mentally Retarded, or both? In just a few months on her HANDLE program, Maria amazed everyone as she moved along a continuum of "diagnoses" from the suspected Autism with Mental Retardation to Asperger's Syndrome; she abandoned her self-stimming behaviors of rocking and flapping unless she was extremely excited; and she also began to negotiate! Negotiations require such flexibility. Changing the rules, changing the premise at times, all with the goal of reaching an agreement with others. Moving into uncharted territory, and not knowing what pattern would emerge. Now that's

---

[23]If you didn't see Ken's airplane, you're probably a linguistically oriented person, one who doesn't instinctively seek visual patterns. I'll phrase the interaction between Ken and his father differently, merely moving my comments on the dad's pause: "His dad began telling Ken the numbers. 'Seven, four, seven,' he said, pausing briefly after the first 'seven.' As his dad was about to continue . . ." I imagine you, too, now see that huge Boeing airplane taking off!

bravery!

It is exactly this kind of bravery that parents of autistic children must muster. They had built for themselves the expectation of a pattern or style of family life that did not include the challenges of raising an autistic child. By realizing that if your child is stuck in a pattern—truly stuck because of some irregular neurophysiological irregularity—then you must break out of your old pattern of behavior and negotiate with your child.

You must find what works.

Why could Maria "come out" while so many others remain "stuck"? Maria's parents diligently and playfully implemented their full integrated HANDLE program with Maria, strengthening her weak systems, enhancing the connections among systems, incorporating many activities to differentiate one body side from the other in movement and to reintegrate the two sides with rhythmic synchronicity. Others do not buy the premise that working on seemingly unrelated developmental activities and changing nutrition could help their child make the behavioral changes they desired so she would fit the pattern they had for her.

Although patterns can help give order to our world, they can be distracting if we need to find order and they give us none. But it is pattern and congruity and constancy that we each seek. That is probably one of the reasons those of us who fall outside the pattern of society are tweaked and teased until we fit the pattern better. The only problem is that we lose our sense of ourselves in the process, because our processing is not understood.

As a child, I spun the wheel of my tricycle around and around, feeling and seeing how the movement of my arms and the resistance of the pedals affect the rhythmic or dysrhythmic movement of the wheel. I began to build a unity of sensory experience. If I was interrupted before this unity occurred, I needed to revisit the experience. Sometimes, just because so many other things in my day had jumbled my senses, I needed to return (to re-treat) to the activity that unified them.

Someone decides that these are perseverative, obsessive-compulsive behaviors. Most assuredly. As I have an obsession to live and a compulsion to do whatever I must to make sense of my world through my sensory systems. And I was allowed to create my patterns and play them through.

Frequently today, however, in attempts to find externally imposed solutions, someone decides if the doctors can't stop the behaviors, not even with psychotropic medication, then maybe a therapist can incorporate them into an activity with some redeeming social value. One problem with this is that the amount of feedback this activity gives is not "right," and this activity has not been generated by the intention of the child who is asked to perform it. If he does not get enough feedback when he performs the constructed activity, he will seek more feedback, and then be admonished for using too much force, for being destructive.

I cry out for all of the children whose self-generated self-stimming behaviors are inhibited before they have served their purpose. Why can't they just continue doing their self-stimulatory activity until they don't need to do it anymore? And if it is truly dangerous, why can't someone devise an activity that will give them just the right amount of energy and rhythm and specific sensory modality input that they need without demanding more of their proprioception or muscle tone or other functions than they can summon up?

The answer to that is simple: Because others are not inside the bodies of these children and adults. Only those who have somehow experienced something similar can really understand. Others can learn to understand, and a rare few may even be able to enter our perceptions energetically and truly know the experience. Then perhaps they can learn to anticipate what it would feel like being Me and doing what they wish Me to do.

Sometimes the answers are so obvious, even though the questions have not been asked. At least not the questions that will provide the answers. Not the questions that look for the pattern.

Diane called me in dismay, sobbing into the phone as she relayed her problem. "Last week, the pediatrician told me he thought my sweet little boy was autistic. I know, I pushed him for a diagnosis, but we just needed to know why Randy hasn't started to talk, and he's almost three. And he won't keep his clothes on! And the most heartbreaking part of it all—he won't ever snuggle up to me or my husband or my mom. He hates being held, and he never gives anyone a hug."

She went on, "But when the pediatrician said he was autistic, I was horrified. I thought there must be something else, not autism, because he also doesn't seem to be growing properly. Well, the pediatrician said only a pediatric neurologist would be able to make the hard and fast diagnosis, so we got an appointment and I just took Randy to him today," she stopped to sob some more.

"He says Randy is either autistic or has a PDD. I don't even know what a PDD is . . . Is that any better than autism?" Before I could explain to her what a Pervasive Developmental Disorder was, she continued, "I need to know what he has and what I can do to help him."

I agreed to drive out to their home to see him. She gave me directions. As I got close, I realized from a strange buzzing sensation in my own head and limbs that I was under some pretty powerful electrical wires. In fact, the family lived in a small development just next to the Bonneville power station, one of the biggest such in the Northwest. I calmed my own systems and drove up to the house. As I parked my car in the driveway, I saw a young woman wearing a sequined glittery white shirt, synthetic stretch pants and running shoes with thick synthetic soles. She was trying to contain a little naked boy, who was gleefully holding a lawn hose and spraying water on himself and the muddy grass through which he sloshed. "There they are," I said to myself.

As soon as Randy's hair began to dry, it also began to stand on end, as if he had spent the entire morning rubbing balloons against his head to create static electricity. Once Randy was dry, his mom carried him into the house, with me right behind. The off-white wall-to-wall carpet was synthetic, as most carpets are today. It was covered with vinyl runners to protect it from stains and wear patterns. The velvet upholstery on the dining room chairs was encased with plastic, as was the soft velvet upholstery on the couch and chairs in the living room. Fairly centrally collected were bright primary color plastic toys—a pounding bench, a busy box, some Legos. Interspersed were a few plush toys, none of which were made of cotton or wool or any other natural fiber.

I interviewed Diane while I continued to observe Randy, struggling to get away from her.

"I know this might seem like an odd first question to ask, but is Randy having a particularly bad hair day, or is his hair usually one big cowlick?"

She laughed, letting go of him. "His hair has always stood straight up, and every picture we have of him shows that."

She suddenly stopped speaking, her lower jaw dropped, and then a small pout developed as she watched her son climb into my lap and snuggle into me.

"It's sure a good thing his grandma isn't here right now," she said. "Boy, would she be jealous."

Diane was obviously jealous, too. But it was simply my clothes. At first Diane didn't want to believe that my totally natural fiber clothing was the magic. But it was hard to refute, especially after she sorted through Randy's clothes and identified that the only ones he ever kept on for even moments were those that were natural fiber.

Exactly why her son was so affected by the electrical energy in his environment, in his total surroundings, I don't know. Perhaps it was that during her entire pregnancy with him they lived under the power lines and in a synthetic home environment. But not all of the children who were born in that little development had his problems. There must have been several other factors, too.

Nevertheless, it was clear that Randy's energy was seriously out-of-sync and he could not process the stimuli—all forms of energy—that were seeking entry through his various sensory modalities. His ears and his eyes and his skin could not form cohesive patterns. Everything was fragmented, and he was responding to chaos with chaos.

In addition to suggesting a number of calming and supportive activities to help Randy relax, I suggested changes in his environment, including replacing some of his glitzy toys with subdued wooden ones. Luckily, they were already building a new home in a quiet wooded area and were scheduled to move in a few months. Randy began to calm down, to find—even to seek—his mom, dressed in cotton sweats and walking around in her stocking feet on the carpet sans vinyl runners. He began to sense the congruity of the rhythms of her body and of her voice. He began to hear her and listen for her and take in language.

By the time they moved into their new home, he almost defied his diagnoses. He continued to make gains. Periodically the mom would call just to let me know how well he was doing. "You won't believe it," she'd say. "He spent the morning happily watching videos and singing along, doing puzzles, and, in front of our neighbor, he showed off how smart he is by identifying the letters and numbers on his wooden blocks."

And then the distress call came!

"Judith, I need your help! Randy has regressed almost back to where he had been. And right now he closed himself in the closet off the kitchen and refuses to come out. He's holding onto the door and screaming, fighting our attempts to get him out. What should we do?"

I had seen their new home, and I knew Seattle. It had been overcast all winter. The windows on the sides of their house let in some light, but were shaded by some wonderful old trees. The windows in the kitchen and family room were smaller so the family had designed skylights to capture every bit of sunshine when they could. Springtime arrived, and with it, the sun. Their precious son was suddenly under bombardment. Without warning, violent rays of light were penetrating the skylights and piercing him and his environment, and his world was again scrambled.

Once again we talked about principles of "HANDLE Interior Design"—the use of color and lighting and materials and space ways that do not stress the senses. This time the modifications were fewer. They let Randy stay in the closet without a fight until they draped sheets from the ceiling to veil the skylights. They talked to him through the closet door, calming him with words like: "It's okay, Randy. Mommy and Daddy are putting up sheets to cover the skylights. They'll shield you from the bright sunlight. You can just stay safe in the closet until we're done. Don't worry, Randy, we'll fix it so it won't bother you again." And when they told him, "Okay, Randy. We're done now and the room is wonderfully dim. No more bright sunlight to bother you . . .." then their brave Randy came out of the closet and began to open again to the world of external stimuli.

Now that his systems were less stressed, we could begin to return to him some of those experiences he had not had—strong sucking when he was relaxed enough to close his eyes to help them work together and process the powerful energy of light without fragmentation. And with that, to form a coherent world where light and sound and touch and movement all interfaced with rhythmic synchronicity to form comprehensible patterns.

I may never know what caused Randy's problems, but I do know that his behaviors and his being clearly demonstrated the area in which he needed help. He needed to be able to have a fluid exchange of energy with his surroundings, not just to have it all impinge upon him until he was so overwhelmed that he could not make sense of any of it. Yes, he did have a pervasive developmental disorder. There was something—energy—that pervaded and disordered his development. But he was a clear communicator. He would not let his areas of disorder be covered up. And with appropriate help, he became empowered to have a full and happy life, yes, even full of sunlight.

Randy's story exposes some patterns that many people would not have identified. From cowlicks to synthetic fibers to electrical energy to chaotic energy in a brain seeking order, and with the order, respite. There are so many patterns to discern, and to discover many of them one must bravely venture into unfamiliar realms. As you do this, know that many others studying autistic behavior are also now breaking old patterns of thinking, with the realization that it is all about patterns. Not isolated events or specific systemic irregularities.

There is a unity to our senses. It must be acknowledged. The patterns will show themselves, and they will be different for each one of us, but there will be patterns in this intertwining series of threads we are weaving now.

10. Energy and behaviors
The importance of grounding

Energy is such an interesting phenomenon. The world of animate and inanimate objects is all formed and moved by energy. Most people rely on sensing the separate energies of light, sound, pressure, touch, movement, pull of gravity, smell, and heat. They then demand their brains take the billions of data they have filtered out and those they have focused on, and organize a cognitive experience of the object and the situation and the relationship. Others feel the wholeness of the energy and know the experience and don't need to focus on disparate details and analyze them. Many autistic children and adults feel this. I know I felt it from an early age and still feel it strongly. The whole is very different from the sum of its parts.

In high school and college I could not be persuaded to take a Physics course, although I loved and excelled in mathematics and spatial organization. Fellow students, teachers and counselors would ask me why I so adamantly refused to study Physics.

"I have better things to do with my time. I study Physics all the time. It's part of the natural observable phenomena of everyday life. Movement and energy. Energy and movement." I knew I was oversimplifying the course content, but I couldn't bring myself to study this observable science when I could instead study Chemistry and Biology and Anatomy and Physiology—those sciences that I felt deal more with the hidden workings of energy.

Oliver Sacks presented some facts of physics and electrical energy in his recent book *Uncle Tungsten: Memories of a Chemical Boyhood.* It's interesting to juxtapose his childhood explorations of physical phenomena with objects and the possible inner workings behind some autistic behaviors. That, again, is the essence of HANDLE: Applied (neuro)science, from the inside-out and the outside-in. Sacks conducted experiments with batteries, using copper and zinc wires. He realized that the chemical activity and the electrical potential were in some sense the same phenomenon. He was particularly intrigued by the Daniell cell battery, that in some seemingly extraordinary way was making electricity all by itself—not by rubbing or friction, but merely by virtue of its own chemical reactions. From this revelation, Sacks went on, in his boyish wonderment, to make batteries, using fruits and vegetables as the conducting media into which he placed two different metals.

Think about the human body. It certainly is an organic medium—a vast number of organic media, in fact, bundled together by energetic forces. Metals also abound in our environment—from the minerals in foods to the pollutants in the external environment. Some people ingest and inhale and absorb through their skin more toxic metals than others because of where they live and what they eat and the type of jobs they hold—pregnant women included. Research, primarily on hair analysis, has shown that autistic children do not seem to process mercury and calcium and other metals and minerals in the same way that normal children do. Mercury seems to be accumulating in their bodies. Could this be the reason that so many children develop autistic behaviors after receiving vaccinations preserved with thimerosal? And if so, where and when does this phenomenon begin and what are safe ways to intervene?

Well, those of us affected more profoundly by these heavy metals try to find ways at least to discharge the excess and aberrant energy building in our bodies, causing us tension, creating noise in our nervous system, jangling our brains. We wiggle and squirm and shake and bang . . .

Head banging is alarming to observers who view it as self-injury and struggle mightily to prevent or stop it. But is it more "injurious" to the person in the spectrum for him to bang his head repeatedly (and usually rhythmically) against a wooden headboard or piece of drywall or to endure the anguish of energy shorting out his system from the inside?

ASD individuals, like all humans, are programmed to survive, and their head banging helps them to do that. It serves a purpose.

Oliver Sacks clarified the function of head banging without even realizing he was talking about human instinctual drive. Also in *Uncle Tungsten,* he described his fascination with a doorbell. When someone pressed on the button outside the house, electrical impulses were set in motion, flowing through the copper wire that became magnetized and caused the hammer at the other end of the wire to strike the bell. This contact broke the circuit and the hammer fell back in place, resting until the next person outside the house again pressed a button.

Doorbells and pressing buttons are excellent metaphors for many aspects of human processing. We have all had our buttons pressed. Most children are adept at finding and pressing one another's buttons. Those of us in the spectrum are constantly having our buttons pressed by virtually everything in our environment.

In the body's electrical system, when our buttons are pushed, the surge of energy needs to be released so we can get respite. So we bang our heads against headboards, or slam our bodies into walls, or pound on tables. And we do it repetitively if our buttons are still being pushed, if we haven't been able to organize our systems to better deal with the surges of energy or if our attempts to protect ourselves from overloading are dishonored.

Might this same phenomenon partly explain why Temple Grandin, like her cows, seeks pressure in order to calm an overwhelmed system, or why a child needs to have constant contact with another person or the wall next to his bed in order to sleep? Could this need for closing an electrical circuit be part of the proprioceptive needs of people in the spectrum and so many other people as well?

Many of the movements that we employ when we are stressed include flapping our arms up and down or waving our wrists. "We" is everyone. It is a remnant of our primary reflex response and surfaces when we are stressed. Those of us in the spectrum engage in these behaviors more adamantly and more often. If sitting, we may try to do the same with our legs, but it's much trickier, so we may just wiggle our ankles. In one way these movements are not helpful because they are basically reflexive, undifferentiated, and therefore disorganized, indicating insufficient cognitive control over impulses.

But the body knows that these movements, as well as gentle rocking movements of the neck, release trapped energy and allow for better flow. Ankle and wrist rotations also activate the diaphragm. Paula Garbourg, whose work aims largely to balance sphincter muscles and also release other deep tissues throughout the body, recommends controlled ankle and wrist rotations to increase diaphragmatic control and bring more oxygen into the system. When out of control, the rapid movements—flailing, actually—can create a state of panic in our respiratory system, and through our vagus nerve and our ANS, cause a generalized sense of danger to our being.

But oxygen is one of the primary fuels the body and particularly the brain require. So why would we do something that would inhibit our ability to inhale an adequate supply? Because the body-brain-mind-spirit has other needs also, and one of them is to reduce the tension in the "high-tension wires" that are connecting our various systems and coordinating responses. Overload causes protective shut-down, in fuse boxes and in the human being, too.

We need to explore this phenomenon called energy. So much research on ASD points to many areas of the nervous systems that are not functioning well, that are out of sync with one another and providing their owners with fragmented and unusual perceptions of the world. What is it that the brain and the nervous systems are processing? Energy. And they require energy to process it. Our metabolic functions are energetic. We are energy and when energy does not flow correctly, some things are cut off, others are burned, yet others may meld in strange ways.

The traditional Hawaiian philosophy of healing, Huna, has seven precepts. The third precept is "energy flows where attention goes." When our attention is scattered or truncated, our energy does not flow, and in a self-fueling cycle, spinning out of control, our energy and attention become ever more fragmented.

One of the ways I help the "electric" children I see gain equilibrium is to offer them copper ankle bracelets. Despite their extreme sensitivity to touch, usually they accept the copper. Why copper and why the ankle?

Copper and peat are two excellent conductors of electrical energy. Many metals are. On high-voltage electrical appliances such as washing machines and refrigerators there is a three-pronged plug. The copper wire that goes into the third prong is referred to as the grounding wire. It takes the excess energy and sends it into the ground. I wear untreated copper every day, to keep me grounded. When my energy is more scattered or frazzled than usual, I need to have more copper on me. I make sure that some of it is as far away from my brain as possible. I may put a lotion with peat or copper on the soles of my feet or wear a copper (or copper/silver/brass) ankle bracelet, usually on my left ankle, since it is my right cerebral hemisphere ("right brain") that usually flies out of control, and cerebral hemispheres relate to the opposite sides of the body.

Copper showed its power in a summer training program I conducted in Seattle in 2002. For eight days, I had been teaching concepts underlying HANDLE assessment, treatment philosophies and practices to a very eclectic group of advanced trainees. A medical doctor and a naturopathic physician were among the students. The class also included two registered nurses, an occupational therapist, five teachers, and one community advocate. They had been challenging me and draining me on many different levels. I was spent. But I kept on going.

The naturopath began to wiggle and squirm in her chair, tipped her head down, used her hand as a visor, and still could not look at me. One of the other students sitting further back, a woman very involved in movement and energetics, also became a little fitful. After a few minutes the naturopath said, politely, "Can you please stop moving your left hand? Every time you move it I see a very strong aura of lights moving also, and they are much too distracting." I stopped moving my hand and went on talking. Soon the woman interrupted again, "I'm sorry, but I guess I'll have to excuse myself. The movement of the aura hasn't stopped, and it's altogether too disturbing and disorienting to me." The teacher in the back nodded agreement.

No one else in the room experienced this phenomenon, but they humored me when I requested that someone go to my office and get a length of copper wire I keep there, readily accessible. I took the copper wire in my right hand and dropped it down to rest on my left foot near my ankle. More than two people in the room screamed as they saw a strong light field—not unlike a bolt of lightning—travel from the top of my head down my body and into the ground at my left foot. It took only a second.

And I continued my lecture, that is, once my students had recovered!

This ability of copper to drain excess and aberrant energy is obviously not a phenomenon unique to me or to the child whose hair would not lie down. Nor is it new. I have realized and relied upon this most of my life, but only in the last 15 years have I begun to apply it to others.

Several years ago The HANDLE Institute began receiving frequent calls from a man in his thirties. He tried to get information on our program and how HANDLE might help him. My front office staff—all two of them—kept comparing notes as to what they were able to glean before the man would hang up in exasperation. He was a native English speaker with no particular articulation problems, but a horrendous speech impediment. He could not complete more than a few words of any thought without jumping into a few words of another thought. He was totally unable to convey an idea through speech.

I later learned that this disorder had plagued him most of his life, but in the comfort of his own home when he wasn't dressed to go anywhere, he could usually speak, just not on a telephone. He had never been diagnosed with anything and was at his wits' end.

He had been able to get enough information to know that I was giving a free, open-to-the-public talk at the Institute one evening the following week. He appeared about 10 minutes before the end of the two-hour talk, knowing his energy was so disorganized he would have been unable to sit still and attend to the talk itself, but desperately wanting to speak with me. I noticed this latecomer, and when he came up to speak with me after the others had left, I knew immediately that this was the man of the dysfluent speech. I also noticed that he was wearing running shoes with thick synthetic soles.

As he tried to communicate his thoughts to me, he became exasperated and leaned onto the table where my overhead projector was still standing. My wooden table—wooden top and wooden legs. As he leaned on the table, his sentences were complete. I heard nearly a paragraph, but then he felt rested again, and he let go of the table.

Gibberish.

The pattern held: normal speech when leaning on the table, dysfluency when not. Glancing again briefly at his feet, I asked him "Have you ever worn shoes that were 100% natural fiber, uppers and lowers—that is, the soles, too?"

Leaning on my table he replied, "Yes, and you know, that's the only time I ever remember feeling grounded."

Immediately I offered him compensatory measures: "You need to wear natural fibers, especially shoes. Leather or rubber or cork or wood soles will all work for you. And until you find those shoes, wear a copper ankle bracelet for grounding." I also suggested that he arrange for a thorough HANDLE assessment to ascertain which of his systems were on overload and shorting him out. And I felt that a naturopathic physician might be able to help him correct nutritional imbalances and other cellular irregularities in his physiological make-up.

"It's really important that you adopt this three-pronged approach[24] if you truly want to recover," I said, "but it will require some work."

He followed through with the evaluations, but was not consistent with the daily activity and nutrition regimens he received. He did, however, buy shoes with natural soles: rubber-soled shoes to wear to work, leather soled shoes for dressier occasions. And at least, to a large degree, he became grounded.

Grounding is essential. Some of us need to feel grounded by having deep

---

[24]The three prongs of the approach were temporary compensatory measures, cellular regulation, and neurodevelopmental reorganization.

proprioceptive input; many by dressing in natural fibers and working on surfaces that are composed of natural materials; others by wearing copper. Some might need to keep small stones or olive pits in our mouths, centering our tongues as we suck.

Bobbie, the young woman who got in touch with her body and her emotions through her HANDLE program, knew instinctively the powers of copper in grounding someone whose electrical energy was disconcerting. But she could not explain to anyone her annoying trait of going into the basement of her home and taking apart the exposed wires to the plug that controlled the electric pilot on the furnace.

About the same time that someone in the family would notice that the furnace was off, someone else would notice Bobbie winding a copper wire around and around her fingers. Her mom knew it was a message. She thought perhaps her daughter wanted rings. She bought her lots of rings. Silver rings. Gold rings. She put them on her daughter's fingers. The same day or soon thereafter, her daughter would bury the rings in the backyard.

To stop the basement escapades, Bobbie's father built a lock-box around the electric cover so the wires would no longer be accessible. Bobbie's erratic behaviors escalated. She rampaged through the house, slamming into things, tossing books and magazines, screaming. She fought sleep and wrestled with her covers all night after she finally did fall asleep.

The afternoon of my first meeting with the family, I gave them 18 inches of copper wire from the local hardware store. With a visible sigh of relief, the young woman put her copper wire on as a proud bracelet, and later her mother got her a more elegant one. Finally, someone understood. But Bobbie's inquisitive mind drove her to remove the copper bracelet about two months later and hide it from her mother. A few days into this experiment were enough. Bobbie felt herself losing the sensory-integration gains she had made. Touch and sound were again painful. She was slipping back into her autism—her need to isolate herself from her world. She knew that experience. The copper bracelet went back on.

Only five months into her HANDLE program, wearing the copper, Bobbie wrote about the "shock for her system." You have already read some of what she said at a later stage. You'll recognize the seemingly scripted opening phrase, I'm sure.

"I love HANDLE. It is the one thing in all the stuff we have tried that has made my life bearable. It has allowed me to open myself up to sensations that really help me to sense the world in a normal way. I no longer have to shut down my systems to cope. I can hear, feel and understand the world around me. This is quite a shock for my system. I hope you understand that people like me are trapped in bodies that torture us. Kind of like you would be tortured not feeling well all of your life. You must understand that we are doing the best we can."

"Trapped in bodies that torture us!" In bodies that do not respond to us, because we cannot allow ourselves to listen to them and because they have somehow begun to short themselves out. Tortured. Now we are finally getting to that part of the autistic experience that is common to all of us who have been there, and even to those who have not. Everyone has experienced moments of intense fright or stress. We know that for a brief moment we have heightened awareness of everything, but if the stress continues, we go blank. We are in a survival mode. We are built to close down from unbearable stress. And we are also meant to sleep, have deep and restful sleep to recoup our energies and to reorganize our thoughts.

Energy, Sleep, Metals, Stress. How do these interrelate? As we look back to those environmental elements that influence the heavy metals in our system and explore this area even more, we need to remember stress in and of itself creates neurotoxicity. So every experience of stress increases the imbalance of metals in our systems as it increases our neurotoxicity. And anything we do to reduce stress helps protect us. The autistic experience, like the human experience, is about self-protection more than anything else.

11. The internal environment
Insidious invaders

The books written on nutrition in general, and on nutritional factors related to ASD in particular, could fill several bookshelves. This chapter is not about specific diets and supplements per se. It is about taking the threads of sensory experiences and finding how they wind through the digestive tract. It is about looking at a total mind-body-brain-spirit connection to food—the foods we crave and the foods we avoid. And the reasons that whole foods are more nourishing than supplements. It is also about the effects of stress on the digestive tract. Nutrition is about much more than food.

Bodies instinctively know what they need for nourishment. So do the many little buggers—microbes—that live symbiotically in the gut and other parts of the body, too. So, why would Andrew—our Andrew whose Theory of Mind shocked his mother—crave exactly those foods his physician knew were detrimental to his well-being and shun those that would nourish him? And why would my son, Matthew, who has only shared the autistic experience as he has seen it played out through me and my clients, instinctively refuse to eat mushrooms or cheese?

In Matthew's case, it's easy. His sense of smell was protecting him from one of his most severe allergies—mold. As a youngster he had not learned that mushrooms are fungi—mold—or that cheese is made through a process of molding. But thanks to antibiotic treatments for ear infections, his body knew he was severely allergic to penicillin—mold.

Andrew's situation was more complex and more challenging. Auditory and tactile hypersensitivities severely limited the list of tolerable foods. Diminished muscle tone made chewing otherwise tolerable foods too challenging, too exhausting. Although already 11, Andrew still did best eating with his hands. Meal preparation and meal times in Andrew's home were no fun. His mom, Jeanette, wanted to prepare healthful food. But Andrew himself—not just his food preferences—was so demanding. Left to his own devices he would sit and rock with a vibrator on his cheeks or in his mouth. Or he would flip through magazines. Until he got bored. Then he might bolt.

What would he eat? Sandwiches. Rice Crackers. Cereal. Pasta. A few fruits. Almost no vegetables. Jeanette tried to provide Andrew a Gluten-Free/Casein-Free diet. But it was a lot of work. And her son was so thin. He had taken glyconutrients for 5 years, and tried other supplements, too. Andrew was pretty good about taking them. And they did seem to help, some. But Andrew remained weak and wan and susceptible to many illnesses. His physician experimented with antifungal medications, thinking that perhaps Andrew's gut was overrun by candida albicans or some other fungus that might explain Andrew's craving for carbohydrates and his inability to absorb nutrients from his food and supplements.

As we worked on his other issues, not focused on increasing the foods he would eat or his basic level of nutrition, Andrew progressed in all areas. Rapidly. Before Jeanette realized how intertwined Andrew's other issues were with his nutritional deficits, she wrote me about their afternoons together, "I think maybe his downtime with me is a chance for him to digest all the new things he's learning and to just kick back."

"Downtime," "new things he's learning," and "digest" all in one sentence!

Gastroenterologists' files are full of patients whose digestive systems went awry because of stress. Anything that stresses any one of our systems stresses all of our systems. Unusual demands at work stress executives and cause ulcers. Inappropriate demands at school stress those of us with ASD and cause digestive problems.

For Andrew to digest new things—new sensory input, new movement patterns, new concepts—was work and he needed to rest after it. Bringing his food to his mouth, chewing and swallowing—these were work, too. Stressful work at that! The tactile sensations and the sound of chewing were irritating. Things that crumbled and melted and sloshed down were easier on his senses. But in order to digest his food, Andrew needed to learn new eating habits.

Because digestion begins in the mouth, food needs to stay there and be processed there. I've mentioned this before. It's worth repeating. Not just with regard to food but also to supplements. Most supplements, swallowed whole, just as foods that are not chewed properly, get to the stomach and intestines and are not absorbed properly. When the physical and chemical processes of mastication and salivation do not occur, not only is the food unprepared for the actions of the stomach, but the stomach is unprepared to receive the food. While we chew, our taste buds inform the brain how sour or salty or sweet or bitter the food is, and the brain signals the pancreas and other organs to send the correct enzymes to the stomach to process this food.

Within a few months, Andrew expanded the foods he would eat because he could. His trigeminal nerve was calmed. He could brush his teeth AND tolerate the feeling of a wide variety of foods on his tongue and gums and palate. His auditory sensitivity diminished and he could accept the sounds of the food in his mouth. His muscle tone increased and chewing was no longer exhausting. His eye-hand coordination improved once he learned to feel and control his fingers and as his eyes developed focal vision. He could use silverware and be proud of his eating habits. Pride replaced stress, and his digestion improved. And with better eye-hand coordination and vastly improved receptive language abilities, he became an active part of the meal preparation process, peeling cucumbers and carrots, setting the table, and helping to clear.

Andrew was not the only member of his family for whom pride replaced stress.

Jeanette wrote: "Andrew and I are having very interactive days. He is so happy with his newfound capacities and doesn't need to resist me so much. He's helping me in the kitchen with very little coaxing. He even helped me to bake cookies from start to finish. We are both so excited and happy that such major shifts are happening."

Writing about Andrew and sandwiches, I reflected also on Imram. A beautiful child, stressed by so many factors. You'll meet him again later. In the food department, Imram's diet was not only very limited, he also would not eat the few foods he might eat unless they were cut just-so. His bread or grilled cheese sandwiches needed to be cut in triangles, with the crust as the base of the isosceles triangle. No other shape would do.

His mother, Nadia, seeing that I understood so many of Imram's quirks, asked, "How do you explain that one?" As she heard my answer, Nadia knew it was right. "Imram," I said, "is extremely sensitive to touch, particularly on his lips and tongue and gums—the areas served by the trigeminal nerve—and also on his fingertips. His mouth can't tolerate harsh sensations or a mixture of tactile sensations. His hands can't tolerate mushy sensations. The triangle solves the problem elegantly. He can hold the firm crust and in so doing protect his hands from the gushy bread and protect his lips and tongue and gums from the harsh crust."

Just as the hands and mouth know how to protect themselves from foods that offend their senses, the body knows to avoid those foods that give it adverse reactions. Some of those reactions may point to allergies and toxic overload, others may point to hypersensitivities to smell or tactility or sound—mentioned earlier. But what about those unusual cravings that many children in the spectrum have, and many other children, too? Does a craving mean that the body has a real need for a certain substance in the food?

Sometimes.

Sometimes, when I am stressed or overtired or both, I crave coffee or dark chocolate. And depending on whether what I want is to relax and sleep or to push beyond the exhaustion and continue working, I NEED, respectively, either a little or a lot of coffee or chocolate. A little provides me a homeopathic-like balancing, returning to my system just enough energy so I can calm down and sleep. A lot provides me enough to go beyond the balance point, to allow me to cognitively override the need for sleep and just exert the excess energy to continue working. Until recently, I thought that self-medicating with caffeine was not related to ASD. As I research more deeply into the field and work with more families, I realize that virtually everything is relevant. So I share the homeopathic effects of caffeine for those of you whose overtired whirling dervish of an ASD child might just be calmed by a couple of sips of coffee or cocoa.

Cravings for sugar and processed carbohydrates, particularly bread, may indicate that parasites, fungi, or bacteria that have set up housekeeping in our intestinal tracts are demanding we feed them what will help them proliferate. That, plus a compromised immune system, is what Andrew's doctor suspected was interfering with his nutrition. Normally we have a balance of microscopic organisms in our gut. They are there to provide a symbiotic relationship: we feed them and they help us to process food so it can be absorbed through the walls of the intestine into the bloodstream and provide us proper nourishment. But if the immune system is weak, and especially if we have taken antibiotics for one of the many infections that those of us in the spectrum are prone to—ear infections perhaps being the most prevalent—then the beneficial bacteria are killed off along with the ones causing the ear infection.

What happens next is that candida albicans, one of the bacteria in the balance, develops an overgrowth—a yeast infection—and this condition of candidiasis or fungal growth of candida can lead to the break down of the mucosal lining between the bloodstream and the gastrointestinal tract. This, in turn, allows harmful toxins and allergens to enter the bloodstream and through it to travel to other parts of the body, producing any number of adverse symptoms, among them a weakening of the immune system. One way to break this cycle is to control the diet, removing yeast and gluten and many other substances. Karyn Seroussi brought this subject to the attention of many parents and professionals as she searched for a solution to her own son's problems.

But there are other factors. Salt is a component frequently overlooked, and American diets are probably as high, relatively speaking, in sodium as they are in sugars and carbohydrates. Salt, in high quantities, kills bacteria and other little bugs in our system. And some of those bugs are necessary for the gut to break down food for proper absorption. So while we may crave salt for other reasons—sometimes because it stimulates the sodium pumps in our nervous system, enabling us to process more rapidly, although perhaps impulsively if our system is not properly balanced with potassium—it may add to the well-documented problems of gut permeability and inadequate nutrition so frequently associated with ASD.

A malnourished body leads to a malnourished nervous system and serious physical as well as behavioral problems. To be properly nourished, we require a balance of foods and water, a reduction of transfatty foods, and an inclusion of balanced essential fatty acids.[25] Generally, the fresher the food and the less the processing, the better it is for our systems. Whole foods are also more valuable than supplements, because they contain naturally occurring enzymes that synergistically work to help the body digest the food. Although some families report that their children have immediate positive results from mega doses of specific supplements, these protocols have not proved effective across the board, and we know nothing of the long-term effects.

Even with regard to whole foods there are diverse opinions and diverse needs. Perhaps one reason that specific nutritional plans do not help everyone is nutrition is not just the food that goes in, it is also how the food was processed and what the body does with that food. One recent theory on why many people in the

---

[25]Essential fatty acids—omega 3, 6, and 9—are truly essential for the health of virtually all of our systems. Their role in neural processing is huge. The white fatty myelin sheath that covers most neural fibers is made primarily of essential fatty acids. The myelin is necessary for smooth and rapid transmission of the neural message, and the thicker the myelin sheath the more rapid the neural transmission. Therefore, fatter neural fibers speed up the processing between the brain and the body and within the various areas of the brain itself.

spectrum appear to be casein intolerant is not that they are allergic to milk, but rather that their systems can't process dairy products that have been pasteurized. It does seem plausible that in the intense heat process involved in pasteurization a cross-linking of protein occurs and various amino acids fuse. Many people with autism have difficulty breaking down and absorbing long-chain amino acids.

However, most people can drink pasteurized milk and eat other products with casein and not have adverse reactions. Others may experience a build-up of mucus in their sinuses which may impact their vestibular systems in one or more ways: restricting movement because of sinus pain, increasing pressure of fluids in the inner ear, altering the neural transmission through the trigeminal nerve and through it affecting the transmission of sound through the middle ear into the inner ear. Reactions to milk vary from one person with ASD to another, so, again, this element alone cannot be The Cause of autism.

So we return again, to weave yet another loop of those intertwining threads of digestive problems, immune-system disorder, sensory hypersensitivities, stress, toxicity. Where do you begin to untangle this loop?

Eastern medical practices are gaining increasing acceptance in the United States. Two of the oldest modalities—Chinese medicine and Ayurvedic medicine—focus on an energetic unity to the systems and the senses. In treating disorders from this perspective, the question of where do you begin to untangle the loop is almost ludicrous. Wherever you begin, you will be working on the whole. And as you are working on the whole, the body will detoxify itself, but you must help in that process.

Detoxification is looming with increasing significance in relation to autism. Yet a number of the families I have worked with have been reluctant to engage in even the simple forms of detoxification that I might suggest[26] because another authority told them that until the child's immune system was stronger or the allergies eliminated, the body would not be able to deal properly with a detox regimen and might respond with increased negative reactivity.

Research shows toxicity interferes with immune functioning, digestive processes and neural functioning. So we really must look at the issues holistically and detoxify the system we are de-stressing and reorganizing while we strengthen its immune response and increase its nutritional base. We cannot work on these elements in isolation. They are interrelated and form a unity.

Homeopathy and HANDLE have a number of elements in common. Both

[26]Some of these suggestions are included in Appendix C.

operate on a holistic basis and are not targeted to specific behaviors, but rather to the underlying cause of those problems, with the knowledge that the same behavior may have different causes in each individual. But the patterns will develop. Also, sometimes, using any method of self-healing, the body-brain-mind-spirit may first respond with a seeming worsening of the condition, as the areas to be healed come to the fore. A number of families have proclaimed that homeopathy cured their children's autism. It certainly could have relieved many of the stressors on various systems—stressors that were interfering with normal systemic processing and producing the autistic behaviors.

I was not fortunate enough to grow up in a time when homeopathy and Chinese medicine and Ayervedic practices were readily accessible in the United States. And both of my parents were trained in the "hard sciences"—Dad in research chemistry and Mom as a nurse also working frequently on research projects. My parents did not believe in allergies. They thought allergies were an attention-getting behavior or some other psychosomatic dysfunction.

But I had many of the nutritional deficits associated with ASD: severe candida overgrowth from very frequent courses of antibiotic therapy; allergic reactions to many inhalants, and to some foods—gluten and dairy and oranges (treated with lead-arsenate during those days when my mother tried to feed me orange juice or oranges).

I avoided dairy as much as possible, other than yogurt (probably seeking the acidophilus and other helpful bacteria to help my poor intestinal tract) and ice cream. We rarely ate bread and cakes at home, and when I did eat them other places, I frequently developed diarrhea, sometimes bloody. I could not process highly fatty foods such as whipped cream, which simply made me gag. And beef or lamb or other dark or fatty meat got only so far in my digestive tract before I regurgitated.

By 1992 I had learned enough about alternative approaches and decided it was time for me to detox, for other reasons, neither related to my allergies and gut problems per se, nor to my remaining behavioral anomalies. By the time I had finished my detox protocol[27] I sensed that I could start to expand my diet. And I was right! The balanced natural detox I had undertaken cleansed my body of elements that were interfering with my immune system and my digestive tract. Virtually all of my former immune and digestive disorders vanished. With my history, I wonder

---

[27]This protocol is provided in brief in the Appendices. However, I advise anyone seriously considering using whole foods to detox to consult a naturopath for guidance. Some of the foods I used to detox may be detrimental to someone else, and the homeopathic remedies I took were prescribed for me, with my personal make-up.

just how many years of "normal life" I might have enjoyed had I embraced the power of gentle detoxing and taken the time to detox earlier.

Others are also coming to the realization that toxicity is a major factor in the varied dysfunctions that cluster under the name of ASD. The M.I.N.D. Institute of the University of California-Davis has recently shifted its focus from seeking a genetic cause of autism to investigating environmental toxicity as causal, since autism is reaching epidemic proportions and genes do not cause epidemics.

The Many Strands

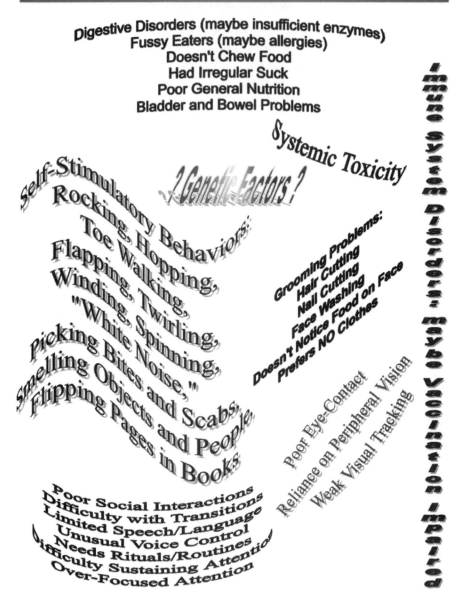

Digestive Disorders (maybe insufficient enzymes)
Fussy Eaters (maybe allergies)
Doesn't Chew Food
Had Irregular Suck
Poor General Nutrition
Bladder and Bowel Problems

Systemic Toxicity

? Genetic Factors ?

Immune System Disorders: maybe Vaccination Impaired

Self-Stimulatory Behaviors:
Rocking, Hopping,
Toe Walking,
Flapping, Twirling,
Winding, Spinning,
"White Noise,"
Picking Bites and Scabs,
Smelling Objects and People,
Flipping Pages in Books

Grooming Problems:
Hair Cutting
Nail Cutting
Face Washing
Doesn't Notice Food on Face
Prefers NO Clothes

Poor Eye-Contact
Reliance on Peripheral Vision
Weak Visual Tracking

Poor Social Interactions
Difficulty with Transitions
Limited Speech/Language
Unusual Voice Control
Needs Rituals/Routines
Difficulty Sustaining Attention
Over-Focused Attention

This chart demonstrates the chaos caused by the numerous strands of disordered systems and behaviors involved in ASD. What HANDLE does, and what this book attempts to do, is examine the various strands, find common threads and reweave the fabric in a cohesive fashion. The fabric may not look beautiful to outsiders, but it will be comfortable and serviceable to those who don it—those of us with ASD.

The Ear and Nutrition

Doesn't chew food

Hypersensitive to sound

Inner Ear / Vestibular System Irregularities

Digestive problems

Stomachaches and bowel problems

Inadequate nutrition

Digestion and Posture

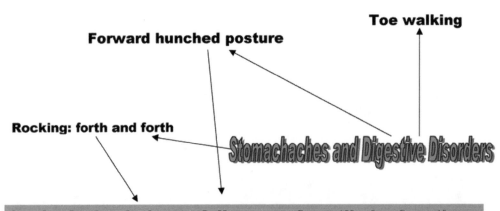

Forward hunched posture

Toe walking

Rocking: forth and forth

Stomachaches and Digestive Disorders

Lack of stimulation to full range of vestibular functions especially the endolymphatic sac

Influences on Visual Functions

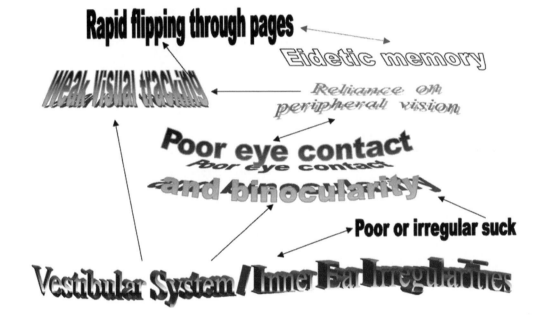

Rapid flipping through pages

Eidetic memory

Weak visual tracking

Reliance on peripheral vision

Poor eye contact

Poor eye contact

and binocularity

Poor or irregular suck

Vestibular System / Inner Ear Irregularities

Muscle Tone and the Ear

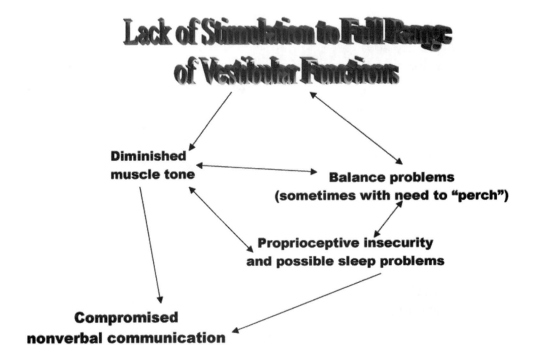

Lack of Stimulation to Full Range of Vestibular Functions

Diminished muscle tone

Balance problems (sometimes with need to "perch")

Proprioceptive insecurity and possible sleep problems

Compromised nonverbal communication

The Importance of Muscle Tone

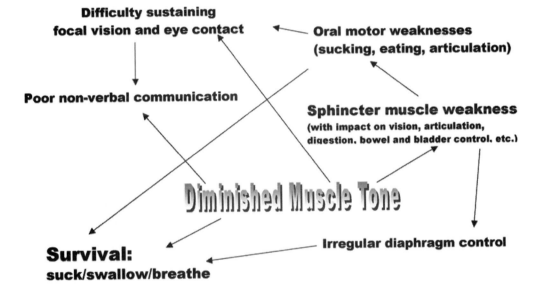

Difficulty sustaining
focal vision and eye contact

Oral motor weaknesses
(sucking, eating, articulation)

Poor non-verbal communication

Sphincter muscle weakness
(with impact on vision, articulation,
digestion. bowel and bladder control. etc.)

Diminished Muscle Tone

Survival:
suck/swallow/breathe

Irregular diaphragm control

The Ear and Language

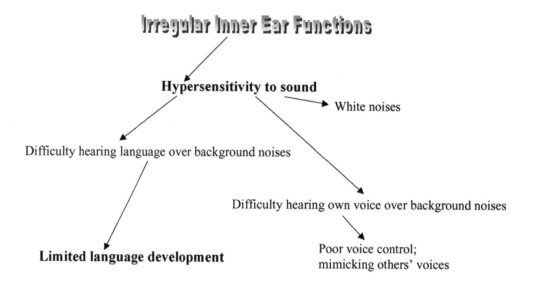

Irregular Inner Ear Functions

Hypersensitivity to sound

White noises

Difficulty hearing language over background noises

Difficulty hearing own voice over background noises

Limited language development

Poor voice control;
mimicking others' voices

Fear and Anxiety

12. Social interaction
The greatest stress

oxins and stress cannot be separated. Most individuals with autism had stressful births and early first days. Many of us also endured stressful pregnancies, with bleeding, stress. or other worrisome events in our first months in utero. Yet, the most stressful situation we face is social interaction. It requires being open to unpredictable sensory input and to be able to respond dynamically, with clear verbal and nonverbal communication, maintaining affect that allows inclusion without derision. The need to share experiences with others whose reality is so different from ours puts stress on all of our systems. And then we are expected to transition smoothly from one such experience to another, as if it were a simple adjustment to make.

Social functioning is the underlying unifying behavior with which individuals diagnosed with ASD have great difficulty.[28]

This is true of me even today, and my sister recently forgot. She was in the midst of an internship, training to become a Certified Practitioner of HANDLE. One event she needed to organize and help present was what we call a Community Information (CI) presentation. I have given perhaps several hundred such presentations, each to a group of relative strangers who have come to a lecture hall or classroom to hear me speak and later to engage in a period of questions and answers. I have no qualms about giving these presentations, and the feedback I receive on

---

[28]Jeanie McAfee, MD, recognizes the immense stress social interaction causes for individuals with ASD. Her work provides parents and teachers alike with wonderful guidelines on how to identify the stress factors in particular situations and how to decrease the negative impact of that stress.

them is that I not only shared my knowledge but also came across with great integrity and concern. So Marlene was shocked by my reaction to her announcement that she had invited some of her friends and colleagues to her home for coffee and a CI, which she expected me to present.

"No! You didn't!" I screamed at her. "How could you do that to me? I can't talk to your friends!" I left the room, crying in frustration and fury and fear. And I began to flap my wrists and twist my ankles and scream at her again. "Don't try to pretend it will be okay. You know I can't do those things. I sure hope you're ready to do a whole presentation yourself, 'cause I won't be anywhere around for this one."

Seeing me move with ease through hours of lecturing and interviews in the past several years, Marlene thought I had overcome my social relationship problems. No, that's wrong; she didn't make the assumption. The truth was that her own fear of presenting in public was so strong that she wanted to practice on friends, because for her the situation would provide comfort and support. So each of us made mindful decisions and visceral choices based on our limitations and strengths. As practiced as I am speaking in a lecture hall, I recoiled at the idea of small talk and chat with an intimate group of my sister's friends. It would be unbearable.

Like children with ASD, I probably would have benefited from coaching in how to develop relationships, not just how to speak and to present material in my realms of interest and expertise.

Steven Gutstein, in his book *Autism Aspergers: Solving the Relationship Puzzle,* gives voice to the true challenge faced by those with ASD. "[Children and teenagers who have autism] never let me forget our basic need to connect with others. I watch in wonder as they cast adrift into the open ocean on a solo voyage to nowhere. I experience their desperation, as they are unable to build even the simplest bridges with others and must cling to their few precious islands of attachment for dear life, fearful of letting go and never finding their way back. And, I know they are the ones who fully appreciate the awesome chasms that exist between us in ordinary life. They are the ones who cherish each precious bridge they must build with such methodical, deliberate effort."[29]

There are many parallels between Relational Development Intervention (RDI)—the program Gutstein designed to guide the child through developmental stages of Experience Sharing—and HANDLE. Both train families to work with

---

[29]Gutstein, P. xiii.

their children in their own homes. Both emphasize working in environments that have minimal visual and auditory distractions. Both rely on developmental stages to guide the suggested activities. The primary difference is that RDI is a behavioral approach, working to teach specific behaviors, while HANDLE is a neurodevelopmental approach, working to reduce the stress that causes us to be adrift and to feel so little safety when we venture across those bridges to the world of others.

The significance of this difference becomes apparent when we examine the developmental stages Gutstein identified as necessary for social interaction (or "experience sharing") or in Greenspan's model[30], "opening and closing of circles of communication." Gutstein's first level, which begins at birth, is based largely on two issues that are problematic for children with ASD: eye-contact and face recognition. The second level, beginning at six months in normal development, involves learning motor patterns, variations of those patterns, and engaging those patterns while taking turns with a partner. These are true developmental stages, ones that reflect neurodevelopment and ones that are difficult to teach if the neurodevelopmental underpinnings are not in place.

Perhaps this is why RDI works so well with youngsters with high-functioning ASD. Their systems are not as multiply challenged as the lower functioning children and adults. And yet, I feel it is more efficient, even for the high-functioning youngsters, to first strengthen the neurodevelopmental systems that must carry the weight of the body-mind-brain-spirit adventures of Experience Sharing so that the child's systems are not stressed in achieving social interaction.

Gutstein is right. The sharing is what it is all about. But from my experience, when the readiness is there, for those who were diagnosed high-functioning or low-functioning ASD alike, training for sharing is not necessary. Once I can be in the same environment as you without feeling stressed, without going into a fright/flight/fight reaction, without knowing my very safety and survival are at stake, I can share. If I am brave enough to remain in this world from one day to the next, then I am brave enough to venture across those bridges when I know the supporting islands are not moving out from under me.

Nine-year-old Seth was one of the bravest youngsters I had met. I was the Learning Disabilities Specialist servicing all three elementary schools in the district where Seth lived. He was the district's most challenging student and the first autistic child to enter a mainstream class. He was high-functioning. He had the ability to

---

[30]Greenspan's Floor Time incorporates an individualized developmental program specific to each child whose family members are taught how to join the child in play, and by so doing, to entice the child to develop the affect to support true social interaction.

communicate verbally. He rarely walked on his toes or flapped his hands. He did, however, maintain a wide-eyed visual hyper-vigilance. And he startled frequently to sounds, because he could not screen out irrelevant sounds. To him they were all relevant. They all gave him clues of movement in his direction—movement that might signal impending tactile assault.

Seth had learned social conventions. He could stand in line, bouncing only slightly until the line began to move. He could wait his turn, ask and answer questions, smile and sometimes laugh when others laughed at jokes. He was one of the best readers in his class. He could help another child read and do his homework. His peers respected Seth's talents, acknowledging his quirky behaviors. But he was high-maintenance. I frequently needed to explain to his teachers one quirk or another. The physical education teacher, in particular, was at a loss as to how to deal with his behaviors. She repeatedly questioned me "Are you sure it's okay to let him sit out if he doesn't want to play dodge ball? Will he really feel okay just running his laps around the gym after everyone else is going out to the soccer field?"

And then one day, in the cafeteria at lunch time, the whole school learned why it was okay and even necessary for sweet Seth to remove himself from the midst of kids and balls moving around him at rapid speeds.

Seth was hungry. His nose was working hard to help him sort out the various aromas coming from the hot lunch line in which he was standing. The line moved forward. Seth took his tray, and began to slide it along the guide rails. He asked for a sloppy joe on a bun. It came with potato chips. The boy behind him said, "Hey, that looks good. I'll have one, too." As Seth's innocent classmate reached forward and took his plate, one potato chip fell off the side. It landed on Seth's right wrist.

Those are the only discernible facts, because next came a free-for-all with sloppy joes and plates and trays and drinks and pies flung by one person or another at whomever seemed to have just thrown something at him. And in the midst of it all, Seth was shrieking at the top of his lungs. The only scream louder than Seth's was that of the child whose potato chip had caused the problem. He was missing a chunk of his left forearm, and the bite mark matched Seth's mouth perfectly.

That was Seth's last day mainstreamed. It had not been possible to teach him what to do in the instance of being so totally focused on his own food, standing in a line, and having a potato chip unexpectedly fall on him. His sensory systems simply were on over-load and he could not engage those cognitive functions that might have pulled him through. He could not say to himself, "Seth, you know that your friend from your class didn't mean for his potato chip to hit your hand. And even so, it's only a potato chip. It's not as if he intentionally hit you with something that could really hurt you."

"Really hurt!" Who knows what really hurts someone else, what stresses someone, and puts him into a fright/flight/fight response that calls forth extra adrenaline and cortisol and keeps the brain from making a nice balanced batch of hormones and enzymes and neurotransmitters to allow for smooth digestive and immune and, yes, cognitive functions.

It is the unexpected assault on our systems that makes dynamic social interaction so threatening, even after we have learned to maneuver through most of them safely and even with enjoyment. It is the need to sit in a particular place so light won't hurt our sensitive eyes or the ventilator's wheeze won't bother us or the tunnel of energy between the file cabinet and the wall won't send shudders through our peripheral nerves. It is the need to control our space and others in our space so we can modulate our actions in keeping with a situation that is threatening to us in ways others just don't sense. For most of us, I feel it is crucial to address as many of the underlying sensory-motor irregularities as possible, to allow us to move more securely into the world of interaction.

Some approaches demand that individuals on the spectrum endure stimulation as part of teaching their sensitive systems to process the world around them. But these approaches put their systems under siege rather than employing Gentle Enhancement. Remembering the assault, these individuals may not feel safe trying yet another approach to move them through the developmental stages to strengthen their weak systems, to heal their bruised ones, and to create new pathways for ones that are not functional. For these individuals, I rejoice that there are creative, sensitive programs whose goal is dynamic interaction and sharing, not just demanding that those of us with ASD become copies of "neurotypicals," at all costs.

Even if we do learn how to bridge so many of the social interactions and share experiences more fully, how many of us will learn to employ with finesse that paradoxical social "no-no" that most people engage in freely—lying. I wonder if deception will ever be something someone in the spectrum can carry off with aplomb until he can actually be in touch with himself, not with the image of himself that others would project upon him. Or is that the ultimate lie? Living in a reflective box, not truly responding to others, but merely reflecting back to them what they want to see.

That's the way I learned to placate my mother, by lying verbally and sometimes emotionally. If my mother were alive today to read this, she would be mortified! Mom was a very truthful person. She kept secrets better than anyone I know, and she truly could not tell a lie, not even a "white lie" without immediately giving herself away by her nonverbal communication. But Mom taught me that the only way around some untenable situations was to tell people what they wanted to hear, whether it was truthful or not.

"Judy, don't forget to come in and tell me about your day before you go to bed," Mom would say each night from her bed where she was reading.

As I entered her room, she would remove her glasses and scoot over in the bed to leave me room to sit beside her. Her face was greasy with highly scented Pond's cold cream. I had to pretend it didn't bother me, neither the odor nor the oozy kiss on the check that Mom expected. I lied, nonverbally. I practiced it almost every night for three years, the whole duration from when my sister went away to college until I did. Before that, Marlene had happily performed what I saw as a grim duty—sharing her day with Mom, so Mom might live vicariously through us. I knew that Mom had had a very difficult adolescence after her family fled persecution in Russia and resettled in Canada. Mom needed to experience the light, social, happy times of teen years through her two daughters.

But at first, when it was my duty to fulfill this function, I didn't get it. Mom would ask me, cheerfully, "So, what did you do today?" And I would answer, "Well, other than normal classes, not much happened in school, but afterwards I went over to Rena's house and climbed onto her garage roof and just lay there gazing at the clouds. One of them was this most amazing looking bird, and as the cloud moved and grew, it seemed as if the warm and fuzzy bird changed into a bird of prey, and just as the wind began to pick up and move the bird/cloud quickly around the sky, I climbed down and went inside because I was afraid it was going to storm any minute."

The truth. But not what Mom wanted to hear. So I needed to pull a script from my repertoire of conversations that I had overheard between my Mom and Marlene, or from television shows. I learned that to be accepted I needed to present myself as someone else. If I told Mom what I really did and felt during the day, we would have a rerun of the days when she asked to read my poetry.

On nights when I was too tired or stressed to step outside myself into the person Mom wanted me to be, and I spoke the truth, she would lash out. "Why are you telling me this nonsense?"

"Because it is my LIFE!" I'd answer. "Because it IS what I did today! Because it IS what makes me happy! I am NOT Marlene. Look at ME, Mom. This is Judy. I'm Just Me, not anyone else. Why can't you accept ME? Why can't you love ME as I am? Why must I be someone ELSE? I CAN'T be anyone else, Mom. I CAN'T!" I screamed, choking on my words and my tears as I ran to my bedroom and threw myself on my bed. Sobbing and kicking, and whacking my pillow into the headboard and the bed as hard as I could, not caring that the foam rubber tore and crumbled as I continued smacking the bed with my pillow and screaming "I can't, Mom, I can't. I'm Just Me, Just Me, Just Me . . ."

Mom knew then to keep her distance. There would be nothing she could do that night to console me, nor could we talk about it rationally in a calmer moment. As much as she loved me and cared for me, Mom simply did not understand me. But she had learned that what I needed from her those evenings were silence and distance.

I know the high degree of anxiety endured by those of us who have learned so many scripts and need to sort through them and match situation to script. It allows us to fit in. Or does it? What would happen if, with all of our neurophysiological differences still greatly influencing our internal makeup, if we did not don the external makeup we have learned makes us acceptable to others? If as we were participating in a social function we didn't exert so much energy repressing our fear of imminent danger of respiratory distress because our girlfriends wanted to experiment with different perfumes or cosmetics? What if we honored our needs to protect our immune systems and to release the energy building up in our heads and our arms?

These needs are not things that go away without being treated, systemically. We can pretend they don't exist, but we do that at a cost. And as young adults and adults desiring intimate relationships, exactly when is the best time to tell someone about all the quirks that our nervous systems impose on us? When and how exactly do you level with someone that your perceptual experience is so different, and that what they have come to know and think they love has been a facade?

We deserve to have lives freer of anxiety and stress, lives in which we can go to sleep in peace and wake up to days of joy. To do that we must get to the root of our disorders, not just learn to cope better.

13. Anxiety
Fright/flight/fight

Some psychotherapists have diagnosed children and adults with Anxiety Disorder, later concluding that Asperger's Syndrome or High-Functioning—Autism or PDD-NOS (Pervasive Developmental Disorder—Not Otherwise Specified) might be the more exact diagnosis. I wonder. I wonder if Autism along the entire spectrum is not primarily an extreme Anxiety Disorder.

Anxiety that began in utero.

Research indicates that most autistic children experienced stress in utero, in the birth process, and/or in the first few days of life. During these early stages of fetal development, stress negatively impacts most of our developing systems. And it only makes sense that the insult to our beings would occur at a time and by a medium that would affect so many developing organs and systems, because it has become clear that autism is a systemic disorder with gastrointestinal, immunological, endocrinological, psychological and neurological complications.

At the Second International Conference on Autism (April 2001), Jeff Bradstreet, pediatrician and medical director of the International Autism Research Center, presented his conclusion that autism should be renamed "toxic encephalopathy." Greenspan prefers to call it a "multisystem developmental disorder."

After experiencing stress in utero, the ANS may take as much as four months to calm down, and during this period, the newborn will demonstrate unusual pupillary response and also prolonged whole body reflexive movements to sound and touch. These fright responses in the body signal the brain to provide more cortisol and adrenaline to support a defensive posture. This then depletes the body's supply of the basic building blocks–amino acids—needed to support our immune system and the production of neurotransmitters necessary for neural transmission.

And if the immune system is not functioning properly, babies fall prey to more diseases that place further demands on already depleted resources. The medication for some of these diseases may cause flora in our intestinal tracts to interfere with proper absorption of nutrients through the intestinal wall. And ear infections compromise the myriad functions that the inner ear and vestibular system support, just when they are needed to develop equilibrium and language.

These infants and toddlers are then held and pricked and given drops that trickle into their nasal and auricular orifices, which irritates and insults them. And the smells of the examination rooms with its bright lights reflecting off the tiles and wash basins and white uniforms are further assaults, together with the ventilation system and the pagers and the squeaking chairs and clanking tables.

No wonder those of us in the spectrum can't heal from the medical diseases that we seem to encounter so often. The continual bombardment of our sensory systems—still so immature and undifferentiated in response to stimuli—causes a constant state of dis-ease, of anxiety.

Our families and caregivers, as well, experience stress and anxiety. Some of their experiences are vicarious, but our distress and their response to it alters their systems, too, because even the nervous systems of adults remain plastic, adapting constantly to environmental stimuli. Part of caregivers' inability to feel what we feel is a natural protective mechanism, whereby they do not allow such disorganized and painful stimuli to be processed. Their inhibitory neurons are working for them.[31]

Now that we are getting close to the crux of the autistic experience, to understand it more fully we need to look at some neuroscientific and physio-psychological elements related to stress and sleep and how they impact the brain and the entire body at various stages in life. For these are the real threads that hold

---

[31]A theory explored at the Weizman Institute in Israel posits that in autism and attentional disorders difficulty focusing may stem from a problem with inhibitory neurons (I-neuron) not doing their job—to repress the level of activity of neighboring neurons, thus preventing the brain from spinning out of control and causing over-excitability. Apparently each I-neuron connects via synapses with thousands of neighboring neurons, and develops fast-switching "if-then" filters or gates that regulate the precision timing and degree of inhibition. The filter is negotiated interactively between I-neurons and their target neurons so that each neuron can potentially be inhibited in a unique way. I-neurons also sense other neurons with which to collaborate on fundamental functions. Additional information is available at www.eurekalert.org/releases/weiznuk011200.html.

this fabric of autism together.

Yes, there are major strands that dominate the fabric—vestibular irregularities, muscle tone problems, visual distortions, proprioceptive disturbances, tactile hypersensitivities, severe auditory overload, resultant language deficits and problems with social interaction, nutritional deficits, immune system disorders, and more. All these reduce our adaptability and increase our stress.

But it is the unrelenting stress that is central.

And to comprehend it from a neurophysiological standpoint, we need to look at the intricate interactions between the ANS and the CNS, at how the thalamus and the cerebellum and the limbic system and the vagus nerve, and other parts with which you will become familiar, relate to and depend on one another in their functions. However, we all understand the effects of unrelenting stress on a functioning system.

On September 11, 2001, when two airplanes crashed into the World Trade Center in New York City, it was a surreal horror. Reactions were worldwide and profound.

Some people responded by rushing to help, in any way they could, with more energy than they knew they had. Others retreated into their homes and themselves, fearful of everything and feeling unsafe anywhere. Millions of people were overtaken by their autonomic nervous systems' response—fright/flight/fight—and struggled to make any sense of the situation while seeking to protect themselves in anyway they could.

Since that shattering day, experts from numerous cultural and professional backgrounds have continued to examine the effects, first on individual behaviors, and then on the human brain itself. We've learned much about the profound impact of anxiety and stress.

Neuroscientists know that after a few hours we recover from short exposures to stress. However, sudden exposure to unpredicted stress is dangerous to our systems; continuous production of stress hormones during periods of overwhelming and unrelenting anxiety weakens immune system responses and floods the body with toxins.

I am not trying to equate the attack on the World Trade Center with the epidemic of autism we are currently facing. But the situations reveal something: a system under stress responds reflexively. The normal flow of information processing shifts. The system needs to protect itself from challenge and attack. After all, the primary concern of each being is survival. When we perceive a threat to our survival, we may strike out, we may turn in, but in either case, we succumb to the program that shifts our body-brain-mind-spirit from the control of higher level cognitive functions and puts it into the fright/flight/fight mechanism of our ANS.

The brain, as our commander of operations, is doing whatever it is doing in response to the stimuli it is receiving from the body. With all of its neural plasticity, this commander can function based only on the information it receives via the cranial nerves and the peripheral nerves of the CNS, and the ANS. These nerves (other than the olfactory nerve) send their messages to the brain via specific brain parts whose job it is to filter information.

The thalamus is the ultimate gatekeeper of most of this information. And the cerebellum (one of the parts of the brain repeatedly implicated in autism) is another filter and sorting station, as well as functioning as a "way station" for information from various senses, particularly those conducted via the auditory-vestibular nerve. Again, it's the cerebellum that integrates the information from the inner ear with that of the ANS to provide us other important information about our security—our sense of body in space and our sense of our internal organs, those smooth muscle organs that the body must protect so we can survive. So now we must explore further the interactions among these systems.

But first, I want to emphasize how each of us, for optimal functioning, is meant to be able to filter out extraneous stimuli and focus in on the relevant information. In *The Shadow Syndromes,* Ratey offers insights into autism as well as anxiety disorders and attentional disorders that only shadow the more serious manifestations of autism. "The one characteristic every shadow syndrome has in common is noise: an internal biologically based, mental white noise."[32] He goes on to say "it is metaphorically akin to the very low signal to noise ratio of a radio channel filled with static. Inside the noisy brain, nothing is clear. The noisy brain cannot separate out stimuli or thoughts, either incoming or outgoing; everything is happening at once . . . Inescapable noise is very stressful—so stressful, in fact, that when researchers investigate stress they typically choose noise as their means to induce stress . . .."[33] He continues relating that in situations of prolonged stress "nothing coheres; thoughts are detached from feelings, and feelings are detached from bodily sensations."[34]

Does this not describe the stress of the autistic experience? Is this not what

---

[32]Ratey, 1998. P. 44
[33]op.cit. P. 46
[34]ibid.

Lincoln Grigsby expressed in his poem? The difficulty filtering and sorting and then organizing and attaching meaning and feeling? So it is important to consider the various stressors on our systems and the filters we have that are intended to help us filter out the noise.

The ANS has three major divisions: the enteric division that deals with the gastrointestinal tract, the parasympathetic division that organizes the responses of our visceral organs when we are relaxed, and the sympathetic division that organizes responses for times of maximal exertion, usually associated with fright/flight/ fight situations. When the brain needs to choose what systems to listen to, it's a no-brainer—the autonomic nervous system wins. If we don't worry about survival, about the needs of our visceral organs, then there's no need to save energy for higher-level functions such as communication and socialization. So whatever it is that signals stress or fright robs us of the capacity to be rational.

The internal noise that Ratey described so well doesn't allow us to engage our higher-level cortical functions and may even push us into midbrain and brain stem functions, so we respond reflexively, engaging the sympathetic division of our ANS. And when the ANS tells the brain it needs to use the body's resources for survival, the pituitary and other areas of the brain respond with a "Yes, sir!"

The parasympathetic system of the ANS ensures that the routine aspects of bodily functioning, such as breathing and sleeping, are carried out. The sympathetic system comes into play when the body encounters a threatening situation. This could be an unexpected explosion of sound or light, the presence of a threatening person, a noxious smell, an increased workload. Translated into the autistic experience, this might mean sucking, or swallowing, or hearing someone sneeze, having bright lights turned on, not recognizing the faces of people in the immediate environment, being led down the laundry detergent isle of the supermarket, being asked to remain visually focused on anything in particular, or any number of other daily experiences. Under these situations, chemicals effect the change from parasympathetic to sympathetic control that elicits fright, usually followed by flight or fight.

The physiological responses that accompany any of these states are designed to support survival. That is, the heart beats faster, perspiration increases, digestion stops, and rates of breathing and blood pressure are changed. The brain shuts down all functions—including rational thought processes—-other than what the body might need in this time of emergency.

These symptoms of fright/flight/fight may be associated with dangers other than those of which we are conscious or those that are apparent to others in our surroundings. They may be the body's response to sensory overload, sensory deprivation or sensory "scrambling."

Think of a child who is sensitive to touch, light and/or sound, his system already in turmoil with the demands of the classroom. He tries to get away from the overwhelming situation by wrapping himself in the curtains. And then he hears the shrill tones of a teacher asking, "How many times do I need to ask you to stop twirling yourself in the curtains?" "Aaaargh," he says inside his head, "when will the noises stop? Why can't I be left to find peace?" Maybe he screams a semi-intelligible "Leave me alone!"

But the teacher needs to preserve order and maintain control, so she reaches out to touch the child through the curtain. This attempt to disentangle the prey from its protective covering is the final affront. His ANS kicks in. He flies into a rage, changing the rhythmic turning of body and fabric into a flurry of fists and legs, kicking and screaming. And, as the curtains and curtain rod are torn from the wall and tumble to the floor, the exposed and frightened child hears the threatening tones in "Now look what you did!" The teacher, also in the throes of an ANS response, needs to gain control of the child and herself, both. But everything spins out of control in a fight reaction to sensory overload.

Another child might respond to sensory overload by becoming hypoactive and non-responsive—a flight reaction (flights do not always need to be outward flights to other locations; they are more frequently inward flights to an unreachable sanctum). Yet another might show unusual pallor in a noisy classroom—a fright reaction.

One family had become quite used to their six year-old's autistic withdrawal from sensory overload—her flight. In fact, Rachel rarely seemed to take in sensory information from her environment. Her eyes and ears didn't focus on anything in particular. Her parents had employed a flurry of aides to try to engage her in activities of one sort or another. Rachel retreated further.

I told them quite simply, "Stop bombarding her with input. First Rachel needs to feel safe and calm, within herself and in her environment. She needs to know that her sensory tolerances are respected. After she relaxes, she will open to experience."[35] I went on to warn them, "She may then show uncontrolled emotions as she learns to feel. But Rachel WILL learn, and she WILL triumph. You must be brave and trusting if you're to embark on this journey with her."

---

[35]There is a children's song—"You Can't Make a Turtle Come Out"—that wonderfully expresses what happens when we poke and prod in attempts to force a creature to come out of its shell. Patience is the lesson. Engagement is the reward.

I taught them several special massages to develop proprioceptive awareness, balance muscle tone, reduce tactile hypersensitivity, and increase awareness of the muscles needed for speech production. I taught Rachel activities to help her eyes focus on objects and people in front of her and to decrease her hypersensitivity to sound. I provided some of her other therapists with new ideas for strengthening her vestibular system and sorting out which parts of her body needed to move in a given response and which needed to be still.

Rachel's program also involved activities encouraging integration of both sides of the body and the brain, incorporating rhythm. Everyone learned to help Rachel release tension and breathe more deeply. They all learned the principles of Gentle Enhancement—to recognize her subtle signs of stress so they could stop when she reached her ceiling of tolerance. Sometimes her tolerance lasted only seconds after she began an activity, and that was okay.

Sensing she could trust me, Rachel softened and accepted most of the activities. Within a week her father wrote to me: "Rachel continues to respond positively to the treatments and exhibits such a profound relaxation response that I am sure they are having a deep effect. I have never witnessed any therapy that produced this kind of response."

This was our major breakthrough. From this point, Rachel continued to surprise everyone with the fullness of her entry into the world as most people know it.

"Rachel has been less perseverative in her verbal and nonverbal behaviors this past week. Her language skills continue to grow, and there has been quite a spurt this past week. Her sentences are more spontaneous and vocabulary is larger. Enunciation is still somewhat indistinct, dysrhythmic and difficult to understand much of the time for those who do not know her well."

And several weeks later, her father wrote "Rachel's development seems to have accelerated substantially. She is using more speech and more advanced speech patterns, engaging in more complex play with dolls. She is now dancing, twirling and responding to music."

Rachel was no longer responding to the world of overwhelming experiences by withdrawing from it! Her senses were open and accepting and processing. But it was too sudden. We had guided her caregivers in Gentle Enhancement. But intelligent and motivated, Rachel herself was impatient to be free of her limited existence. She now wanted it all. But she was not yet ready.

In the same letter, after sharing his delight in Rachel's dancing, her father continued, "In the last five days, Rach has been a huge behavior problem— willful, screaming, demanding, etc. She is constantly perseverating verbally (which is extremely difficult to listen to). Is this kind of pushing back behavior a normal part of this process? You warned us that she might cry more often." And he admitted, "I am not reacting to this all that well and am fighting to regain control and probably not doing a great job."

This wonderful, supportive father had his wish. His daughter was no longer unresponsive and nonverbal. And, like most parents, he wanted her to move forward and do all of those things that other six and a half year-olds do. But Rachel's newfound sensibilities were just that. Newfound. Not yet strong enough for consistent use. She still needed times to retreat back into her earlier comforts. She would continue to move forward into the world, when she was sure of her footing.

"Rachel is not ready yet," I told her dad, "to have it assumed that she's integrated these changes for natural flow. She seems to be asking for 'down-time' and an opportunity to plateau. Plateaus are a natural part of learning, accepted when 'normal' children need to reorganize and recoup strength for the next forward surge."

"The most likely explanation is that she's going through a process of serious reorganization and asking for help to find boundaries for the new Rachel. I trust that you and Barbara will find the wisdom and compassion (as well as the love) to provide these boundaries without it seeming punitive. Let Rachel know that she's being brave to move through these stages, and to do it so rapidly; that it's difficult for all of you to know how to respond, and that you too are a little uncertain but are there for her. Let her know the boundaries you're establishing are to help all of you move through this period of her growth in communication—not just in talking. Let her know you read her loud and clear, and you'll continue to be her loving father. As an important part of that job, you'll set some boundaries to help all of you feel more secure.

"And, no, this isn't an expected response to the program. However, each person has unique responses to the reorganization of internal systems. Frequently when the body is healing itself rather than being treated as an enemy that must be conquered and contained—as it's recognizing its weaknesses, and healing and integrating—there are behaviors that may appear untoward, much like a fever as the reaction to fighting off infection."

It was not just Rachel whose systems needed help to respond reflectively.

Her marvelous, understanding father also caught himself reacting out of frustration because his own sensory systems were overloaded—overloaded by Rachel's momentarily spinning out of control. Now her father was feeling ungrounded, seeking support so he could respond rationally.

Fright/flight/fight reactions affect everyone, not just those of us with ASD. There are so many parallels between the experiences defined as autistic and those that signal other disruptions of attention and learning, and those that just demonstrate human responses to stress. And, again, it's the ANS, and primarily the sympathetic division of this system, that's programmed to take over in times of stress.

The sympathetic nervous system, serving as the body's first line of defense, has implications that are both profound and mundane. If a person experiences a situation as threatening for whatever reason, her sympathetic nervous system takes over. With more oxygen sent to the muscles rather than to the higher cortical levels of the brain, little attention can be given to actual events or thinking. She can't respond in a fashion deemed reasonable or appropriate by others.

This phenomenon explains many disorders sometimes called psychosomatic. Stomachaches and digestive problems are real (and may be caused by the 'shutdown' of the digestive system in order to concentrate on sending emergency rations to other muscles). Headaches can occur when not enough oxygen reaches the brain; feelings of nausea from lack of cortical synchronization of visual-vestibular-proprioceptive input; muscular pain caused by tension. And a number of other things, all due to effects of stress.

The behaviors that many people with ASD naturally engage in—turning off parts of the body-brain-mind while rocking, focusing on seeming nothingness and making white noises—are not unlike more traditional ways to relieve stress. Picture a child at recess, swinging while humming without even realizing he is humming; a couple at the end of a long day of work, sitting on the porch on a glider, listening to music and gazing into nowhere, relaxing enough to be able to enjoy dinner. Think about the millions of people around the world who learned to meditate, sometimes using a mantra to help them tune out the here and now in order to leave thoughtful mind and physical body behind for several moments of respite.

Meditation. For 30 years accepted by the Western medical profession as one of the best ways to reduce stress and gain more self-awareness and mental organization. All the time, altering the physiological and biochemical effects of stress, reducing plasma cortisol and, arterial blood lactate, and facilitating other neuroendocrine changes.

Keeping in mind this picture of meditation as we view the ANS response, it should be clear how innately wise self-stimming behaviors are for people with ASD. But when the stress remains constant because of sensory overload, this altered state, in some ways simulating a meditative state, becomes dysfunctional. Imagine trying to engage in meditation while seated on a pillow of cacti amidst a throng of scorpions under an unrelenting sun. The two conflicting states of severe sensory stress and attempts to escape it through meditation would be unbearable, and would play havoc with the biochemicals that are part of the autonomic nervous system's response patterns.

The major biochemicals that effect the change from parasympathetic to sympathetic control are adrenaline and cortisol—the stress hormones. Increased production of these substances during stress interferes with the ability to concentrate, learn and remember. This again points to similarities between ASD and other disorders, such as attentional problems and learning difficulties.

In addition, adrenaline and cortisol are two of the body's chief defenses against allergy and infection. If they are constantly being produced and utilized as a response to stress, the body's reserves are depleted, so there isn't enough to support good immunity and balanced response to potential allergens. This may result in increased vulnerability to viruses, over-reactivity to certain medications, and heightened sensitivity to certain foods or food additives.

All of these symptoms are becoming recognized as part of the multi-faceted problems inherent in ASD.

Allergies and immune system disorders further weaken the system and have a negative effect on behavior and concentration as well. As part of the cortisol response to stress, the body first produces elevated levels of sugar that are carried in the bloodstream, and to counter the blood sugar, then produces more insulin. This cycle can lead to diabetes, but more often we see it manifest as hypoglycemia, a condition that exacerbates swings in mood and performance. When this situation of chronic sympathetic nervous system response occurs in infants and young children, their immunity, digestive processes, nutritional levels, and basic functions are weakened before they've had a chance to develop most of those skills and brain functions others take for granted.

The state of fright/fight/flight also elicits reflexive responses in children and adults alike. Unexpected stimuli, such as sudden noise, light, movement or even alteration of body position might reactivate the Moro reflex, supposedly inhibited at 2-4 months of life. In this state, the individual's behavior will be typically reflexive in nature and driven by the need to survive, rather than showing reflective thought or reasoning.

When Carlos entered the center where I was waiting with two of my interns, he shuffled through the door, accompanied by two aides—one who assisted him at school and one who monitored him at the group home where he'd been living for a few years. Carlos was large for 13, and yet small, insignificant in his attempts to hide himself from his environment. He hunched over inside his hooded coat on a warm day, watching the floor as he moved. He had brought with him his favorite toys: plastic coat hangers and an electric cord. He crouched, his back to me, spinning the cord over the coat hangers, lost in the patterns.

He didn't say a word, although occasionally he muttered some sounds. He shuddered if my interns or I or either of his aides as much as twitched. He jumped backwards, still stooped, when the aide in front of him repositioned himself in his chair. Every unanticipated movement frightened this strapping youth. He was utterly terrified.

But I understood, and it was because of my understanding that we were able to work with Carlos for four hours that day, and no one was bitten or kicked or slugged by this quiet fearful teen. Carlos had a long history of abusing others. At school his aide contained him in a private small room with no furniture and only a bare overhead fluorescent light. Rarely was anything more dangerous than a magazine in the room with them. Yet every day Carlos assaulted the aide, usually only once or twice inflicting injury, although he waged assault more frequently than that.

I observed Carlos's pallor, his posture, movement patterns, and darting use of his eyes, rarely resting on anything but his cord and coat hangers. I watched him pick up on everything in the periphery, jumping at every unanticipated movement. Yes, I said that already, but I meant EVERY unanticipated movement. If his aide tipped his head to scratch his neck, Carlos startled. If the other aide crossed or uncrossed her legs, Carlos jumped.

Yet I was soon able to move slowly and freely, telling this youngster who would not look at me and had not yet spoken "Carlos, I appreciate your being here and trusting me. I know it's taking a great deal of courage on your part to be in the room with me and everyone else. I hope you'll feel safe here. We won't touch you. And before I move I'll warn you. I'll say 'Carlos, I'm going to uncross my legs now and stand up because I want to see what you're doing with your cord and hangers. I won't touch them and I won't touch you. But you will feel me looking over your head to watch.'"

I began to tell him when I felt the others were about to move, and had them take my lead. They were awkward, stammering as they tried to narrate their movements. "Carlos, I'm about to move my arm, my right arm, and cross it over to my ear, my, uh, left ear and, oh yeah, I'll be tipping my head a little sort of with my left side down. Then, let's see, I guess I'll be moving my right hand up and down to scratch that left ear."

No incidents. No assaults. Carlos no longer felt frightened by our every movement, and the movement of every shadow. He stood up, his color became richer. He was relaxing out of a fright/fight/flight reaction. He would have energy for some higher level responses, for processing and responding. For the first time, Carlos was about to gain control of himself, and not be governed by a run-away ANS.

The parasympathetic and sympathetic divisions of the ANS have a great deal of autonomy in the way they perform, with the CNS exerting little control. Indirectly, the ANS is very much involved in our behavioral responses to emotions such as fear, anger, rage, panic, pleasure. These emotions are triggered by brain centers, primarily in the limbic system. Without mediation by our cerebral cortices—the areas in our brains where we engage rational thought—messages sent from the limbic system to the autonomic control centers dictate many of our bodily responses.

These autonomically-controlled responses then produce further sensory input, which in turn contributes to a continuation of the emotional response. In fact, more than 80% of the fibers of the vagus nerve (one of our twelve cranial nerves, and the one that services most of our internal organs) process sensory information, and many of those relate to comfort and discomfort in the gut. Through cyclical interaction among various nerves, emotional responses escalate unless the higher brain centers are able to intervene.

An individual like Carlos, caught in a physically and psychologically debilitating spiral of fright/flight/fight, with the accompanying hormonal changes and reflexive reactions that help to maintain the stressful situation, is unlikely to have the energy to regain cortical control. Outsiders can't use normal logic with someone in this situation, although I mediated for Carlos using logic based on neurological function. Carlos needed me to do this, because he could not mediate with himself until the reaction was assuaged. But without knowing what is causing the reaction and being able to make the necessary changes in the environment to provide respite, there is no relief from this insidious cycle of fear, of stress, of anxiety.

One ANS response to stress that is particularly harmful when it occurs over an extended period is a change in breathing patterns. Breathing is the activity governed by the ANS that we perform more times per day than any other. And just as earlier I mentioned that Movement and Life are synonymous, so are Breathing and Living. When the quality of our breathing changes, the quality of our life changes as well.

Most people with autism don't breathe deeply or rhythmically. They are almost always breathing under the influence of stress. When breathing is shallow and dysrhythmic, we don't expel toxins through our breath, and the rest of our body needs to deal with them somehow. Because breathing also affects the cells in the wall of the gut and the liver, in fact the cell walls of every cell in our body, the effects of prolonged stress on gut permeability and on internal cleansing become obvious.

One of the primary state changes that HANDLE practitioners watch for is a change in breathing patterns. When these occur, employing the principle of Gentle Enhancement, the activity—diagnostic or therapeutic—is stopped for that session. When individuals tell us, "No. I can do more," we reply, "I know you can, but your body has signaled it needs to stop now, or we'll be working against our goals." In diagnostic sessions, we have learned what we needed—that the particular function performed in the particular situation is stressful. In performance of treatment activities, we know that the body-brain has felt the impact of the particular activity, and to push beyond would only shut down the very systems we are trying to strengthen.

Sandy, the young woman who moved from nonverbal to hyperverbal so rapidly, had a behavior that most people viewed as a tic. To me, it was a sign that she needed to become aware that her breathing was changing. Her diaphragm would move up and down, as if it were massaging her vagus nerve and trying to calm down a yet unheeded response of overload. When I saw it, I would ask her, "Sandy, do you feel your diaphragm going up and down?"

"Oh, yeah," she would respond.

"Well, we need to figure out what is stressing you now, so your breathing can return to normal."

"I need a snack," was one of her common responses.

"Well, it's a good thing you can tell what your body wants. Now you just need to remember to feel when your breathing starts to change, so when I'm not around, you can still keep on an even keel."

"Okay," she would say. And eventually, she did learn to read her own state changes before her ANS took over.

Another important state change sign to observe is the sudden tensing of muscles, any muscles not actively involved in performing a particular activity. Examples: Extension of the fingers, tensing of the jaw, holding the eyelids open wide without blinking. When we are in fright/flight/fight reactions, more blood and oxygen are sent to the muscle spindles in those muscles that we feel need to support us at the moment, as long as the supply of the basic building blocks we need for cortisol and adrenaline production are available. I've said that before. It's important enough to repeat.

The initial tensing response to acute stress and reduced tonal response to prolonged stress may help explain why the baby who will later be diagnosed with autism responds to touch and sound and other stimuli by arching and hyper-extending, displaying high tone in infancy. As he grows, though, his muscle tone begins to diminish, not to the normal tone of relaxed readiness to respond, but to hypotonicity. A sort of signal that "under siege, my supplies have given out and I am giving up."

The metaphor of being under siege is not new in the description of autism. Clara Claiborne Park titled her remarkable account of her autistic daughter Jessy's childhood as just that—*The Siege*. Park, however, put Jessy under siege to elicit specific responses. And there are a number of behavioral approaches to treating autism that advocate "besieging" as an effective parenting and teaching technique.

From my experience, viewing the underlying neurological causes of ASD as the siege, HANDLE's approach to treatment is different.

In the HANDLE paradigm, as we work with individuals who need to learn to protect themselves from stress, initially we are their stress-o-meters. We watch for state change signs, and tell them what we see, what it means, and why we need them to stop doing a particular activity NOW. As I did with Sandy. Eventually our clients—those with autism and those with other disorders of behavior and learning—begin to recognize their own state changes as they are occurring and to modulate their behaviors. This is a remarkable feat for an individual with autism. But it is a necessary one.

Some people—those who can sustain visual focus for prolonged periods and meld information from several senses at once without needing movement or proprioceptive input to provide feedback—might learn to control their states employing techniques such as neurofeedback, seeing the response so they might then connect it to the internal sensations they are feeling.

I much prefer being able to read out my various state changes without reliance on equipment. It allows me to protect myself from environmental stress in almost any situation, to do what I need to control my environment and my participation within it.

But this is not enough. We need also consider the role of the limbic system in stress. After all, it is this system, the seat of our emotional responses, that screams "Yikes! Get me out of here!" And the body-nervous systems may respond by moving out of the path of physical danger or closing off the threatening stimuli. Each of the major components of this system that loops around deep inside our brain has separate but interrelated functions.

The thalamus—currently considered by some as central to attentional disorders—is a good place to begin our tour. Although the thalamus is structurally located in a part of the brain called the diencephalon, it has so many direct connections to the limbic system that now some neuroscientists include it among the structures of the limbic system. It acts as the relay station for all senses other than our sense of smell. The thalamus waits until it has received the necessary and sufficient information from various senses before opening its gates and sending the information onwards—some to various portions of the cerebral cortices and other to the hypothalamus, our next stop in the limbic system. When the thalamus gets flooded with information it may release it unfiltered. When it gets disparate information from various senses and cannot form a coherent energetic sense, it may disregard the information. In either case, the higher cortical areas and the hypothalamus get erratic messages that almost defy interpretation.

The hypothalamus—also recently included in discussions on the limbic system—has received information from the thalamus. This information is about the regulatory functions, and so the hypothalamus provides input to both the ANS and the pituitary gland. It regulates functions such as body temperature, hunger, thirst, waking and sleeping states, and it can trigger enormous feats of strength in perceived emergencies. It's the signal of a stressed hypothalamus at work in conjunction with the amygdala (which we will soon visit on this loop) that turns the passive, low-tone, self-stimming child into the enraged super-strong lion who defies containment when he perceives a threat to survival.

Although the pituitary gland is not considered part of the limbic system, we will visit it briefly on this loop. The pituitary has long been called "the master gland" because it's considered to regulate the timing and amounts of hormonal secretions. During puberty its activities cause the rush of raging hormones that anyone who survived adolescence (or survived life with an adolescent) will have a hard time forgetting. When the timing signals to the pituitary are relatively regular but the input from the body is irregular, it's no wonder so many people in the autism spectrum are out of control during puberty.

The amygdala, a long-recognized part of the limbic system, links areas involved with cognition with those of sensory processing. A major function of the amygdala is to protect us from being overcome by noxious fumes and the like; it receives unfiltered information directly from the olfactory bulb. Recent research indicates that the emotional significance imparted through the amygdala brings focus to salient aspects in our perceptual field, and therefore may be responsible for our interest in and ability to deal with perceptual tasks such as face recognition.[36] Amygdala is the area of our brain where we store memories of fear and send a learned response to fear to the prefrontal cortex of the brain for action, bypassing rational control centers.[37] So we get the lion on the rampage, as irregularities of the prefrontal cortex have long been associated with anti-social behaviors.

The hippocampus (what a wonderful name to remember for those of us who rely on visual imagery) receives combined input from the thalamus and from the emotional messages derived largely by the amygdala. The hippocampus' apparent functions are to store short-term memory somewhere, anywhere, in the brain, and, luckily, another of its functions is mapping—internalizing maps of geographic areas and the like. It functions best when it also helps us build a short-term map of where it stored that information before deciding if the information is necessary for long-term retention—a reorganization process that occurs usually when we sleep.

Since so many of the savant characteristics of people with autism relate to mapping, and to immediate memory for echolalic speech repetition, this area of the limbic system may be more dependable for those of us in the autism spectrum. However, the input the hippocampus gets from the thalamus may be out of kilter with what the rest of the world views as reality (Temple Grandin associates memories with places, not with people). And the emotional tone associated with these perceptions may be fear or rage. So perhaps many of our memories, too, are best forgotten, because they may return us over and over again, perseveratively, to painful situations. We may choose to block memory.

---

[36]Grelotti, DJ, et al

[37]Thompson, RF., et al

The remaining structures in the limbic system are the cingulate gyrus and the basal ganglia. The basal ganglia direct impulses between the cerebellum and the frontal lobe of the cerebral cortex, thus helping to control bodily movements and to develop motor planning. That is, if the cerebellum's Purkinje cells (those great big cells that receive such strong hugs from the climbing fibers) agree to relay outgoing messages, since they alone have the responsibility for that. But in order to operate with accurate information, these cells need to receive the information that the olivary bodies process, and that information comes largely from some of the cranial nerves.

So now we have a number of threads, all intertwined again, and including information that needs to come to and from both sides of our body and our brain. The cingulate gyrus, part of the limbic system, lies immediately over the corpus callosum in our brain. And it is the corpus callosum that serves to integrate the information between our right and left hemispheres in another connection, in addition to those connections that are channeled to and through the thalamus and amygdala in particular. The cingulate gyrus apparently also plays a role in our ability to voluntarily control the sphincter muscles in our bladder, and as such may some day be implicated in general sphincter muscle control, the unity of which we explored earlier.[38]

We have taken a circuitous route, on the track of how reactions to fear through our limbic system and into our prefrontal cortex impact our autonomic nervous system with its influence on our immune system and digestive system and ability to rid our body of toxins. And we have also just connected a part of the limbic system with that one function that is infamous for embarrassing us in moments of extreme fright and other distress—voiding our bladders, sometimes also our bowels, when the limbic system is spinning frighteningly out of control.

But remember that this path in the brain itself began with the thalamus, the sensory relay station. So where does the thalamus get its information? Or did it begin with the olivary complex? Perhaps if we can provide it meaningful, organized input we can break the cycle.

The thalamus receives its information from 11 of the 12 cranial nerves and also from the peripheral nerves that give us sensory-motor feedback from our body below our neck. Just to make the loop more seemingly hopeless to untangle, the

---

[38]Recent independent studies performed by Dr. David Lewis at the Harborview Medical Center in Seattle, Washington, in conjunction with the University of Washington, show that one of the HANDLE activities, frequently prescribed in one of several variations, ensuring Gentle Enhancement—the activity called Crossed-Arm Bounce—activates the cingulate gyrus. The research was presented at the October 2003 conference of the Society of Nuclear Medicine in Anaheim, California.

ANS can be considered part of the peripheral nervous system. And what about that one stray cranial nerve? Which one is so bold as to send its information somewhere other than the thalamus? The olfactory nerve. The one that is so integrally tied to our emotional responses and memory, and is meant to be active, as our smoke alarm, even when we are asleep. The olfactory nerve sends its information directly to the amygdala, where we sense fear and hit the panic button.

So we need to somehow calm these nerves and help them send integrated information to the brain. But the sad news is that once your limbic system is operating from a sense of anxiety, overall arousal is increased, making you better able to detect potential threats in your environment. This is great for you, but for those of us who are overly sensitive to those threats, increasing the irritation we already feel sends us further and faster into a fright/flight/fight reaction.

In the last couple of years, controversy has arisen between two researchers. Jocelyne Bachevalier, professor of neurobiology and anatomy, University of Texas Health Science Center, surmised from her work with monkeys that early damage to the amygdala is a probable cause of autism. Monkeys whose amygdala were lesioned at age two months showed most of the characteristics ascribed to autism: avoidance of social interaction, ritualistic behaviors, and what appears to be absence of face recognition. The characteristics continued into adulthood.[39]

David Amaral, professor of psychiatry and neuroscience, University of California-Davis, who has been researching the role of the amygdala, disagrees with Bachevalier, because he found that similarly lesioned monkeys, while avoiding social interactions, were extremely vigilant to other monkeys in their cages. He concluded that this was therefore not an appropriate model for autism, because those in the autism spectrum would demonstrate indifference to others. He felt that the lesioned monkeys exhibited signs of intense fear rather than an inability to read social signals.[40]

This research, with its apparent contradictions, actually provides strong support for my hypothesis that stress and fear are the culprits—stress and fear that develop at a very early age, probably in utero, at birth, or during the first few months create the symptoms and alter the development of our systems. Stress and fear that cause us to watch those in our environment with hyper-vigilance. Stress and fear trigger the sympathetic branch of the ANS to take over.

John Upledger, an osteopathic physician, feels that it is the balance between

---

[39]Meunier, M, and Bachevalier, J. 2002

[40]Black, H. 2001

the sympathetic and parasympathetic branches of the ANS that results in the best preventive medicine and that this balance must be considered in any successful program to enhance health. When the sympathetic division is constantly engaged and expending energy, the result is chronic stress without the replenishment of our resources.

So, acknowledging that most individuals in the autism spectrum are operating with hyper-vigilance and from fright, and that their sympathetic nervous systems are overworking, we need to find a way to break this cycle, not by providing scripts to help them make it through a particular situation in a robotic fashion, but by truly relieving the fear and stress. How do most of us find the resilience to deal with our fears and start a new day refreshed? WE SLEEP.

Maybe one way out of this exhausting self-perpetuating cycle of overwhelming disorganized stimulation that elicits fear is through the respite of sleep. Sleep, after all, is a time of rest or reorganization to help strengthen the learning experiences of the day. What's more, if we can sleep, perhaps we can dream and awaken the creative spirit, so tomorrow will not be just another day of self-protection and performance of rote activities.

14. Sleep
The essential peace

There are two extremely important concepts we have not yet broached. The first is resiliency and its interdependency on sleep, and the second is boundaries.

Resiliency is a necessary aspect for emotional and physiological growth. It is more important, even, just for remaining what some might view as static. "Static" is a concept I have a hard time applying to a living system or to anything in our energetic system, certainly not to our nervous system, which is in a state of continual adaptation to the myriad stimuli and experiences of daily life. Everything is in a constant state of change and adaptation. Even if our adaptation is to dig our heels in and say, "You can't make me," we have been changed by the need to face the event and decide. Even rocks change—their shapes change through erosion and other natural forces, and their composition changes as new layers of minerals are added or vegetation growing on them depletes some minerals and deposits others.

Human beings require a great deal of resiliency to move through the experiences of one day and into the next. Our brains and nervous systems and immune systems have the capacity for considerable resiliency. We need to be resilient to move from our early reflexive behaviors through reactive ones to responsive ones that include having weighed the elements and decided how to act or not act. Our response can be reflective, resistive, receptive. When our responses begin to be repetitive, regardless of changing input, we are in a state of regression, and are beginning to return to reactive or reflexive behaviors. (The chart on the following page demonstrates how we cycle through many of these Rs of neurodevelopment). It is

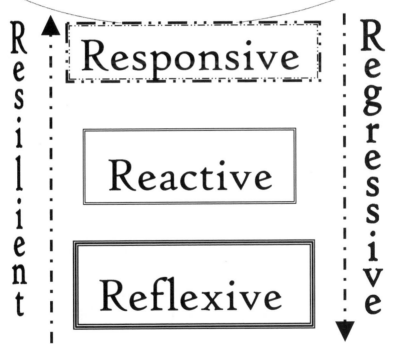

Reflective   Resistive

Receptive

Resilient ↑ Responsive ↓ Regressive

Reactive

Reflexive

resiliency that carries us upward, to our greatest potential.

There are several elements that nourish our resiliency. One is that intangible thing called love. Although most of us in the spectrum do not demonstrate love the same way most other people do, and at times our parents may be concerned that we don't know how to love and be loved—we do feel the energy of love. We just don't know how to organize around it.

Another element is nutrition, and we have already looked at several reasons those of us with autism most likely have a poor nutritional status—from improper chewing of our foods to candida, from allergies to sensory overload and stress, from nutrients our mothers did not get during their pregnancies or from supplementation or medication they did ingest.

An area we haven't yet explored more than cursorily is crucial to resiliency. *Sleep.* Studies show that the vast majority of people with autism have sleep problems. Almost all of my autistic clients have sleep disorders. And these problems of sleep are not purely related to the need to block out the sounds of the refrigerator's motor humming or the lights from the neighboring houses or the smells of the yard where rain has just fallen or the touch of the sheets on the bed. There are many causes of stress to our systems, and these may change at different stages in our lives, as we will see.

Scientists have been studying sleep for a very long time. Certain facts appear with consistency. Most adults spend 25-35% of their lives sleeping. Most infants and young children spend about 50% of their time asleep. Premature babies are asleep about 75% of the time.

There are two forms of sleep: Rapid Eye Movement (REM) and Non-Rapid Eye Movement (NREM) sleep, with REM accounting for 10-25% of sleep time for most people.

Sleep serves a number of important functions. NREM sleep restores the body and REM sleep reorganizes and restores brain processes for flow, structure and storage of information, and nurturing creativity. In infants, who are born with all of their brain neurons but whose synaptic connections among neurons are just beginning to grow, sleep is particularly significant in this process, and it appears that the growth of the synapses occurs during REM sleep.

The synapses allow information to be shared between one neuron and others. Without functioning synapses our brains would be virtually inoperative. Irregular synaptic relay causes disorganized perceptions and difficulty in responding to stimuli, and many forms of disordered behaviors depending on the locations and severity of the deficits.

The major factor that interferes with sound sleep is stress. The Institute for Natural Resources (INR) suggests keys to managing stress. The first key is to recognize the body's stress signals and then to identify what causes the stress. The INR suggests reducing stress by listing priorities, pampering yourself, acknowledging major life events as sources of stress, learning to say no, having fun, and building your resistance to stress through diet, exercise, and adequate sleep. Other suggestions: Pace yourself to save energy, have a strong support system, accentuate the positive, laugh often.

Most people in the ASD are stressed. They awaken each morning stressed, they go to bed stressed. The sensations that surround them while they sleep stress them. Their attempts to pamper themselves and to say NO are frequently deemed behavioral problems, even when they want to choose whether or not to sleep in pajamas, with blankets, with music, with another person. Most of their attempts throughout the day to reduce stress are negated by the realities of the world that bombard them, wanting faster responses to more and varied input, calling attention to the negative aspects of behaviors; nutrition is poor and exercise is just not going to happen, because of energy depletion as well as problems of balance and coordination and muscle tone.

Fortunately, in sleep, when we can pamper ourselves, the body-brain unit tries to compensate us as much as it can for the stress of the day. One way this happens, it has been found, is that people in the spectrum (as well as those with Down Syndrome) spend much less time in REM sleep than other people. *Whew!* At least in sleep, the body has some time to restore itself and rebuild its resources for the demands of yet another day.

But that means that the brain-building, mental-organizing, creativity-boosting benefits of REM sleep are primarily lost to us. And because most of our dreams occur in REM, and because the more you dream the more you develop a cohesive perceptual sense of yourself and the world, it's probable that those of us in the spectrum have more immature dreams and as such rarely find ourselves in our dreams.

I wonder if I could have known that when I wrote these two lines fifty years ago:

"But strange it may seem to those of right mind
That in these sweet dreams myself I can't find."

I do know that when we interview families on sleep behaviors, we get many unusual responses. We hear most commonly: difficulty falling asleep (sensory overload), needing someone else in bed in order to sleep (proprioception), needing music or other white noise in order to sleep (specific auditory hypersensitivity), not tolerating bedclothes (tactile hypersensitivity), sleeping so soundly that nothing wakes her up (NREM sleep and most of that delta to restore the bodily resources).

Of course, many people outside of the spectrum have sleep problems. In the last several years, researchers have increased their understanding of the brain mechanisms that promote sleep. Because the brain and body have many sleep enhancing substances, any of them could be deficient or out of balance in ASD. Melatonin is the substance presently proving itself an effective "natural" aid to sleep for restless autistic children and their sleep deprived families as well.

Although researchers still debate whether the autistic brain has too much or too little melatonin, because melatonin naturally promotes normal sleep and stabilizes circadian rhythms, many families have experimented with this substance. It can be purchased over-the-counter in many health food stores but is best prescribed or at least monitored by a physician who knows what other supplements and/or medications the individual in question is taking.

Of the several families I know who have tried melatonin for their ASD children, the reviews are mixed:

"We didn't really notice any change at all in the first week. And since it was just one more thing to try to get into that mouth and down that throat, we had to choose our battles and melatonin lost out."

"Wow! What a difference! Almost immediately the sleep problems were just gone."

I don't recall ever hearing a family say that the melatonin made the sleep problems worse, fortunately. But on more than one occasion I did hear from the families that had seen a positive shift, "Somehow, it seems that after a month or so on the melatonin, sleep started to become a problem again." Some families reported that although with melatonin, initially sleep was no longer an issue, other behaviors did not improve. However, other family members were better able to cope with the self-stimming and constant white-noise and other behavioral issues because THEY were more rested.

"What do you think was going on?" some parents asked me. "Why did melatonin not continue to help with the sleep issues?"

"It probably worked initially because Connor so badly needed sleep that it duped his brain into feeling that at last it had what it needed for restful sleep. And, of course, in one sense that was correct. But I think that because all of the stressors of daily life were still impinging, working against the relaxation response and causing a continued build up of neurotoxicity, after a short period the brain was again overrun by the anti-sleep factors. Doctors might explain this phenomenon as 'tolerance set in,' meaning that the body became accustomed to a particular dosage and now needs more. No one knows if a higher dose of melatonin might help now, but no one knows what untoward effects higher doses might have either. I think we need to keep working on reducing the stressors and balancing the body-brain-mind-spirit naturally. I know it's more work to do your HANDLE program faithfully than to pop a pill, but I think the results you'll get will be more 'complete' and therefore lasting."

In this whole debate, we need to look further than just "sleep," as it is the absence of REM that may be most significant. And REM sleep probably will not happen until the body experiences less stress and depletes fewer of its resources during the waking hours.

So again, we are back to stress, and how we can diminish it. And this brings us back to the thalamus' inability to filter the information it is receiving from the cranial nerves. Those nerves neurologists generally check to see if they are intact or not, and rarely know how to help when they are not.

Most people with autism have several cranial nerves that are not operating properly. We have already singled out the auditory-vestibular nerve for its role in filtering and processing sounds as well as information from the body in relation to gravitational pull, bodily position, muscle tone, speed of movement. It also plays a role in visual tracking and even reading out nuisances of control over the muscles that control the positioning of the eyes, and as such their ability to converge and diverge.[41]

Most people know very little about these nerves and how they service us. Processing between these nerves and the muscles they innervate should be automatic. All we should experience is ability to open and close our eyes, direct our

---

[41]For those of you who want to know, the cranial nerves that control these muscles are the oculomotor nerve, the trochlear nerve and the abducens nerves. They, in turn, share information with the auditory-vestibular nerve regarding the positioning of the eyes and tension in these muscles. The oculomotor nerve is the one that also commands the sphincters of the eyes—the eyelids and the iris, which controls the dilation and constriction of the pupils, in conjunction with information received from the ANS. Exploration of the profound connections among these cranial nerves and the others and the thalamus and other areas of the brain would add some to our discussions here, but I feel it would derail us from our focus. I trust that those of you with strong sympathies for the hypoglossal and glossopharyngeal and accessory and facial and optic nerves will excuse my not digressing further to include these in this volume.

gaze, and filter excess light as needed. But imagine now that you are in my body as a child, or in Donna Williams' or in the body of my five year-old client who had been diagnosed with autism in his native land—a land of intense sunlight and endless miles of white sand and stucco buildings that reflect light.

A few months after I met them, Nadia, his mother, showed me two photographs of Imram.[42] In the one taken shortly before I met him, the pain in his face was visible, as he tried to protect himself from light and yet work somehow to bring his eyes to converge and look at the camera. This was the countenance that he presented to the world before he and his mother implemented his customized HANDLE program. The photo clearly shows the pain and fright of living in a confusing and assaultive world. Tactile and visual input were disorganized for him. His muscle tone was irregular and providing him confusing messages. His reflexes were not fully integrated most likely due to his living in an unrelenting state of sympathetic nervous system hyperactivity. He could not adequately judge foreground and background in his visual-spatial world. He misinterpreted or ignored nonverbal communication. And his trigeminal nerve was so sensitive that he avoided most movements of tongue and jaws—little chewing and speaking, lots of drooling, and, you may recall, sandwiches only if cut into triangular quarters.

In the second photo, taken after Imram and his mom had followed his HANDLE program for two months, it is obvious his pain is gone, and focusing on the camera is effortless.

These were not the only changes. One month into their HANDLE program, Nadia wrote: "Imram came up with a couple of very good sentences last week which I wrote down as milestones to remember:

1. 'Mamma, listen to me.' (with his elbow perched on the table, like a businessman) 'I want to see Spiderman on ABC Family.'

2. 'Mamma, I said, make me bread with cheese.'"

And, knowing what to appreciate, Nadia added. "A little bossy I think, but, hey, at this stage I'll take anything!"

She continued, "Two people I see socially also called to tell me how much of an improvement they have noticed in him. They weren't aware that I was working with him. They said he seems so much happier and that he came up to them and started talking and it was very clear. That was great encouragement."

---

[42]Initially Imram's mother wanted to share these photos with the world, to provide hope for others. Before the book was published, she retracted her permission. The reason? Imram was now so "normal," that she dared dream he would lead a normal adult life. Nadia feared that publicity about his autism diagnosis might one day hurt him socially or vocationally.

And just about the time the second photo was taken, Nadia wrote again: "I have seen a great improvement in his speech and social behaviors. He is still behind others his age though but we are hoping he will catch up."

After six months on their HANDLE program, Nadia again shared: "Imram is doing well and his speech is really developing. I see a great improvement in him over last year when he refused to play with anyone, go to different classrooms, let anyone touch him, go on field trips and would just speak one word if he needed anything. He is now playing with a few friends at school, sharing, telling stories, singing songs and playing ring around the rosy."

Despite her exuberance over these wonderful achievements, Nadia was still shocked to SEE the difference in her son—the obvious relaxation of his face. Hidden behind the visible relaxation was the release of tension in his cranial nerves, released to function normally to service speech and eating and to allow him to relax and enjoy life.

The reason? We developed a program for him that relieved the stress on his cranial nerves, provided them organized input, and employed Gentle Enhancement to strengthen the weak systems without stressing them. Stressed systems do not get stronger.

What were the activities his mother diligently performed with him? Face Tapping. Ear Muffs. Side to Side Tips. Beastie Back Roll. Peacemaker Massage. Two-Finger Spinal Massage. Skull Tapping. Jiggle Bridge and Sternum and Navel. Hug and Tug. Seated Clapping Game. Buzz Snap. Hoop Mazes. Suspended Glow Ball. And she made sure he sipped two ounces of water through a Crazy Straw two or three times a day with his eyes closed.

Implementation of this formidable list of activities, each with its peculiar name, required less than 20 minutes per day.[43]

But regardless of the particular causes of the disorder or the therapeutic regimen undertaken to resolve the problems, in my experience, the only way out of the vicious cycle that robs us of our resiliency to adapt to new situations and to develop more functional synapses and begin to leave our autism behind, most of the time, naturally, and to sleep—the only way to accomplish this naturally is by respecting the vulnerabilities of the individual. That is the true significance of Gentle

---

[43]The list of HANDLE activities is not a standardized program for every child we see with autism. But the principles of the activities are. Determining which activities are appropriate for which person at which stage in his development, and in combination with what other activities is far from a trivial decision when you remember that we are working with a stressed system, and an error in judgment on the development of a program may shut down those very systems you wish to strengthen. You can find some of these activities described, and read the principles behind these and others, in the appendices.

Enhancement.

One of the most common signs that anyone's system gives us that their internal organs are stressed is that their ears turn red. Many people have learned from a popular book such as *Is This Your Child?* by the physician Doris Rapp or from someone else versed in allergies, that red ears signal an allergic reaction to something. Well, yes. That may be. What it definitely is, is an early warning sign of stress.

To understand this reaction we need to look briefly once again at the vagus nerve, that cranial nerve that provides sensory information about what is going on in so many of our internal organs, particularly the gut. The vagus nerve surfaces at three locations on our bodies: the anus, and each outer ear. So, we generally check ears to see if there is irritation, although many parents who learn of this connection look at us in surprise, saying, "We always wondered why his anus was so red most of the time, and there were no ointments or no baths, nothing that could soothe it."

Stress to the system has both unusual and profound consequences. It interferes with the body's physiological balance, impairs higher level cognitive functioning, robs the body of chemicals needed to protect it from environmental offenders, and promotes return of primitive reflexes that can contribute to the individual's difficulties in coping with sensory stimuli. And it interferes with our ability to relax and to sleep. And that, in turn, thwarts our resiliency, our ability to regroup and face situations with new-found strength, to respond adaptively.

So until we can resolve the stressors on the ANS, including those affecting the enteric system, we have not resolved the issues of autism. Because the interactions among stimuli, behavior and the brain are dynamic and the brain is plastic, behavioral interventions may alter those parts of the brain that are creating (or perhaps, more correctly, responding to) anxiety in specific situations—instance by instance—allowing the person to control the physical manifestations of anxiety, but the nervous systems are still in a state of hyper-vigilance and excess tension—of anxiety.

Look at the photo of the two boys in the photo on the following page. One boy is truly relaxed. The other is *trying* to relax. One boy is not autistic; the other one is. His anxiety gives him away. From the photo, we have no idea if he can speak, or if he toe-walks, or it he has a weakened immune system. Yet if we look, we can see that he is in the spectrum.

There are different stressors affecting us at different stages in our life. I can't possibly review all of them—sensory, nutritional, hormonal, environmental, medical, emotional—nor take you on in-depth research journeys into each develop-

The boy on the left is truly relaxed. His muscles are supporting his body against the pull of gravity but without tension. His smile is natural. He is looking at the camera without squinting. For the boy on the right, none of this is true. He is tense. He is trying to relax, but he can't. He is straining to hold his head forward despite his weak muscle tone. He is trying to smile. He is working hard to focus on the camera. Relaxing isn't easy if you are autistic.

mental stage. However, it is important to see what some of the stressors are at different stages in development, stressors we can weave into this ever more intricate, disparate, warped fabric.

The prenatal experience is probably the most important to consider, and the one that we will look at the least, as it is too immense for the scope of this book. It involves all of the factors in Mom's life, and Dad's, too—factors that influence genetic makeup, maternal health, and general well-being. These include: the environments in which they work(ed) and play(ed) and live(ed); how many phthalates Mom ingested by microwaving her food in plastic containers or absorbed through her skin and nails by using nail polish and perfumes[44], how much aspartame she included in her diet[45]; whether or not they put in new carpeting as they were preparing for their new baby.

---

[44]Many plastic infant toys were removed from the market when research, some of it conducted at the federal Centers for Disease Control and Prevention (CDC), proved that the phthalates in these plastics is extremely neurotoxic.

[45]Little-known, but well-documented studies, spurred on in part at the insistence of Ralph Walton, MD, Chairman of The Center for Behavioral Medicine, show clearly that when aspartame interacts with digestive juices it converts to formaldehyde. One source for additional information is www.holisticmed.com/aspartame/abuse/methanol.html.

More generally, we look at the pregnant woman's basic nutrition and nutritional supplementation, recently implicated as one of the environmental factors that decides which genes turn on and which stay silent, thereby altering the expression of those genes, without altering the genes themselves (this makes exploring a genetic basis for autism that much more challenging). We also need to consider the pregnant woman's age and her enthusiasm about this pregnancy; the type and amount of prenatal medical care and dental care she receives; the degree of stress she endures during the pregnancy. All of these and more affect the developing fetus.

And then there's the perinatal or birth experience itself. Variables include: type of delivery (post-term, premature, breech, C-section, induced, suctioned, forceps, prolonged labor, continually monitored). Now that we understand the fragility of the cranial nerves of a fetus or newborn, we see the importance of a gradual transition into the world; we recognize the problems caused by sound that cannot be filtered out, the possible toxic effects of medication, and stress in whatever way it impinges on us—then we can understand why the experiences during these few hours of a baby's life are so critical.

The neonatal stage cannot be overlooked. Today industrialized societies tend to over-stimulate children of every age, but this can be most detrimental in those first few months of life, when the infant's systems have not yet learned to filter and focus. Hospitals have a cacophony of noises and bright lights and probes and so many other sensory intrusions that infants must learn to shut off because the overload is much too much. At home, parents have learned that black and red in contrast to white are the most stimulating colors, so the nursery and toys literally reflect these colors, frequently in high gloss. And music has been proven to be good for developing brains, so a radio or CD player is on in the nursery, competing with the television in the living room and the conversations and arguments in the kitchen. The infant is lying on brand new permanent-press sheets that release formaldehyde, and if it is winter, he is in a flame-retardant, synthetic sleeper with his feet encased, ensuring that his neural energy will not get released and that he will not be able to freely exchange toxins with the universe.

And he is placed on his back to sleep, so that his eyes are always exposed to light (those of us with light-sensitive eyes get little protection from closed eyelids), and he cannot begin to integrate many of his primary reflexes, so he continues to respond reflexively. He is fed baby food containing high amounts of salt and sugar and preservatives[46], and milk that has been pasteurized, and he is vaccinated against ever-so-many things, and exposed to so many pollutants.

He is shampooed and bathed with highly aromatic products, and powdered with others, and encased in disposable diapers. And then he begins cutting teeth! More stress to the nervous system. And during this period, if he is breastfed, what is his mother eating and drinking and feeling as she nurses? This is such a critical developmental time, and think what it is like for the child who will be diagnosed (or diagnosable) as in the spectrum; remember that he had more than one of the prenatal and perinatal factors influencing his ability to cope with the continual bombardment of neonatal life.

Then come the toddler/preschool years. Now he moves around on his own with other people moving in the same space. He is expected to walk and learn to feed himself and speak and play with other children and become toilet trained, and have more vaccinations, and eat more "regular people food" and watch TV and ride a tricycle and take stairs, and an endless list of other things.

Is it any wonder that at this stage of development, those of us who have not yet let you know we were autistic, now show you? We do not have the wherewithal to organize ourselves in this vast array of sensory challenges. We are simply overwhelmed and stressed, and until we can get respite and get organized we can't calm down our overwrought systems and have the energy and other resources available for all of these coordinated and cognitive and social and communicative behaviors.

Although it is in early childhood that most of us with autism are recognized and diagnosed, our real challenges and those of our families have only begun. The school years and adolescence are perhaps the most difficult times of all. And there are choices our families need to make for us: Should we be mainstreamed or placed in self-contained special education classes or facilities, or should we be home-schooled until we are able to participate more easily in group situations? How much social stimulation is right? What academic demands should be placed on us? What enrichment should be offered us? How can they control our special diets when we have lunch and snacks in school? Who will help with our toileting? How many illnesses will we be exposed to?

Mostly, who will understand and protect and nurture us?

Suppose we make it safely through the elementary years, with understanding teachers and protective classmates. Then the storm! Puberty! We have not yet be-

---

[46]Research at Duke University Medical Center is showing that early nutrition has a profound effect on the production of pancreatic enzymes later in life, not only relevant to the rise of early-onset diabetes, but also to the autism-secretin connection posited by some.

come fully acquainted with our bodies and our feelings until now, and they have been almost predictable, for us. We knew that we would overreact to everything at school during the days the marching band practiced on the athletic field. We could anticipate the sounds and lights in the auditorium and beg out of the assemblies. We knew we had better get an aide or a friend to help us transition through the hallways between classes and on the playground during recess. We knew how much energy we needed to get through a day. We knew where our elbows were in relationship to our shoulders—well sort of.

But now things are changing. The adolescent is growing not just taller, but his whole body feels and even sounds different. His voice is changing, and it resonates differently through his bones.

And then, *everything* changes. Moment to moment, day by day. Nothing is the same. All of the behaviors he learned to control are no longer under his control. He is driven by a wild rage of something called hormones. He can't tell you it is because of the hormones that he is suddenly attracted to women's breasts and needs to resist the urge to feel and smell them. He had barely learned to develop eye-contact, and now he is embarrassed to look at them for fear he will look at the "wrong" place. He is torn between his need to maintain his autism—his aloneness—and this biological urge to be with others.

And the worst thing is that once again, we autistic people just plain don't know who we are, and we don't have any real friends with whom to talk about all of this, even if we could put it into words. We are again, totally out of control. And we are too big for Mom or Dad to figure out how to restrain us and protect us. Our hormones are telling us we want independence. But to be independent means to be self-regulating, and although autism and autonomous may share that "self," ASD teens do not have the capability to be autonomous.

The fright is unimaginable. The retreat–the flight–is how most of us handle this stage. Some of us fight. All of us stress our systems because we are stressed. And these stresses go unresolved throughout adulthood for most of us, unless we figure out or someone else does for us, that there is a unity to our senses and our sensibilities. If we are high functioning, we will find or create a profession that utilizes our strengths and protects us against our vulnerabilities, but they will still be there to haunt us if we do not recognize their root and treat them, respectfully, but treat them nonetheless.

As I summarized in *The Churkendoose Anthology* section entitled "Who will protect us from our vulnerabilities?":

"I see as the central challenges for children and adults who fall within the spectrum . . . their central nervous system sensitivities are so many and their enteric nervous system and immune system may be so weak, that their autonomic nervous system is continuously stressed, just trying to brace against constant bombardment from a hostile environment. Sometimes as they protect themselves, they close down to activities, and it may be the behaviors they do not exhibit that provide us the biggest clues into the puzzle of their developmental profile. Not the presence of rocking and hand-flapping, but the absence of a full range of rocking or the inability to move one hand without the other. Not the biting and swallowing of Styrofoam cups and the gnawing of shirtsleeves, but the lack of chewing food. Not the tantrums over having their nails cut but the blocking of sensations on their faces or the seemingly high tolerance for pain in general. These are some of the many clues we must uncover if we are to help unlock these children from the traps of their own irregular systems."[47]

[47]Bluestone (2002) P. 91.

15. Boundaries
Within and without

Being released from confinement can be an extremely threatening experience. Confinement of any kind represents structure and boundaries. Remember Rachel, who suddenly found herself able to interact in new ways with her environment, having new experiences impinge upon her, and having no idea where her boundaries were? And remember the child whose plaintive "Where are you now, Mama?!" I can still hear, crying out from fear that he did not know where he was, where he began and ended. Autism provides people a strange sense of boundaries and lack thereof.

We limit our repertoire of topics for conversation, of activities we engage in, seemingly compulsively. We have a strange fascination with doorways and doors. Opening and closing doors. Trying to run through an open doorway to we know not where and needing to feel heavy weights or another person's presence to define where we are in space. We obsess about the exact alignment of our trophies, yet we scatter them wildly in a moment of intense frustration.

Eight-year-old Bobby was one of 12 children in a self-contained special education class I taught in 1968. He was the only one who was autistic. One child had Down's syndrome, most of the others had severe learning disabilities and attentional disorders and some were hyperactive. Most had difficulty with impulse control and boundaries. To protect Bobby from their intrusions into his world and to protect them from Bobby's violent reactions when his boundaries were crossed, I needed to establish a clear boundary around Bobby—something always there and always visible, yet mobile to allow Bobby's movement, and adaptable as Bobby needed less protection.

A giant hula hoop did the trick. Everyone in the school knew they did not cross this high-profile, tangible boundary. Bobby could see it surrounding him and feel safe. He carried it with him through hallways and onto the playground. It was his shield. And every few weeks, as Bobby's sense of security increased, I snipped away an inch or so of its diameter. Before the end of the school year, Bobby was able to step out of his hoop and walk into a circle activity with the group, clasping another child's hand and truly joining us, with a smile, although not yet a word.

Safety comes first. Boundaries help us feel safe.

I recall a session during which one of my interns was reviewing a videotape, looking for a certain event in my assessment of a new client. She narrated to me what she was seeing. "He's opening the door. He's closing the door. Opening. Closing. Opening. Closing." It was five year-old Spencer who was experimenting with the difference between inside and outside of our evaluation space. Finally satisfied, he was able to leave the portal and join in some activities. He was exploring, testing, learning where he was and where he wasn't.

Greenspan finds that each child must first develop a strong and separate sense of self in order to empathize. He must be able to form those boundaries that separate self from other and to identify what he feels before he can make the projection that will let him walk, proverbially, in someone else's shoes.

This is yet another aspect to the sense of boundaries. I do not need to physically transgress your space and get in your face to understand how you feel. I can project myself there once I know where I am and how I feel. So here we are again, returning to proprioceptive and tactile senses helping us to get in touch with ourselves—our feelings and our boundaries—and helping us understand and respect others. The skills of respecting boundaries can be taught, but it usually requires a seemingly endless list of "don'ts"—don't go into the kitchen, don't touch other people's things, don't stand so close to that child's face. Or a more restrictive list of "do's"—do sit still in the chair over there, do exactly what the other children do, do what your group leader asks you to do.

One of my fears in teaching boundaries in this way is teaching "compliance." Complying with an externally imposed set of rules can be a very helpful skill, as long as the person imposing those rules is ethical and moral. We need to develop our own sense of boundaries, of what is right for us to do and wrong for us to do in certain situations. We need not be stimulus bound nor compliant. Life continues to present us with new experiences, with expanding or contracting opportunities. Our boundaries must be elastic to allow us to make it through all of these situations, even though we are hardwired for fear—primarily through our ever vigilant amygdala, protecting us from those who would disregard our boundaries.

We have already looked at some of the challenges of change, of transition, of that first passage down and through the birth canal or suddenly out through the surgical opening of a C-section. Transitions to where? Fear of the unknown causing sympathetic nervous system responses. Stress.

Many adults with ASD have jobs that provide them boundaries. Cubicles to work in. Routinized activities. Predictable interactions with others in meetings across large tables. Vocational choices directed by a unique set of abilities and challenges.

Current research is showing that the cerebellum plays an important role in the ability to shift attention among various stimuli and is therefore involved in our being able to adapt to changes in our environment readily or becoming stimulus bound. Bound. Boundaries. How we are able to process stimuli in our environment determines our sense of boundaries and our ability to understand those many elements of social interaction that relate to boundaries. How close should I stand to you? How far away must I insist you stand from me? How much is too much? When is it my turn? What are the exact rules of the game? These are all elements that we can be taught, but we learn them effortlessly when our senses are organized.

At the close of the 20th century the whole experience of visual boundaries shifted for children in highly technological countries. They stopped experiencing a regular shift from the infrequent close confines of books and construction toys and televisions to the expanse of outdoor play and kite-flying and cloud-gazing. Their days became filled with hour after hour of close visual work, with disregard for the fact that the normally developing visual system matures late and requires frequent shifts from near-point to far-point focus. Classrooms and homes became more cluttered with visual stimuli, and time outside of the house translated too frequently to going to shopping malls and play-spaces with brightly colored plastic barriers and slides and balls and lights.

This must have a profound effect on how their brains process perimeters and expanse—boundaries.

For some children in the spectrum, this shift was a mixed blessing. They could experience many activities through virtual reality that they could not experience in reality due to their sensory-motor challenges. We have yet to see how these children transition from experimenting with movement and proximity on a computer screen or videogame to real-life interactions with people moving through shared space.

We may discover that these virtual experiences provide a safe way to practice reacting to situations that in real life the peripheral nerves, cranial nerves, cerebellum, thalamus, vestibular system, and other parts of our brain and body would otherwise recoil from. Perhaps we will find that many of these children's parents also shifted from reality to virtual reality and their greater enjoyment of the virtual experience is part of the problem. It's too soon to know if these experiences are helpful in ultimately extending boundaries even though they constrict them in the moment.

This is just one of the many areas we still need to research. I think it should be evident that the boundaries of the research into the cause of autism and the cure for autism also need to expand, exponentially, and not limit our ability to resolve this puzzle, to change the epidemic proportions of this challenging dis-ease. We will do this as family members and researchers and educators and physicians and therapists and as autistic individuals, too, working together. As we work together within a framework of elastic boundaries, we will at times feel very vulnerable. We will be entering territories we have not yet explored and we will not know if we can trust a guide. We'll sense others trespassing on turf we considered our own. It will be challenging. But it is the only way to a solution.

We will all learn to hold hands and share resources—one person has the flashlight, and another the shovel, one the reserve food supplies and another the two-way radio. To resolve a problem with so many interwoven threads we must explore the threads and the patterns, knowing they are all part of the fabric, all forming the boundaries and at the same time leading the way to the door. In and out. In and out. In and out. Until those of us in the spectrum feel free to go out into the real world, into which we can meld without disturbing the boundaries or breaking the patterns of the larger fabric of society.

*C*onclusion

Type in the words "autism" and "treatment" on a search engine on the Internet, and you'll get over 210,000 matches! The approaches vary from biomedical to behavioral, from working with splinter sensory mechanisms to sensory integration. There are "mainstream" approaches and "alternative" approaches. Some approaches rely on supplements, others on high-tech equipment. The array of approaches knows no boundary.

Although this book is about autism spectrum disorders and provides theories that tie together the many threads, I do not imagine I have all of the answers, nor did I come to answers without looking into other approaches. The complexity of autism demands that we look at it from many angles. It also demands, however, that we integrate the information we glean so that families can get help with the heartbreaking reality of having a child with significant difficulty relating to them and to others. This seeming absence of relating, and the fear that it will never develop, is devastating beyond description.

Most approaches that do not focus on the nutritional/neuroimmune/ physiological basis of autism focus on aspects of social functioning because that is the unifying difficulty for individuals diagnosed with ASD. The contention is that children with ASD need to be taught how to develop relationships, not just how to speak and to learn scripts.

After moving together through the labyrinth of the body-brain-mind-spirit, we should agree on one thing: We will not achieve sustainable functional goals by treating one area. We must look at the whole being-experience as fully as possible. Nor can we go back in time and undo the causative factors that produce an autistic existence. As research is amassed in the next several years, I am certain we will learn of many toxins and other substances and experiences that in combination are in fact stealing our children's futures and, with them, our own.

Our society will develop more gentle and thorough ways to detoxify our environment and ourselves. And simultaneously we will undoubtedly create new dangers, to be discovered 50 years from now. As we discover the solutions to existing problems and know we are creating new poisons yet to be identified, does it still make sense to study individual systems, individual problems—digestive, nutritional, immune system, cerebellar, limbic, etc.? Probably. There is more to learn and more to prove to those who want such an array of evidence before they can adopt an holistic approach.

Bower and Parsons (2003), in their exploration of the role of the cerebellum, conclude that just such an openness to a systems approach is necessary, and that the concepts we have held about brain structure and function are on the verge of change in the direction of a holistic approach. "It is clear that how we think about this brain structure–and how we conceive of the brain as a whole—is about to change."[48]

In 1986, Levinson posed a challenge to find just such a holistic, systemic solution when he stated "Valid scientific theories are always interconnected with an unlimited and unrecognized number of variables, and thus have no confining horizons. Therefore, the number of unexpected clinical insights increases in proportion to the validity and scope of the working theory."[49]

In this framework, an acceptable approach to a problem as profound as autism will need to satisfy the requirements of sound neuroscience as well as the immediate needs of concerned and desperate parents and caregivers. But since this book has shown that what we call autism is a dis-ease—an autonomic nervous system response to severe stress—any viable approach to autism must respect the ANS. Even in the instance of the loop that appears to be the most self-contained and therefore a good starting point—the loop that encompasses toxicity and detoxification procedures—the ANS comes into play.

Detoxification alone will not produce sustainable results. Because stress reduces breathing, and in turn robs the body of one of its means to detoxify, and because stress causes neurophysiological imbalances, we cannot detox, not really, without dealing with the underlying elements that cause stress.

Nothing stands alone. The brain and body are in a constant state of interaction. We do not know if the areas of the brain found to be abnormal in individuals

---

[48]Bower, JM, and Parsons, LM. *P. 57*

[49]Levinson, HN. P. 225

with autism were the cause of the disturbed behaviors or if the brain, with its plasticity, is responding to environmental factors, beginning from prenatal or perinatal
experiences. So where to begin?

While we are waiting for conclusive biomedical research that may provide
preventative measures, we need to work with what is. And even after there may be
a means to prevent further incidence of autism, we will still need to address the
problems of those who already are enmeshed in the autistic experience.

For those whose lives are in the spectrum, HANDLE begins with non-
judgmental evaluation of neurodevelopmental functions and is guided by the underlying treatment modality of Gentle Enhancement. Treatment with Gentle Enhancement, not just in the connotation of therapy, but in its full meaning of how to interact with one another.

- Ascertain the problem areas—as many as possible—and do so openly
  with the entire family involved. Not to fix blame. There is no blame.
  (My mother is not to blame for having a stressful pregnancy and introducing me to many toxins. Nor is my dad to blame for performing work
  that put me at risk during my most critical developmental stages.) No;
  the purpose is simply to identify what you need to work on and why.

- Focus on the problems the individual with ASD demonstrates, while
  acknowledging the courage of that individual to wake up each morning
  and start another day knowing the problems will be there and the world
  will be unforgiving, unrelenting.

- Take care not to force stressful activities just because someone said they
  will be helpful. Remember also, social groups are systems, and when the
  family system is stressed in the implementation of a treatment program,
  that stress works against healing.

- Remember that all behaviors are there for a reason. Do not mask symptoms and control behaviors until you know what they are there to tell
  you. They may be the only clues or the best clues you have.

- While working to heal underlying problems, adopt temporary compensatory measures to increase FUNctionality and reduce stress. These will
  include environmental modifications (e.g., lighting changes, corrective
  lenses, grounding with copper, anti-allergenic diet, humidifier for white
  noise and a HEPA air filter to improve the air quality), and also behavioral

modifications (e.g., allowing fidget toys; reducing the amount of close visual work; providing time and space to unwind, literally and figuratively; permitting breaks or naps as needed).

- Keep in mind that the cranial nerves, particularly the auditory-vestibular nerve and the trigeminal nerve, need soothing and regulating. This may require a combination of activities to innervate and organize the stimulation to them as well as methods to calm them.

- Begin to work on weak systems, developmentally, taking great care not to stress some weak systems while trying to enhance others. Sucking through a straw. Engaging in activities on the floor or in a beanbag. Incorporating safe human contact—safe in the eyes of the beholder.

- Reduce demands on multiple systems whenever possible. Perform activities that require visual focus while lying down or sitting in a corner, so that visual vigilance for tactile and proprioceptive insecurities will not interfere.

- Do not single out one system for work now, and others later; the brain and body will work to reorganize themselves as they see fit. This reorganization process defies prediction, because the body-brain-mind-spirit will set its own priority. Remember: humans do not first develop balance and then muscle tone, but both in concert.

- Review the state change signs discussed here, and add your own as you learn them. Watch for any and every state change and STOP an activity when you notice a state change. This is how the ANS gives signs. If we ignore them, we pay a price.

- Assume that each person wants to achieve! Motivation is innate. Experience can strengthen it or weaken it, but as long as we are alive we are motivated.

HEAR WHAT I AM DOING[50]

Carolyn Hunsinger

Please, mom, <u>hear</u> what I am doing; see what I am saying.
The world is a crazy, confusing, scary place for me.
I can't do the things other kids do—my body doesn't work right.
But inside, I'm just like other kids—I need to be loved and appreciated;
I need to belong, to fit in; I need to contribute, to be useful; I need to be heard and understood; I desperately want you to be proud of me.

I want to tell you my needs, my feelings, my thoughts, but they get trapped inside me because I <u>can't</u> get my mouth to say the words. There gets <u>so much</u> piled up inside me that sometimes it just blows up everywhere. And I know you're disappointed in me, and you get angry at me, and somehow, it's <u>all my fault</u>.

My actions speak so loudly, you can't <u>see</u> what I am <u>saying</u>. Yet, my actions <u>are</u> my saying. <u>My body says what my mouth can't</u>. I act out my feelings, but often, the acting out is such a problem that my <u>feelings</u> go unnoticed. But I have no other way of telling you my feelings.

I want to cooperate, to succeed, to contribute, to feel good about myself, but to do that I must be heard.

Please, mom, <u>hear</u> what I am doing; <u>see</u> what I am saying.

[50] Reprinted by permission of the author.

$\mathcal{F}$inal thoughts

I s there a program that is right for autism? Of course not. Autism is only a construct, and constructed by those who are looking at parts. Looking from the outside-in. Not having the coordination of a construction project manager. And, as you were reading this book, I would be very surprised if you did not find your cousin (diagnosed with Attention Deficit Disorder), your neighbor (diagnosed with Bipolar Disorder), your teacher (diagnosed with Anxiety Disorder), your therapist (diagnosed with Irritable Bowel Syndrome), yourself (always suspected of being a little ODD—Oppositional Defiant Disorder) in some of the quirky behaviors. What we call autism is not an isolated "disease." It is the concentration, the quintessence of the disordered body-brain-mind-spirit. Disordered from earliest experience and yet still valiantly trying to relate to this world.

After weaving this cloth and trying it on in front of you, I now wonder if I was ever autistic. According to most diagnostic criteria, definitely.

Was it my deafness, providing me respite from the onslaught of yet one more form of sensory overload that helped me forge ahead into the world more normally? Most likely.

Did my disciplined periods of dietary and nutritional watchfulness coupled with gentle but thorough detoxification contribute to my healing? Most assuredly.

Did my ability to find and move through activities that served my own developmental needs, despite the inappropriateness of some of these behaviors—did that allow my systems to develop and integrate and does it still provide them release of built-up tensions? Undeniably.

Am I autistic now? I don't think so.

Even though my preferred modalities are solitude and written expression, and uncontrollable silliness and deep input rather than light touch, and my scripts and photos and rituals are still essential parts of me? No. I am not autistic.

How do I know for sure? Because the label is not who I am. I am who I have always known I was. I am Just Me. And finally very proud of that, with all of the quirks that are part of me. I am Just Me.

And I believe I will live to see the day when, through understanding and early intervention, the world will no longer batter people whose perceptual experiences are fraught with fright, so that such people can bravely conquer their hidden demons and move forward to true sharing, without the need for being taught how to be fluid.

An approach such as HANDLE can enhance development, gently, and with that allow us all to be. Just to be.

Just Me.

Appendices

Gentle Enhancement

BENEFITS:

Autism Spectrum Disorder is an extreme anxiety disorder that includes basic survival and everyday human functions interrelated with fright/flight/fight responses, so working with individuals on the spectrum must incorporate respect for their perceptions, for their tolerance of stimulation, passive and active, internal and external. That is the essence of Gentle Enhancement, which is the key to resolving the many issues of individuals with autism, and resolving them at their roots. Resolving problems at their roots allows for continued developmental growth without a need for continuous coaching for each situation the person may confront later in life or in another environment. Gentle Enhancement respects the person and his perceptions. It builds on the neuroscientific research that overloaded systems shut down. Gentle Enhancement is the basic therapeutic modality of HANDLE.

PROCEDURES AND PRECAUTIONS:

1. Monitor each and every activity in a therapeutic program and in the events of daily life as well (to the degree that it is possible). Watch for the following signs of stress or of a State Change—that is a signal from the body that it is experiencing distress in one or more of its foundational survival systems. The signals we observe most often are:

   a. Reddening of the ears and/or the anus

   b. Change of facial color (pallor or flushing)

   c. Change in breathing rate or depth

   d. Change in muscle tone (increased tension or flaccidity)

   e. Loss of visual focus or glassing over of the eyes

   f. Worsening of an activity once it is becoming integrated

   g. Complaints of nausea, dizziness, disorientation or other somatic concern

2. Stop any activity as soon as you see the first sign of a State Change. Do not wait until the body-brain-mind-spirit has progressed to a state of com-

plete overwhelm, meltdown, or shut down.

3. Alter elements in the environment if you suspect they may be causing the state change. Some of the more common stressors are:

a. Shrill or unexpected sounds

b. Bright or fluorescent lights

c. Strong odors, especially those used to mask other odors

d. Crowded spaces with threats of movement and tactile invasion

e. Preponderance of synthetic materials (toys, clothing, carpeting, etc.)

f. Foods frequently found to be allergens to people with ASD

g. Environments with a lot of young or active children, because they usually include all of the above factors

An Activity Sampler
For
Autism Spectrum Disorders

A NOTE TO OUR READERS

The activities presented in this appendix include the variations that are most frequently suggested for those people with ASD. Variations exist which may be more appropriate for those with other conditions such as stroke, Tourette's Syndrome, etc.

While I hope you receive benefit from employing these activities, a full assessment and individualized program by a Certified Practitioner of HANDLE will yield best results. Your HANDLE program may include some of the activities shown here, and will undoubtedly include additional activities selected and tailored to your specific needs which will be modified and updated throughout your six month follow-up plan in keeping with your progress.

Accentuation Stomp

BENEFITS:

This activity develops a high level of integrative functions, enhances differentiation of movement, reinforces laterality, provides rather intense proprioceptive and mild vestibular stimulation, and can increase muscle tone. It can also help to stimulate many reflexology points on the soles of the feet, thereby helping to balance bodily functions such as digestion, elimination, etc. The Accentuation Stomp is frequently used to strengthen a weak hemisphere of the brain: for non-verbal individuals stomp once on the right leg to stimulate the left hemisphere (i.e. speech and language centers); for those who focus on details, stomp once on the left leg to stimulate the right hemisphere (i.e. centers involved with the whole picture).

MATERIALS:

1. It is useful to have an assistant to help you sustain rhythmic movement and to monitor your performance in general.

2. For some variations you may need a chair the appropriate height so that both of your feet comfortably reach the floor.

3. You may require a wooden dowel at least three feet long.

PROCEDURE:

1. Stand in an unobstructed space.

2. Stomp twice on your _____ leg. Then smoothly transfer to stomp once on your _____ leg (once on the right leg to stimulate the speech and language centers for non-verbal individuals, or once on the left leg for those who require greater stimulation of their right brains).

3. Repeat this pattern until it becomes smooth and rhythmic with four beats to a measure, and each stomp receiving one beat with a rest on the fourth beat: L,L,R, rest L,L,R, rest or R,R,L, rest R,R,L, rest.

VARIATIONS:

1. Once you can stomp rhythmically, have a helper observe your perform-

ance, and note any extraneous movements and learn to quiet them. Extraneous arm movements can be quieted by holding a wooden dowel with both hands.

2. When you can sustain the stomping pattern without extraneous movement, try to sing a familiar song or count while continuing the stomping.

3. This activity requires good balance as well as muscle tone and moderate endurance. If your muscle tone or balance is weak, or if you have other challenges in performing this activity, you can perform it seated.

4. Your assistant can help to move your legs until you integrate the stomping pattern.

5. Saying (or hearing your helper say) "Right-right-left" as you stomp increases the integrative nature of this activity.

Blow Soccer

BENEFITS:

This activity is designed to provide mild to moderate stimulation of the facial nerves and muscles, to encourage the binocular functions of convergence, divergence, and visual accommodation, to gently stimulate the vestibular system and to strengthen interhemispheric integration. The ring or sphincter muscles of the lips and body are also strengthened with this activity, and breath control (and drool control) are developed.

MATERIALS:

1. For blow soccer you can use two twist closures for plastic bags (or paper clips bent into a "U" shape) taped to the area where you want the goalposts. You may use other materials, of course, to form the goal posts or wickets (masking tape, rolled in the middle and sticky on the ends, works well).

2. You may need to place a straight edge on each side of the field to keep the ball from going out of bounds

3. The "ball" used in blow soccer needs to move easily but not uncontrollably. A piece of cotton or a small wad of tissue paper fashioned into a ball will work well. "Berry beads" or cherry pits are the best "balls" for this activity.

4. If breath control is poor, initially you will need something easy to blow.

5. You will need a partner for this activity.

PROCEDURE FOR BLOW SOCCER:

1. Tape each goal post on opposing ends of the table.

2. Position the two players on opposite sides of the table behind the two goal posts.

3. Place the ball in the center of the playing field.

4. On the count of three, each player begins to blow the ball toward the

opposite goal, and to defend his or her own goal. No hands are allowed on the playing field.

5. You should decide how many goals (for example, three) determine when the game is over. Establish as many formal soccer rules as you wish. Note: For both blow soccer and blow croquet, we like to add another rule: "The game is cancelled on account of rain" whenever too much saliva is on the playing surface (from drooling or unintentional spitting).

VARIATIONS:

1. To increase or decrease the amount of vestibular stimulation, encourage more or less head tipping as you work to angle the trajectory of the ball.

2. Playing on the floor, rather than at a table, increases the amount of head tipping and therefore adds more vestibular stimulation.

PRECAUTIONS:

1. The competitive nature of Blow Soccer can motivate some people, but for others it can decrease the fun. Use common sense to decide what is best for you.

2. When muscle tone and/or general motor control is weak, small children may benefit from sitting on their caregiver's lap so that they are free to concentrate on the game.

3. Because this activity stimulates the vestibular system, among other things, take special care that someone monitors you for state changes such as dizziness, facial flush, reddening of the ears, etc.

4. Because of the vestibular component, don't play directly after eating, and stop at least 20 minutes before performing a risky job—which could be riding a bike, driving, or going up and down a flight of stairs.

5. Be careful not to hyperventilate, which may mean taking breaks from the game, even if you are having fun.

Crazy Straw

BENEFITS:

Drinking through a crazy straw can help to improve many functions including interhemispheric integration, binocular functions (eye teaming and focal vision), light sensitivity, sound sensitivity, articulation, bowel and bladder control, and tongue and lip control for articulation.

MATERIALS:

1. You will need a crazy straw—one of those plastic straws with lots of curls or twists and a small diameter, and a clear drink that you enjoy. The twists and turns of the crazy straw create more resistance in sucking.

2. For some people whose ears are very sensitive, a regular straw should be used instead of a crazy straw, because you have to suck so much harder through a crazy straw that it might be painful.

3. Water is the recommended beverage, since it is essential for healthy brain and body functions. Also, it is easiest to clean a crazy straw used only for water.

PROCEDURE:

Hold the straw in the center of your mouth, and sip and swallow, allowing a rhythmic pattern to develop if you can. You will benefit more from doing this with your eyes closed.

PRECAUTION:

If you have a tendency to, or a history of, crossed eyes, be sure that you look at a distant object while drinking.

VARIATIONS:

1. If you cannot swallow thin liquids, use a thick beverage and drink it through a regular plastic straw.

2. When there is a fear of aspiration, sucking is still possible with an activity such as using a straw to create enough suction to transfer small bits of colored paper from the table to make a mosaic on a larger piece of paper. Or use the straw to pick up a light object such as a paper napkin, and transfer it from one side of your tray to the other.

3. If you cannot yet suck through the straw, wait until you have enjoyed Face Tapping for several weeks, then try again. Meanwhile, watch others drinking through the Crazy Straw.

ADDITIONAL PRECAUTIONS:

1. Be sure to rinse out the straw well after each drink, so harmful bacteria do not build up in the loops.

2. If you are pregnant, do not engage in this intense sucking, as it may stimulate contractions.

MORE ABOUT THE BENEFITS OF USING A CRAZY STRAW:

When you examine the importance of sucking in human development, it is truly profound. Not only do we suck for nourishment, but also in sucking we do many other amazing things:

- We integrate the two sides of our mouth and cheeks and thereby stimulate the two cerebral hemispheres in a coordinated rhythmic fashion. This enhances our interhemispheric integration in general. We rely on interhemispheric integration to be able to process language, balance our instincts with logic, and so many other functions frequently compromised in neurobehavioral disorders as well as in brain injury.

- As we suck, many of our cranial nerves are stimulated, and they in turn help regulate many aspects of our vision, including the ability of our eyes to converge—that is, focus together on a target.

- One reason that people become light sensitive is that the two eyes do not team in their processing of the visual images, which of course is based on perception of light and darkness. Another is that the pupils have a reduced degree of reactivity to light. Drinking through the straw enhances these functions and thereby reduces light sensitivity.

- This activity works in many ways on the ear and its myriad of important functions. Stimulation of the trigeminal and facial nerves directly stimulates structures in the middle ear also. We are all familiar with how chewing gum or sucking on hard candy helps people to tolerate the pressure change in their ears during take-off and landing on flights. And through a connection in the part of the midbrain called the colliculus, visual focus directs auditory focus.

- Increasing tongue and lip control and coordinated breathing supports our ability to speak with good articulation.

- As related in her book, *The Secret of the Ring Muscles*, Paula Garbourg (dubbed "Dr. Paula" by appreciative patients) discovered that when we strengthen any set of sphincter muscles (such as the lips and also the esophagus) we strengthen all the sphincters in our body (such as the pupils of the eyes and the bowel and bladder) too.

- Sucking also stimulates the pituitary gland for balanced production of hormones, including the human growth factor hormone.

Face Tapping

BENEFITS:

This activity awakens, organizes, integrates and relaxes the trigeminal nerve, one of the twelve pairs of cranial nerves. This may produce many benefits, including increased facial muscle tone for nonverbal expression, integration of facial and general tactile sensations, alleviation of headaches, etc. It also supports speech production as well as hearing and vision, and may give rise to a sense of calmness. It also helps to open the sinuses, alleviate TMJ, increase circulation to gum tissue, and support energy channels.

MATERIALS:

You will need just your hands or the hands of a helper.

PROCEDURE:

1. Tap using two fingers on each hand and rapidly and rhythmically <u>alternating</u> from one hand to the other. The tempo of this tapping would approximate the beat in *Twinkle Twinkle Little Star*. The energy involved in each tap should be enough to produce a sound if you were to tap on a tabletop—your goal is to stimulate the nerves that are situated between the skin and the bone. You will know that the tapping pressure is right if you feel a tingling or a sense of vitality to the face after tapping, but no discomfort or pain. Adjust the tap (or guide your helper to tap) to your comfort level.

2. The tapping pattern should always be the same, so the brain eventually begins to anticipate the stimulation. Here is the recommended sequence, which is also portrayed in Figure 3 on the following page:

   1) From the temple along the eyebrows, to the midpoint between the eyebrows, up to the hairline and return by the same path to the temple.

   2) From the temple down across the top of the cheekbone to the bridge of the nose and back to the temple.

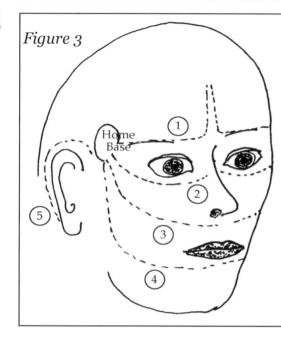

Figure 3

Home Base

Start and Stop at Home Base, at temples:

1. Across brow to midline up to hairline and back.

2. To bridge of nose and back.

3. Across cheek to mustache area and back.

4. Down sideburns and under lip and back.

5. Behind ear following imaginary eyeglasses and back.

3) From the temple down along the bottom edge of the cheekbone, along the upper gum line (the "moustache area") and in to meet just below the nose. Then return to the temple, tapping.

4) From the temple downward to the rearmost corner of the lower jaw then forward on the gum line of the lower jaw to meet tapping hands in the space between the lower lip and the chin. Return, tapping, to the temple.

5) From the temple around behind the ears, where the eyeglass arms would rest on the bone, very close to but not touching the ear. Return, tapping, to the temple. This last pathway is not on the trigeminal nerve proper, but rather enhances hearing via bone conduction.

VARIATIONS ON FACE TAPPING:

1. If you tap your own face, it may help to do it in front of a mirror or across from your helper who is also tapping on her face.

2. If someone helps you, find a comfortable position for this activity.

3. Tap on the route through a cool cloth placed over the face if you find the face tapping uncomfortable even after reducing the intensity of the tap.

4. If you have long fingernails, you can use the knuckles of your first two

fingers to tap with instead of fingertips, but you will get a less focused sensation using knuckles.

5. Until you are comfortable with the tapping, try rolling a HANDLE massage ball or a room temperature tangerine on the "route" of the tapping.

6. If you have a sinus condition or toothache, reduce the intensity of the tapping, but do try to tap, as it may help to promote sinus drainage or improve the health of the gums.

7. If you are sensitive to smell and a helper is implementing Face Tapping for you, make sure that she is not wearing highly scented hand lotion or sleeves that are scented by fabric softener, smoke, or any other scent you find offensive.

Hoop Mazes

BENEFITS:

This activity enhances the vestibular system, with the main emphasis on proprioceptive aspects of that system. It also benefits differentiation of response—an advanced aspect of reflex inhibition. The goal of hoop mazes is to increase your ability to respond automatically and efficiently to dynamic changes in proprioceptive and visual stimuli. Individuals who have difficulty moving through a crowd, sharing boundaries, moving through the house without bumping into things or people, or moving in a coordinated way in team sports will particularly benefit from this activity. Those who always move quickly, and may lose their balance when they slow down, will benefit from experiencing planned, deliberate, controlled movement.

MATERIALS:

1. You will need one or two hula-hoops and a helper.
2. You may also need cushions or an air mattress for some variations.

PROCEDURE:

1. Your helper will hold one hoop so that the job of moving through it is challenging but possible for you, starting with the hoop nearly vertical and the lower edge at about knee height.

2. Move through the hoop without touching the hoop with any part of your body. No diving through the hoop: Move slowly, smoothly and deliberately (crawling is allowed and even encouraged). Then return through the hoop from the opposite direction. Four or five passes (with several seconds of recovery time between passes) through the hoop is enough for one day.

3. When it becomes easy to move through the hoop vertically, your helper can vary the position of the hoop to make it more difficult. Maintain a given level of difficulty until there is little or no challenge for three days in a row.

4. Now you are ready to try the variations, below, arranged in order of difficulty.

VARIATIONS:

1. Use two hoops, parallel and about two feet apart.

2. Use two hoops held at an angle to one another, either enmeshed in one another or separated by several inches.

3. Perform the activity on an uneven surface such as sofa cushions or an air mattress.

4. Stack cushions so that there is a difference in height, and perform hoop mazes on these.

5. Add other objects to make an obstacle course, such as furniture that you must pass under, around or through.

6. Be creative, and think up some of your own variations. But be safe.

PRECAUTIONS:

1. For individuals who are frail or otherwise at risk from falling, have the area surrounding the maze protected with cushions, and have adjacent objects on which to lean if necessary.

2. Always monitor state changes as you employ Gentle Enhancement.

Hug and Tug

BENEFITS:

This activity enhances interhemispheric integration (and with that, language, memory, and a myriad of other functions). It also supports articulation. In addition, it is useful in promoting differentiation of fingers, one from the other, and from one hand to the other. Hug and Tug strengthens muscle tone of the fingers; stimulates Reflexology points for the brain, sinuses, jaw, mouth, eyes, and inner ear; integrates tactile sensations in the hands; enhances proprioceptive input in the fingers and hands; and may also calm and focus the individual.

MATERIALS:

You will need only your own hands and possibly the hands of a helper/caregiver.

PROCEDURE:

Figure 4

1. With your arms resting on a supportive surface or placed lightly against your lower ribcage, interlock your index fingers, holding your hands so they meet at the midline of your body. (See Figure 4.)

2. Squeeze and pull with your interlocked index fingers—one relaxes as the other pulls, then the other relaxes and the other finger pulls. Both of your hands and arms remain virtually motionless and relaxed—only the fingers are moving a bit.

3. Repeat the back and forth pull-release three or four times as the index fingers stay hooked together.

4. Unhook your index fingers and interlock your middle fingers, and repeat.

5. If you are at least four years old, you may want to continue with your ring and little fingers.

6. No matter how old you are, end with a hug and tug for your thumbs.

VARIATIONS:

1. Allow your helper to engage and manipulate your fingers, each hand separately first and then both hands together, with your hands crossed at midline. To accomplish this, with your finger interlocked with your helper's, the helper gently presses on the nail of your finger as it is wedged between her index and middle fingers. At the same time she presses with her thumb on your index finger joint closest to your hand, while giving the hug and tug squeeze. (See Figure 5.)

Figure 5

2. Your helper may do this hugging the fingers of both hands simultaneously and then releasing; or she may guide one hand to squeeze and pull while the other allows itself to be pulled, alternating active and passive roles first one hand and then the other. (See Figure 6.)

Figure 6

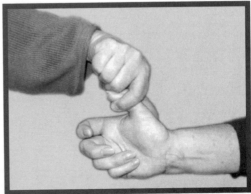

The technique for manipulating your thumbs is the most challenging to perform. (See Figure 7.)

Figure 7

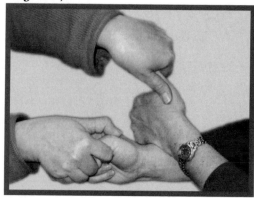

3. You may perform the squeeze and pull with both hands simultaneously, rather than alternating roles. (See Figure 8.)

4. Coordinate squeezes of interlocked fingers with phrases or words.

Figure 8

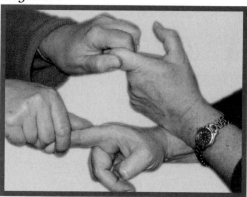

Skull Tapping

BENEFITS:

This activity enhances interhemispheric integration, and also provides gently organized stimulation of the sensory-motor cortex. It brings energy, blood flow, and oxygen to the brain to increase general alertness.

MATERIALS:

You can do this activity by yourself, although it is best if a helper can do it for you. All that is needed is a pair of hands (preferably with short fingernails) and the ability to move them in an energetic rhythmic alternate movement pattern so that the result is a tap and not a push.

PROCEDURE:

1. Using two fingers on each hand, tap your head with rapid movement and whatever degree of firmness is comfortable, alternating hands rhythmically and moving in "baby steps".

2. Start at the base of the skull, just <u>above</u> where the head joins the neck. Tap with one hand on either side of an imaginary midline from back to front (to the hairline in the front) and then back to the base of the skull. (See Figure 9 on the following page.)

3. Pick your hands up and move them to the spot in the center of the head where the fontanel, (a baby's soft spot) was. Now each hand taps from center down to just above the ear, and back. Each hand taps on its own side so that the skull is getting alternate stimulation on the right and left sides, both with two fingers marching side-by-side (not one above the other) so that the tapping stimulates both the sensory and motor cortices. (See Figure 10 on the following page.)

4. Pick up your hands, and place them again at the base of the skull. Repeat the first tapping pattern from back to front and front to back.

5. Upon completing this tapping pattern, hold the fingers of both hands at the stopping point for approximately two seconds before releasing.

VARIATION:

If Skull Tapping is too intense a sensation for you, you may initially roll a slightly textured air-filled ball on your head in these same areas, or rub the scalp as if you were getting a dry shampoo.

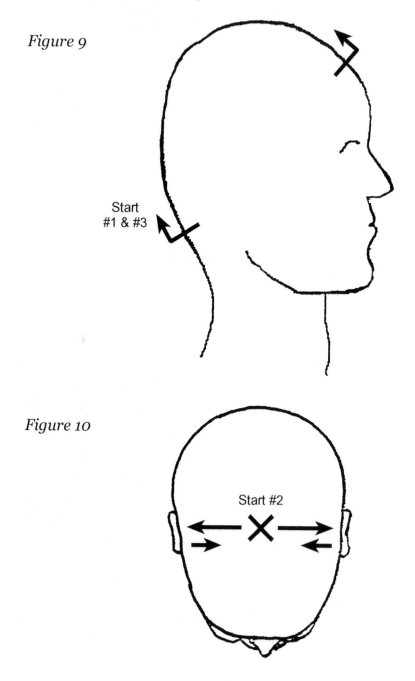

Figure 9

Start
#1 & #3

Figure 10

Start #2

Two-Finger Spinal Massage

BENEFITS:

This massage stimulates the Autonomic Nervous System, thereby helping to regulate the body's responses to vital activities such as respiration, circulation, digestion, etc. It modulates reactions to stress and other threats to comfort or survival. As such, it also regulates pupillary response, decreasing light sensitivity.

MATERIALS:

You need a caregiver who is able to modulate the strength and pressure in two fingers of his hand. Short fingernails are preferable.

PROCEDURE:

1. Generally this activity is performed with you lying on your stomach on a comfortable surface, but you can also benefit from this massage if you are standing or sitting comfortably, and there is enough space for your helper to stand behind or beside you.

2. Slowly, with his index finger and middle finger on one hand, your helper will place a finger on either side of your spine beginning where your neck joins your shoulders.

3. With whatever amount of pressure feels good to you, your helper will slowly drag his fingers beside your spine to just below your waist.

4. Then your helper will turn his hand (or bend his fingers) so that he can drag it again, evenly and comfortably, back along either side of your spine to your neck.

5. Your helper will repeat this massage two more times, or more, if you insist.

NOTE:

This activity may be done over a shirt or sweater, as long as you can hold the fabric taut so creases do not interfere with the smooth motion intended.

VARIATIONS:

1. Some people enjoy this massage performed in the downward direction only. Since the goal of the activity is to calm over-stimulated systems, the Two-Finger Spinal Massage should be performed in whatever manner is most comfortable to the recipient.

2. To begin with, your helper may need to perform the massage on a doll, pet, or family member until you feel comfortable accepting it.

Vestibular Stimulation

BENEFITS:

Activities that enhance the vestibular system also enhance the auditory functions of the cochlea, since those two systems share the same fluids and are part of an integrated system in the inner ear. This system is extremely important for everything we do and is one of the systems that is central in understanding and treating autism spectrum disorders.

PROCEDURES AND PRECAUTIONS:

The slow and controlled HANDLE activities specifically designed to enhance vestibular functions are deceptively simple and at the same time very powerful. I won't describe precise activities here, because Certified Practitioners of HANDLE customize the range and speed of motion, the amount of support, the other stimulation in the environment, and the number of repetitions of each movement—usually beginning with only one repetition and increasing very slowly over days and weeks to perhaps four or six repetitions in all.

HANDLE vestibular activities rely on no special equipment, are usually performed on the floor or in the lap of the caregiver, and must be monitored with Gentle Enhancement in mind. The activities also isolate each of the three axes of the semicircular canals to strengthen each without demanding that all three axes respond to treatment on the same timetable.

If anyone reading this book attempts to perform slow, controlled vestibular activities with anyone—especially with someone on the autism spectrum—understand that you do so at your own risk. Watch for state change signs and stop the activity immediately at the first sign of any state change. Also, make sure that you plan to engage in slow, controlled vestibular stimulation such that the activity occurs at least 20 minutes after eating and at least 20 minutes before engaging in any dangerous activity (such as going up or down a staircase, riding a bicycle, using a sharp implement, playing near a street or on an uneven surface, walking through a crowded space with sharp-cornered furniture, etc.).

NOTE: *A Certified Practitioner of HANDLE will be able to help guide an integrated HANDLE program incorporating the appropriate type and degree of vestibular stimulation.*

Detoxification

BENEFITS:

Toxicity as a core issue in Autism Spectrum Disorders is a focus of concern. Because stress creates neurotoxicity, because our environment has been flooded with ever-increasing toxins, and because many instances of autism are triggered by contamination with heavy metals such as mercury, it is crucial to incorporate some form of detoxification protocol in any program attempting to ameliorate autistic dysfunctions.

MATERIALS AND PROCEDURES:

There are many types of detoxification procedures a given family may implement, depending on the availability of affordable protocols and professional guidance. The procedures below can generally be employed without great expense and without interfering with other measures a family is currently applying. Most naturopathic physicians could help guide you in how to balance these various suggestions and which ones might be best for your particular situation.

WHOLE FOODS: Certain foods are known to remove toxins from the body, while others are known to support the systems and organs through which those toxins pass as they exit the body. Some of the foods and how they help are listed in the chart below.

FOOD ITEM	DETOXIFICATION FUNCTION
Raw Potato or Asparagus	Draws toxins out of almost anywhere in the body
Carrots	Flushes out free radicals in the blood stream
Garlic	Boosts the immune system during detoxification
Beets or Dandelion Greens	Cleanses the liver
Parsley or Watermelon	Cleanses the kidneys
Water	Flushes the system

STEAMY BATHS/SHOWERS OR SAUNAS: Steam helps to loosen toxins within the body and to excrete these toxins through the skin.

A ROUGH TOWEL OR LOOFAH: Rubbing the moist body with a rough, natural fiber material helps skin—our largest organ—exfoliate and release toxins.

TEAS: There are a number of readily available teas that assist with detoxification, and a few teas that are available only through private distributors.

REFLEXOLOGY: Applying this form of Chinese Medicine at home, gently, can help to reduce stress and the neurotoxicity it produces, enhance the liver, kidneys, pancreas, intestines and all our other organs and through this, assist in detoxification.

CASTOR OIL PACKS: Edgar Cayce and his followers utilize this procedure fairly routinely. Information on this procedure is available at http://www.are-cayce.com.

The Uncharted Territory of Just Raising Ivy[51]

A HANDLE STORY

BY CHARMA JONES

Ivy's first birthday is all a blur to me now. Pictures are the only things that bring back faded memories of that special day. She was smiling, laughing, having fun, dancing to the words of "Happy Birthday." Kisses to all.

So much has transpired since then. As I am sure it is with most parents of autistic children, there has been so much work, so many struggles and so many sleepless, tearful nights. We could write a book on that alone.

And the uncertainty—will she ever talk, walk, read? Will I ever hear her beautiful voice say those beautiful words, "I love you too, Mom?" What will she do when I am gone? Who will take care of my sleeping child? I supposed that these questions would never be answered, so I shoved them far back into my mind. Besides, I was already flooded by the day-to-day toils. "Get off of the refrigerator, please. Don't smack your head on the sidewalk. I'm sorry she's screaming. Ivy, you need to wear clothes, we are shopping." All were everyday declarations. And the one most said, "She doesn't talk."

Although it was years ago, I would swear it was just yesterday. It all seems to blur together—the chaos of the numerous appointments and the uncharted territory of just raising Ivy.

This is something about Ivy. And something about how she became the beautiful kindergartner that is now fully functional and seeking out approval from peers. At this very instant, she is looking into my eyes asking, "I want a cookie, please?" She still speaks most of her words in broken English, but she is only six, and she WILL learn. HANDLE is the oil that got all Ivy's gears moving.

Twenty months into Ivy's life, I thought I had gone crazy. "Am I just imag-

[51]*The Uncharted Territory of Just Raising Ivy* is reprinted by permission of the author from <u>The Churkendoose Anthology: True Stories of Triumph over Neurological Dysfunction</u>. Copyright © 2002 The HANDLE® Institute.

ining that she was talking last week? Singing Winnie the Pooh? I'd swear she was playing and smiling just last month at that movie we went to see." Her pediatrician assured me that this was a stage, and that all kids stop talking at some point. Eight months passed and still the pediatrician asserted that the stage would break. He would not listen to my concerns about the sleepless nights, the constant rocking, head banging and screaming bundle of frustration that had become Ivy. I didn't understand how that could have been a stage. That "stage" has lasted for four years.

Ava, Ivy's older sister, had not gone through this. With Ivy, it was impossible for me to enter a shopping center. Ivy would immediately panic. We began walking everywhere because Ivy could not stand the car ride. I could not stand to see her in so much pain.

It was cold season on the west coast of Washington State. Sure enough, with me working in the public schools, I caught a cold and gave it to Ava. We ended up at the pediatrician's office. When we got there, I discovered that our pediatrician was on vacation. "Oh great! Can we please be seen by someone else, then?" They said they would try. I signed in just as Ivy was jumping from the counter to the floor. I picked her up and went to the waiting room.

While we waited, I was thinking... she never hears me. She has to be deaf. My mother had mentioned it to me a few times and I wondered if she was right.

Soon they called our name. I think Ivy's screams made them hustle a bit. In came a woman pediatrician I had never seen. (To tell you the truth, I cannot find her name on any of Ivy's files. If you are she, thanks a million, you listened.)

Ivy was running around the room and throwing herself into the wall. The pediatrician stared at Ivy. I quickly tried to divert her attention to Ava, who was indeed diagnosed with a cold. "It will pass," the pediatrician said. "Ivy, on the other hand, seems to have a behavior problem. Do you have a communication problem with her?" I explained that I felt she was deaf, and yes, Attention Deficit Disorder runs in my family and I am dyslexic. She made a quick call and had asked if I could be at an appointment a month later. "Yes, I can." The appointment was with a child psychologist. I felt both unsettled and relieved at the same time. Finally, someone is going to tell me my child is deaf. We will get the needed surgery and it will be all better.

In January of 1998, at the age of two years and eight months, doctors at Mary Bridge Hospital diagnosed Ivy with "severe language deficits." A formal cognitive evaluation could not be completed "given her young age and active, impulsive behavior." Words of the Pediatric Psychologist. This made me ill, as I knew there was something more. And so I went on a learning excursion.

I had been told not to be a "renegade parent." I feel strongly that if I hadn't, Ivy would not be where she is today.

My learning took us to the Tacoma Learning Center. Evaluations ensued. The evaluation report contained these words, "self injurious, short attention span, self stimulating behaviors, no interest in peers, reduced eye contact." Ivy was 33 months old and she was assessed at a developmental age of 21 to 22 months: social skills, 24-month level, language development, 23-month level, independence, 35 months level, motor skills, 20-month level.

But, they were a great group of people there. They started Ivy in sensory therapy and this was the hardest time for me. Having your child in "the program" meant you met with the therapist (for the big people.) During these sessions, Ivy was in the classroom getting her therapy, and I was so worried because she was without me. The therapist, however, turned out to be the voice of reason. He reminded me that I am a person, even without Ivy stuck to my side, and counseled me to find myself so that I could be a better parent for Ivy. Thank you so much, Joel, for all your help.

In February 1999, we moved to Iowa. Before we left, I threw out Ivy's pacifier and let her watch me. She seemed to be fine, so that was the end of the pacifier. Maybe we were both ready to move on. When we got set up in Iowa, we decided to give potty training a try. We were persistent and it paid off.

In August, we were seen at the University of Iowa Hospital and Clinic. I had heard great things about them being the foremost authority on the study of developmental delays. More evaluations followed and they told me the same thing that I had heard from every other doctor, "She seemed to have a communication and behavior problem, with autistic tendencies."

At this time, Ivy was sleeping only three hours at night, and did not take a nap. When I brought this up to the team, their only answer was drugs. My husband and I were very opposed to this. No one seemed to have any answers for us, not even advice on dealing with her blatant disregard for any authority.

We looked into numerous therapies and "miracle cures." I was feeling frustrated that she was coming up on school age with no hope that she would ever attend. But, we did receive a letter from the school district stating that she was to attend. I called the district to let them know that this was impossible. I laughed and I cried, and they didn't believe me until they saw her. She soon started her first "special education" class.

We had learned that persistence was the way to teach Ivy. We could get her to eat, use the toilet and say "no." We started trying to get her to write her name, but she always wrote it in mirror image, no matter how insistent we were. Her behavior and actions were still harsh, and we still had no answers for "what was making her do this."

Angie Knowles and Denise Richardson were her special education teachers. They were super. They taught her sign language for potty, so we knew. Teaching Ivy to sign seemed to help her a little with communication. Angie and Denise were always searching for answers to our never-ending questions. One of them mentioned the Early Developmental Intervention unit, where Barb Kaufmann was applying the HANDLE approach to neurodevelopment. Angie had had experience with it with another autistic student. She said we might look into it.

We called and made an appointment. I swear the anticipation almost killed me that week, as it always did when we found a window for our closed box little girl. My husband was worried about my high hopes and had always consoled me after our letdowns. Ava asked if they were going to give her another shot to make her all better. All I could do was hold Ava and listen to her go on about how much she loved her sister even though she bit, hit and tore up her things. Ivy always did have a great support group in her sister, grandparents, parents and friends.

The office had a treadmill in the waiting room. I was immediately aware of it because I recognized it as something from which Ivy would jump. Barb Kaufman came to the door and said, "Come on back. Just let her act like herself." All I could think was, "Great, Ivy will have her hog-tied in a second." But, I must have sensed something in Barb that comforted my frustration, aggravation and pain. Ivy must have also because she went to Barb and sat in her lap. It made me cry. Ivy never went to anyone. Barb gave Ivy a pad of paper and she started scribbling. Barb spoke with us—and with Ivy. This was impressive. Until now, I was the only one that spoke **to** Ivy, not about her. Ivy soon finished her picture with her famous mirror image name. I asked Barb why she does that, not expecting an answer. Barb replied with, "Both sides of her brain are working separately and not together." Barb went on to explain how some autistic children can feel threatened by their environment. Their systems are, in essence, jammed. She then explained the vestibular system and how Ivy seemed to be dealing with tactile hypersensitivities, vestibular irregularities, proprioceptive weakness, light sensitivities and probable difficulties with binocularity. WOW! I was in awe, not at the medical terms, but at the fact she had an answer.

I was so relieved. Someone knew what was going on! Then it hit me she might have a solution. She picked Ivy up out of her lap and looked into her eyes. She told Ivy and me that there is a therapy called HANDLE, and if Ivy is ready we will start getting her system undimmed so that it will make her feel a little more comfortable with us. I had been trying to force Ivy into my world, but didn't stop to think that I might need to come into her world to walk her into mine. We made a follow up appointment.

That night, Tim, my husband, and I talked about what Barb had said. We were both relieved at her explanations of why Ivy is the way she is, how HANDLE can work for her and, better yet, why it works. We started that week. Barb gave us some things to do at home like Face Tapping, which proved to be an amazing tool, and joint compression.

Goodness, she was able to control her jumping around! And, she was not

Ivy, now able to express herself, share fully her unique characteristics and relate to the world.

throwing herself nearly as much. Ivy also noticed her need for these activities, coming to me from time to time grabbing my hands and tapping her face, or giving me her balled up fist so I would squeeze it. I started to comprehend why certain behaviors happened, and better yet, she started to understand me and what I was asking. Ivy soon had no need for the 3D glasses and special colored highlighter. Her brain was working in the right direction. We knew because she wrote her name in the correct manner all the time.

We soon stepped up into craniosacral therapy. I will never forget the first time Barb had Ivy's head in her hands. After a few minutes, Ivy looked straight into my eyes and said, "Please help me, Mommy." Barb and I both cried. The following sessions were filled with the alphabet verbally, and signing it with both hands simultaneously. Words followed soon.

All aspects of HANDLE have made a difference in Ivy's life. Recently, on a family trip, Ivy stayed in her seatbelt the entire trip to Mississippi. While there, she befriended a gecko that she found. She slept with him that night in her hand. She was so gentle, finally comprehending her own strength. Ivy's list of successes is a long one, if you will bear with me. She is now in full time kindergarten, mainstreamed in public school. Her eye contact is remarkable on down to her eye contact with herself in the mirror as she administers her hairspray and barrettes in the morning. She washes her face, brushes her teeth and dresses herself. She seeks out conversation with peers. I watched her one day walking down the hallway of her school, talking with a boy in front of her. She walks beside me in the grocery store grabbing groceries for me, with not even one scream from her. Her emotions are under control.

The best improvement yet, or benefit I should say, is that we had a son. At first, we were concerned with how Ivy might be with him due to her past violent behaviors. When we brought him home and she looked at him, "Ohhhhhh baby boy" came from her mouth. Then she sat and held him for the longest time, kissing him and, if you can believe it, she re-changed him after watching me change his diaper. By the way, every night when I put her to bed at 7:00 p.m. she tells me, "I love you too, Mom." And for that I have to say, "Thank you so very much to Barb, for bringing my daughter back to me. It is so nice to listen to her sing 'Winnie the Pooh' once again."

Clinical Procedures

EVALUATION:

The HANDLE evaluation begins with an intake questionnaire and a verbal exploration of history and presenting concerns. The Certified Practitioner of HANDLE guides the two-hour assessment, in the presence of the client's parents, caregivers or support persons, in a manner that is non-judgmental, non-stressful and affirming.

Throughout the evaluation, the HANDLE practitioner engages the client in a series of varied activities while noting response patterns and analyzing strengths and weaknesses in the client's processing. The practitioner employs observational assessment, rather than standardized testing, to ascertain which functional areas are inefficient, which are obstructed.

Following the evaluation phase, the client enjoys some free time, while the practitioner develops a comprehensive profile of the client's core neurological processing. This neurodevelopmental profile traces presenting concerns back to their origins, through the paths of vision and audition, proprioception, kinesthesia and vestibular functioning, to the most foundational level of touch, taste and smell. It incorporates the processes of attention, differentiation, lateralization and integration as well. The root causes of perplexing behavior and poor learning patterns are brought to light, and a picture of the dynamic interaction of neurological functioning emerges.

The practitioner then uses knowledge of the client's developmental history, including gestational influences, nutrition, allergies, other special health problems, and more, to ascertain the total environment in which these roots developed. These factors, too, become part of the profile, not to place blame, but to discern if other procedures or complementary health measures should be explored. This comprehensive profile then provides a roadmap to guide the creation of a therapeutic treatment plan unique to each client.

PRESENTATION OF RESULTS:

The client and family receive a thorough discussion of the results, an explanation of the recommendations and skilled guidance in the implementation of their program. The practitioner may also make nutritional recommendations or suggest temporary environmental accommodations, such as reducing extraneous sounds in the surrounding or altering lighting, as necessary. HANDLE provides clients virtually all the special tools required for implementation of the activities.

THE HOME TREATMENT PROGRAM:

Each program is customized for effective application in the client's home or other supportive setting. Videotapes made of the clinical sessions provide a tool for easy reference at home. Programs generally require less than half an hour daily. The recommended activities are simple to perform, and can be done as a sequence or broken into several clusters, depending upon individual preferences and schedules. Some activities may require support from a caregiver. The focus is always on Gentle Enhancement to strengthen the client's neurological functioning without producing stress. To this effect, some programs incorporate Mental Rehearsal to allow a client to progress by watching others perform specific activities.

FINE-TUNING AND PROGRAM REVIEWS:

Within two weeks of starting a HANDLE home-treatment program, a fine-tuning session ensures understanding and correct application of the activities. It also provides an opportunity to adjust the program to the client's progress. Additional program review sessions are recommended every four to six weeks. Many clients see significant results within the first few months, but we encourage each client to benefit from six-months of fine-tuning. If an in-person visit isn't possible, your practitioner will work with you to find an alternative such as videotape and an e-mail or phone discussion.

ADDITIONAL SUPPORT:

Most clients achieve their goals through the home-implemented programs. Occasionally, clients may benefit from therapy sessions with their practitioners, or other on-site work to determine issues of mismatch between the client's system and the general environment. Certified Practitioners of HANDLE are dedicated to meeting whatever level of support our clients need.

IS HANDLE RIGHT FOR YOU?:

To help you decide if the HANDLE approach can address your concerns, we offer additional information at community presentations, on audiotape, by e-mail and telephone and on our website. In addition, we can provide you with contact information for Certified Practitioners of HANDLE, as well as phone numbers of clients who have been through their HANDLE program and are willing to share their thoughts on the process and the results. To find out more, contact us at:

The
HANDLE®
Institute
International, LLC

1300 Dexter Avenue North, #110
The Casey Family Building
Seattle, WA 98109

Phone: (206) 204-6000
Fax: (206) 860-3505
Email: support@handle.org
Web: www.handle.org

References

Abo T., and Kawamura T. (2002). *Immunomodulation by the Autonomic Nervous System: Therapeutic Approach for Cancer, Collagen Diseases, and Inflammatory Bowel Diseases.* Retrieved January 1, 2003, from http://www.blackwell-synergy.com/links/doi/10.1046/j.1526-0968.2002.00452.x/abs/

Adolphs R., Baron-Cohen S., and Tranel, D. (2002, November 15). Impaired Recognition of Social Emotions Following Amygdala Damage. *Journal of Cognitive Neuroscience, 14* (8), 1264-74.

Amen, D. G. (1995). *Windows into the A.D.D. Mind: Understanding and Treating Attention Deficit Disorders in the Everyday Lives of Children, Adolescents, and Adults.* Fairfield, CA: Mind Works Press.

American Psychiatric Association. (1994). *Diagnostic and Statistical Manual of Mental Disorders* (4th ed.). Washington, DC: Author.

Anderson, J. (1998). *Sensory Motor Issues in Autism.* San Antonio, TX: Therapy Skill Builders.

Attwood, T. (1998). *Asperger's Syndrome: A Guide for Parents and Professionals.* Philadelphia: Jessica Kingsley Publishing Co.

Autism: New Knowledge of A Brain Key Control. Retrieved January 1, 2000, from the American Association for the Advancement of Science EurekAlert web page: http://www.eurekalert.org/releases/weiz-nuk011200.html

Ayres, A. J. (1979). *Sensory Integration and the Child.* Los Angeles: Western Psychological Services.

References

Baron-Cohen, S. *Theory of Mind in Normal Development and Autism.* Prisme, 2001, 34, 174-183.

Baron-Cohen, S., Wheelwright, S., Spong, A., Scahill, V., and Lawson, J. (2001). Studies of Theory of Mind: Are Intuitive Physics and Intuitive Psychology Independent. *The Journal of Developmental and Learning Disorders, Special Edition, 3*, 1.

Bauman, M. L., and Kemper, T. L. Eds. (1994). The *Neurobiology of Autism.* Baltimore MA: The Johns Hopkins University Press.

Benbadis S., and Rielo, D. *EEG Atlas: Normal Sleep EEG – Rapid Eye Movement Sleep.* Retrieved December 24, 2002, from http://www.emedicine.com/neuro/topic690.htm

Black, H. (2001, October). Amygdala's Inner Workings: Researchers Gain New Insights into this Structure's Emotional Connections. *The Scientist, 15* (19), 20.

Bluestone, J. (2002). The *Churkendoose Anthology: True Stories of Triumph over Neurological Dysfunction.* Seattle, WA: The HANDLE Institute.

Bluestone, J. (2001). *The Fabric of Autism.* Presentation at the Best of the NW, Autism Society of Washington Annual Conference in Yakima, Washington.

Bluestone, J. (2003). *Principles of Attention, 2nd ed.* Seattle, WA: The HANDLE Institute.

Bower, J. M., and Parsons, L. M. (2003, August). Rethinking the 'Lesser Brain'. *Scientific American, 289* (2): 50-57.

Bradford, N. (2000). *The One Spirit Encyclopedia of Complementary Health.* New York: Hamlyn Publishing Group Ltd.

Chelimsky G., Boyle, J. T., Tusing, L., and Chelimsky, T. C. (2001, July). Autonomic Abnormalities in Children with Functional Abdominal Pain: Coincidence or Etiology? *Journal of Pediatric Gastroenterology and Nutrition, 33* (1), 47-53.

Cohn, D. (1995). *An Introduction to Craniosacral Therapy: Anatomy, Function, and Treatment.* Berkeley, CA: North Atlantic Books.

Colburn, T., Dumanoski, D., and Peterson-Myers, J. (1997). *Our Stolen Future: Are We Threatening Our Fertility, Intelligence, and Survival? A Scientific Detective Story.* New York: Penguin Books.

Condon, W. and Sanders, L. (1974, January). Neonate Movement is Synchronized with Adult Speech: Interaction Participation and Language Acquisition. *Science, 183,* 99-101.

Diet Affects Genetic Expression, Study Finds. Retrieved August 4, 2003, from http://www.abc.net.au/news/newsitems/s915753.htm

Edelson, S.M. *The Cerebellum and Autism.* Retrieved April 4, 2002, from www.autism.org/cerebel.html

Eliot, L. (1999). *What's Going on in There? How the Brain and Mind Develop in the First Five Years of Life.* New York: Bantam Books.

Gackenbach, J. *Sleep and Consciousness.* (1994, May 19). Lecture presented at Smithsonian Institute. Retrieved December 24, 2002, from http://www.sawka.com/spiritwatch/sleepand.htm

Garbourg, P. (1997). *The Secret of the Ring Muscles: Healing Yourself through Sphincter Exercise.* Garden City Park, NY: Avery Publishing Group.

Goddard, S. (1996). *A Teacher's Window into the Child's Mind: And Papers from the Institute for Neuro-physiological Psychology.* Eugene, OR: Fern Ridge Press.

Goldberg, M. *A New Definition of Autism.* (1997). Retrieved January 13, 2003, from http://www.neuroimmunedr.com/Articles/Autism___PDD/New_Definition/new_definition.html

Grandin, T. (1995). *Thinking in Pictures and Other Reports from my Life with Autism.* New York: Doubleday.

Greenspan, S., and Wieder, S. (1998). *The Child with Special Needs: Encouraging Intellectual and Emotional Growth.* Cambridge, MA: Perseus Publishing.

References

Greenspan, S. (2001). The Affect Diathesis Hypothesis: The Role of Emotions in the Core Deficit in Autism and in the Development of Intelligence and Social Skills. *The Journal of Developmental and Learning Disorders, Special Edition 2001, 3* (1), 1-45.

Grelotti D. J., Gauthier I., and Schultz, R. T. (2002, April). Social Interest and the Development of Cortical Face Specialization: What Autism Teaches us about Face Processing. *Developmental Psychobiology, 40* (3), 213-25.

Grigsby, L. (2003). *The Light Within.* Fairfax, CA: Author.

Groh, J. M., Trause, A. S., Underhill, A. M., Clark, K. R. and Inati, S. (2001, February). Eye Position Influences Auditory Responses in Primate Inferior Colliculus. *Neuron, 29,* 509-518.

Gutstein, S. E. (2000). *Autism Aspergers: Solving the Relationship Puzzle.* Arlington, TX: Future Horizons.

Hannaford, C. (1995). *Smart Moves: Why Learning is not all in your Head.* Arlington, CA: Great Ocean Publishing.

Harvard Mental Health Letter. *How Autism Looks.* Retrieved January 13, 2003, from http://www.health.harvard.edu/medline/Mental/M0103b.html

Harvey, M. T., and Kennedy, C. H. (2002). Polysomnographic Phenotypes in Developmental Disabilities. *International Journal of Developmental Neuroscience, 20* (3-5), 443-448.

Hoshino Y., Kumashiro H., Yashima Y., Tachibana R., Watanabe M., and Furukawa H. (1982). Early symptoms of autistic children and its diagnostic significance. *Folia Psychiatric Neurology, 36* (4),367-74.

Hunsinger, C. (1996). *Hear What I Am Doing?* Rainer, Washington: Author.

Jamal G. A., Hansen S., and Julu P. O. (2002, December). Low Level Exposures to Organophosphorus Esters May Cause Neurotoxicity. *Toxicology, 27* (181-182),23-33.

Jennings, D. E. *Autonomic Nervous System (ANS) Function and the Breath.* Optimal Breathing. Retrieved December 24, 2002, from http://www.breathing.com/articles/autonomic-nervous-system.htm

Kanwisher, N., Stanley, D., and Harris, A. (1999, January). The Fusiform Face Area is Selective for Faces not Animals. *Brain Imaging Neuroreport, 10* (1), 181-183.

Kaufman, B. N. (1993). *Son Rise: The Miracle Continues.* Tiburon, CA: H.J. Kramer, Inc.

Kehm Equipment Incorporated. Retrieved December 25, 2002, from http://www.workingcomfort.com/Respirator_Accesories/deluxe_banana_oil_kit.htm

Kranowitz, C. (1998). *The Out of Sync Child: Recognizing and Coping with Sensory Integration Dysfunction.* New York: Skylight Press.

Lathe, R. and Le Page, M. *Toxic Metal Clue To Autism.* Retrieved July 31, 2003, from http://www.newscientist.com/news/news.jsp?id=ns99993842

Levinson, H. N. (1986). *Phobia Free: A Medical Breakthrough Linking 90% of all Phobias and Panic Attacks to a Hidden* Physical *Problem.* New York: MJF Books.

Lewis, D. H., Bluestone, J., Savina, M., Krohn, K., and Minoshima, S. (2003). *Imaging Brain Activation and Synaptic Plasticity in Recovery from Chronic Traumatic Brain Injury (TBI).* Presented at the 28th Annual Conference of the Western Regional Society for Nuclear Medicine, Anaheim, CA.

Martin, L. A., Mittleman, G., and Goldowitz, D. *Cerebellar Neuropathology and Autistic Behaviors: Exploration of a Mouse Model System.* Presented at the NIH/ACC 2001 Conference. Retrieved December 24, 2002, from http://www.nichd.nih.gov/autism/abstracts/goldowitz.htm

McAfee, J. L. (2002). *Navigating the Social World: A Curriculum for Individuals with Asperger's Syndrome, High Functioning Autism and Related Disorders.* Austin, TX: Future Horizons, Inc.

McKelvey, J. R., Lambert, R., Mottron, L., and Shevell, M. I. (1995, July). Right-Hemisphere Dysfunction in Asperger's Syndrome. *Journal of Child Neurology, 10* (4), 310-314.

Meunier, M. and Bachevalier, J. (2002). Comparison of Emotional Responses in Monkeys with Rhinal Cortex or Amygdala Lesions. *Emotion, 2,* 147-161.

References

Mercola, J. *Pasteurized Milk and its Link to Autism* Retrieved October 3, 2003, from http://www.mercola.com/1999/archive/milk_linked_to_autism.html

Myles, B. S., Cook, K. T., Miller, N. E., Rinner, L., and Robbins, L. A. (2000). *Asperger Syndrome and Sensory Issues: Practical Solutions for Making Sense of the World.* Shawnee Mission, Kansas: Autism Asperger Publishing Co.

National Institute of Mental Health. *Anxiety Disorders Treatment Target: Amygdala Circuitry.* Retrieved January 13,2000, from http://www.nimh.nih.gov/events/pranxst.cfm

Oetter, P., Richter, E. W., and Frick, S. M. (1988). *MORE: Integrating the Mouth with Sensory and Postural Functions.* Hugo, MN: PDP Press.

Ozonoff, S., Dawson, G., and McPartland, J. (2002). *A Parent's Guide to Asperger Syndrome & High-Functioning Autism: How to Meet the Challenges and Help Your Child Thrive.* New York: The Guilford Press.

Panksepp, J. Melatonin - The Sleep Master: An Emerging Role for this Over-the-Counter Supplement in the Treatment of Autism. (Reprinted from *Lost and Found: Perspectives on Brain, Emotions, and Culture,* Bowling Green, OH: Bowling Green State University). Retrieved April 5, 2003, from http://www.autism.org/melatonin.html

Park, C. C. (2001). *The Siege: A Family's Journey into the World of an Autistic Child.* New York, New York: Back Bay Books.

Pecci, E. F. (1977,January). *Minimal Brain Dysfunction in Children.* A lecture delivered at the 10th Annual Medical Symposium of the A.R.E. Clinic, Inc., Scottsdale, AZ.

Pelphrey K. A., Sasson N. J., Reznick J. S., Paul G., Goldman B. D., and Piven J. (2002, August). Visual Scanning of Faces in Autism. *Journal of Autism and Developmental Disorders, 32* (4), 249-261.

Purves, D., Augustine, G., Fitzpatrick, D., Katz, L. C., LaMantia, A-S., and McNamara, J. O. (Eds.). (1997). *Neuroscience.* Sunderland, MA: Sinauer Associates, Inc.

Rapin I. (1991, May). Autistic Children: Diagnosis and Clinical Features." *Pediatrics, 87* (5 pt. 2), 751-760.

Rapp, D. J. (1991). *Is This Your Child?: Discovering and Treating Unrecognized Allergies in Children and Adults.* New York: William Morrow.

Rapp, D. J. (1996). *Is This Your Child's World? How You Can Fix the Schools and Homes That Are Making Your Children Sick.* New York: Bantam Books.

Ratey, J. J. and Johnson, C. (1998). *Shadow Syndromes: The Mild Forms of Major Mental Disorders that Sabotage Us.* New York: Bantam.

Rudin, D. and Felix, C. (1996). *Omega 3 Oils.* Garden City Park, NY: Avery Publishing Group.

Sacks, O. (2001). *Uncle Tungsten: Memories of a Chemical Boyhood.* New York: Vintage Books.

Schauenstein K., Rinner I., Felsner P., and Mangge, H. Bidirectional Interaction Between Immune and Neuroendocrine Systems. An experimental approach. Retrieved January 7, 2003, from *http://www.ncbi.nlm.nih.gov:80/entrez/query.fcgi?cmd=Retrieve&db=PubMed&list_uids=1328993&dopt=Abstract*

Scientific Fact, Industry Fiction: The Chemical Industry Archives, A Project of the Environmental Working Group. Retrieved January 7, 2003, from http://www.chemicalindustryarchives.org/factfiction/

Scientific Research on Maharishi's Vedic Approach to Health: Part I *TRANSCENDENTAL MEDITATION Introduction and Overview of Research.* Retrieved December 12, 2002, from http://www.t-m.org.uk/research.shtml

Seroussi, K. and Rimland, B. (2000). *Unraveling the Mystery of Autism and Pervasive Developmental Disorder: A Mother's Story of Research and Recovery.* New York: Simon & Schuster.

Siegel, B. 1996. *The World of the Autistic Child: Understanding and Treating Autistic Spectrum Disorders.* New York: Oxford University Press.

Stein, K. *Why the Purkinje Cell?* Retrieved December 12, 2002, from http://www.eventhorizon.com/samples/live_science/purkwrld/

References

Stitt, B. R. (1997). *Food & Behavior: A Natural Connection*. Manitowoc, WI: Natural Press.

Thompson, R. F., Garcia, R., Baudry, M., and Vouimba, R. M. *Brain's "Fear Center" Identified*. Retrieved December 17, 2002, from http://www.excelinstitute.com/articles/fear%20center.htm

Thrower, D. *MMR and Late-Onset Autism -(Autistic Enterocolitis)- A Briefing Note*. Retrieved January 18, 2001, from http://www.whale.to/vaccine/thrower11.html

Tomatis, A. A. Thompson, B. M. (Trans.). (1997). *The Ear and Language*. Montreal: Stoddart Publishing.

Tougas, G. (1999, March). The Autonomic Nervous System in Functional Bowel Disorders. *Canadian Journal of Gastroenterology, 13 Suppl A,* 15A-17A.

Treffert, D. A. *Asperger's Disorder and Savant Syndrome*. Retrieved December 25, 2002, from http:www.wisconsinmedicalsociety.org/savant/aspergers.cfm

Treffert, D. A. *The autistic savant*. Retrieved December 25, 2002, from http:www.wisoncsinmedicalsociety.org/savant

Trepagnier, C., Sebrechts, M. M., and Peterson, R. (2002, June). Atypical Face Gaze in Autism. *Cyberpsychology and Behavior, 5* (3), 213-217.

Twachtman-Cullen, D. (2003, January). The Effect of Theory of Mind Deficits on Communication and Social Behavior in Individuals with ASD: An Introduction. *Autism/Asperger's Digest,* 16-19.

Upledger, J. E. (1996). *A Brain Is Born*. Berkeley, CA: North Atlantic Books.

Waterland, R. A., and Jirtle, R. L. (2003). Transposable Elements: Targets for Early Nutritional Effects on Epigenetic Genetic Gene Regulation. *Molecular Cellular Biology, 23,* 5293-5300.

Waltz, M. (2002). *Autistic Spectrum Disorders: Understanding the Diagnosis and Getting Help*. 2nd ed. Sebastopol, CA: O'Reilly & Associates, Inc.

Welsh J. P., Yuen G., Placantonakis D. G., Vu T. Q., Haiss F., O'Hearn E., Molliver M. E., and Aiche,r S. A. Why do Purkinje Cells Die so Easily After Global Brain Ischemia? Retrieved December 12, 2002, from http://www.ncbi.nlm.nih.gov:80/entrez/query.fcgi?cmd=Retrieve&db=PubMed&list_uids=11968459&dopt=Abstract

Wheeler, M. (1998). *Toilet Training for Individuals with Autism and Related Disorders.* Arlington, Texas: Future Horizons.

Williams, D. (1992). *Nobody Nowhere: The Extraordinary Autobiography of an Autistic.* New York: Avon Books.

Wing, L. (1981). Asperger's Syndrome: A Clinical Account. *Psychological Medicine, 11,* 115-129.

Ziegler M. G., Ruiz-Ramon P., and Shapiro M. H. (1993, July-August). Abnormal Stress Responses in Patients with Diseases Affecting the Sympathetic Nervous System. *Psychosomatic Medicine, 55* (4), 339-346.

Zimmerman, A. W., and Gordon, B. (2001). Neural Mechanisms in Autism. *The Journal of Developmental and Learning Disorders, Special Edition, 3* (1), 119-132.

Index

A

adrenaline
   role in fright/flight/fight, 130
   as defensive agent, 138
adults
   coping mechanisms, 164
   plasticity of nervous system, 132
   work environment, 164
Affect Diathesis Hypothesis, 76
allergies
   as cause of stress, 175
   defense against, 138
   example (Mathew), 106
   food, 15, 176
amino acids, 130
amygdala
   as information channel, 144-145
   early damage to, 145-146
   link to olfactory bulb, 144
   role in face recognition, 144
   memories, 144

research into, 146
ANS *see* Autonomic Nervous System
antibiotics, effect of digestion, 109
anticipation, 42-43
anus
   relation to vagus nerve, 156
   reddening of, 156, 175
anxiety and social interaction, 14, 129-147
Applied Behavior Analysis, 3
ARI *see* Autism Research Institute
ASD (Autism Spectrum Disorder)
   alternate names for, 129
   chart depicting causes of, 114
   description of, 175
   diagnosis, 7-8, 159
   risk factors for, 2
   sleep, REM, 150
   social interaction and, 121
   stress, 151
   summary of challenges, 160-161
     see also autism/autistic people

Index